Meeting the Moment

Meeting the Moment

Socially Engaged Performance, 1965–2020, by Those Who Lived It

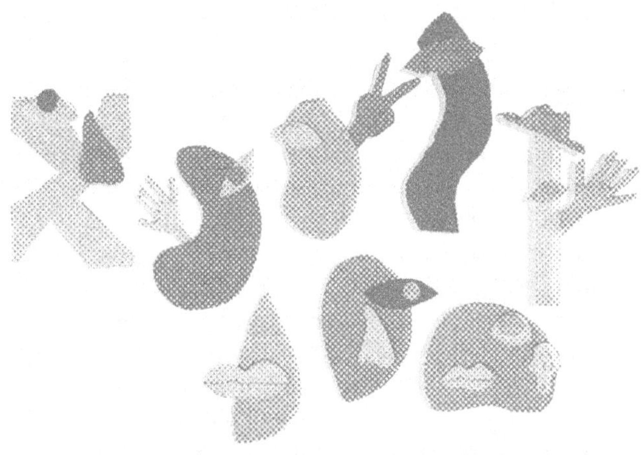

Jan Cohen-Cruz and Rad Pereira

New Village Press • New York

Published in the United States by New Village Press
bookorders@newvillagepress.net
www.newvillagepress.org
New Village Press is a public-benefit, nonprofit publisher
Publication Date: May 2022
First Edition

Library of Congress Cataloging-in-Publication Data

Names: Cohen-Cruz, Jan, 1950- author, interviewer. | Pereira, Rad, 1989– author, interviewer.

Title: Meeting the moment : U.S. socially engaged theater and performance, 1965–2020 : conversations with people who've lived it / Jan Cohen-Cruz and Rad Pereira.

Description: First edition. | New York : New Village Press, 2022. | Includes bibliographical references and index. | Summary: "Composes the recollections of socially engaged theater makers and performers to discuss the challenges and adaptations of the field. Meeting the Moment explores experiences of a diverse range of progressive theater and performance makers in the U.S., in their own words, since 1965. These performers, often unknown beyond their immediate audience, articulate diverse influences. Curated stories from over 75 interviews and informal exchanges offers insight into the field and point out limitations due to discrimination and unequal opportunity for performance artists over the past 55 years. They also reflect on how artists are educated and supported, what content is deemed valuable and how it is brought to bear, as well as which audiences are welcome and whether cross-community exchange is encouraged. The book's voices from the field point to more diverse and inclusive practices and give hope for the future of the art" — Provided by publisher.

Identifiers: LCCN 2021060577 (print) | LCCN 2021060578 (ebook) | ISBN 9781613321546 (paperback) | ISBN 9781613321560 (ebook) | ISBN 9781613321577 (ebook other)

Cover design: Juan Pablo Rahal. *Cover illustration:* Izzy Sazak
Interior design and composition: Leigh McLellan Design

EARTHMATTERS

Feel the floor beneath your feet

The layers of Earth beneath that floor

What's there? Who's there? Why?

We honor the ancestors, past, present, and future, who are with us, present in spirit through their guidance and influence on our words, actions, stories, and understanding.

We honor the blood and the bones without which this land as we know it would not be possible: the hundreds of vibrant, complex polylithic Native nations that have been stewarding these lands from time immemorial; the enslaved Africans and their descendants who built this country and its cultures with their bodies, minds, and spirits; and the many waves of (im)migrants who arrived and continue to arrive on these shores to add their hands to the care of this place we all share.

We offer our care and gratitude to the land, water, and air.

We invite you to reflect with us on the many histories/presents/futures of socially engaged theater and performance from 1965 to 2020 on Turtle Island, the country currently known as the United States. We are guided by community wisdom; our evidence is some of the people who have lived it and our intention is to uplift many simultaneous realities of this field.

Contents

Foreword

by Carlton Turner

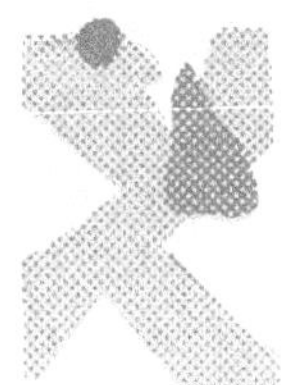

I am the son of Emmett and Genevia Turner. I was born in Mount Vernon, New York, and raised in Utica, Mississippi, on the unceded territories of the Natchez, the Chahta Yakni (Choctaw), and the O-ga-xpa Ma-zho. My family of schoolhouse teachers, Christian preachers, builders, growers, bridge makers, plantation owners, storytellers, and cultural producers have lived in this community at the foot of the Mississippi Delta for eight generations.

I don't recall when my work as a cultural producer began, but I do remember I began to think more consciously about my contributions during my college years at the University of Mississippi. It was there, in 1996, that my brother Maurice S. Turner II and I decided to form the group M.U.G.A.B.E.E., an acronym for Men Under Guidance Acting Before Early Extinction. Our sound was part Harlem jazz, part southern gospel and jook-joint blues, and indelibly influenced by the emergence of hip-hop as a global genre. Our process of making and sharing and community building was influenced by John O'Neal, Hollis Watkins, Nayo Watkins, Fannie Lou Hamer, Alice Lovelace, Linda Parris-Bailey, the Highlander Research and Education Center, and Alternate ROOTS, among others.

I don't remember when or where I met Jan Cohen-Cruz, but I feel like as long as I have known Alternate ROOTS, I have been within her sphere. Many of the artists interviewed for this book are now or have been my mentors, teachers, collaborators, and friends. Being part of the ROOTS family exposed me to a community of artists and practitioners that has become my foundation for learning and growing my own work. Jan has made a gigantic contribution to this field and to making sure that the work has been documented and shared across both academic and community spaces, providing a consistent platform for learning, critique, and refinement. I feel like Jan is always asking the same questions. Why do we do this work? And how can we, in understanding the collective why, evolve our work?

I have not yet had the opportunity to meet Rad Pereira in person, but I have learned from the powerful voice they have etched on the pages of this manuscript. Rad honors the long precolonial, cross-cultural tradition of this work, reminding us that the values of collective action, community healing, and creativity are ancient practices that undergird the foundation of our contemporary community cultural development landscape. And in communities of color, this work has traditionally been about advancing cultural practices; it has now become our primary methodology for surviving white supremacy.

This book intentionally complicates attempts to narrowly define socially engaged performance. It centers the voices of practitioners to understand more about their pedagogy, experiences, values, and work. Those voices emanate from the manuscript to create space for a dialogue across the various ways of practice, from which emerges a more complete picture of how this field grows and why the work of these artists is shaping the next iteration of stories and influences.

In 2017, my partner, Brandi, and I founded the Mississippi Center for Cultural Production in my home community. This space, which focuses on community-centered design, cultural production, and community development, uses food and story as binders for collective transformation. This institution is grounded in many of the values and theories of change written about in this book. I consider it required reading for our continued growth. Thank you, Jan and Rad!

In Solidarity, Carlton Turner
Utica, Mississippi, May 30, 2021

Foreword

by Jill Dolan

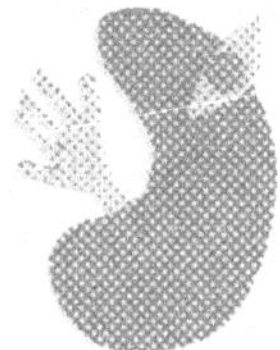

Reading these accounts of creative, entrepreneurial, socially engaged performance over the last five decades brings me a great deal of joy. The isolation of the COVID-19 pandemic year, which demanded we stay physically distant from one another, clarifies the urgent need for the physically present, intimate, local yet widely resounding performance art to which Jan and Rad testify and which they honor here.

These artists' dedication to staging meaningful live interactions with impact beyond the moment sings from these pages. More than ever, we need this work to remind us of the possibilities of our common humanity, which is perhaps best realized in physical proximity, where we can experience moments of potential by breathing, together.

The political moment also bespeaks the need for such a deep and detailed account of these decades of performance focused on social change. After four years of the most divisive, destructive presidential administration in American history, the United States has few models for engaged civil discourse and argumentation.

The performance work *Meeting the Moment* recounts offers strategies for face-to-face interaction born in curiosity and creativity, respect and joy. These artists make performance in communities where their commitments run deep; their art determines to make a difference within the specifics of place in ways that extend profitably elsewhere. We need these exemplary stagings of argument and disagreement, alignment and accord. We need live performance to show us how to embrace the possible. Performance allows us to imagine the potential of the future, even as we debate the best way forward, standing beside one another, engaging one another's palpable humanity.

When I teach courses about theater and social change, students inevitably wonder how the possibilities offered by live performance, situated so inexorably in a particular time and place for a unique collection of spectators, can promote more widespread cultural transformation. I urge them to take the long view, represented here by the collected testimony to performances that did just that.

The project of achieving real social equity across every metric of power is historic, attenuated, and inevitably intergenerational, as this book attests. Social change ebbs and flows, advances and retreats, as we continue the fight for real equality. I appreciate performances that urge me to experience *now* through a determined illustration of a *when* and that move my own and others' imaginations from the *as is* toward the more hopeful, capacious contours of the *as if.*

Rabbi Abraham Joshua Heschel, the great human rights activist who linked his arm with that of Martin Luther King, Jr., in the 1965 Selma to Montgomery civil rights march, spoke of the need to adopt an attitude of *radical amazement.* Heschel said, "Our goal should be to live life in radical amazement . . . to get up in the morning and look at the world in a way that takes nothing for granted. Everything is phenomenal; everything is incredible; never treat life casually. To be spiritual is to be amazed."

The stunning performances recounted in this book promote pleasure and wonder and offer incremental pathways toward lasting social change. I hope as readers, spectators, and artists, you are radically amazed and heed their clarion call.

Jill Dolan
Princeton, New Jersey, June 2021

Introduction

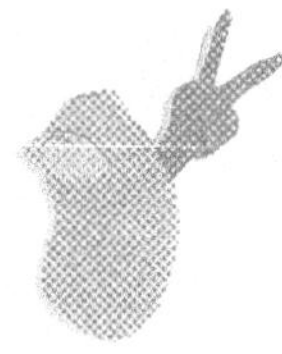

A richly diverse range of socially engaged theater and performance has regularly appeared at places all across the United States, often unknown by anyone beyond its immediate participants. Sometimes the cause has been a lack of information—teenagers, for example, making work together on justice themes, had no idea, and were not likely to learn in school, about the long tradition of political theater. Sometimes it is terminology—people who identify with social practice, creative placemaking/placekeeping, ensemble theater, or grassroots or community-based performance do not realize that they have a lot in common with one another. It may be the place-based nature of the project, made for its specific locale. Race, class, and cultural differences have kept people apart, with few artists from one tradition knowing much about the practices of the others, with the exception of a largely white Euro-American canon that formally educated artists were supposed to have studied but that, as defined, has outlived its historical moment.

Jan was motivated to write this book to connect these instances of socially engaged theater and performance, explore parallel concerns, and interrogate differences during the period that I have been following it, 1965–2020, through the reflections of practitioners who have lived it. While there have always been artists working directly in relationship to

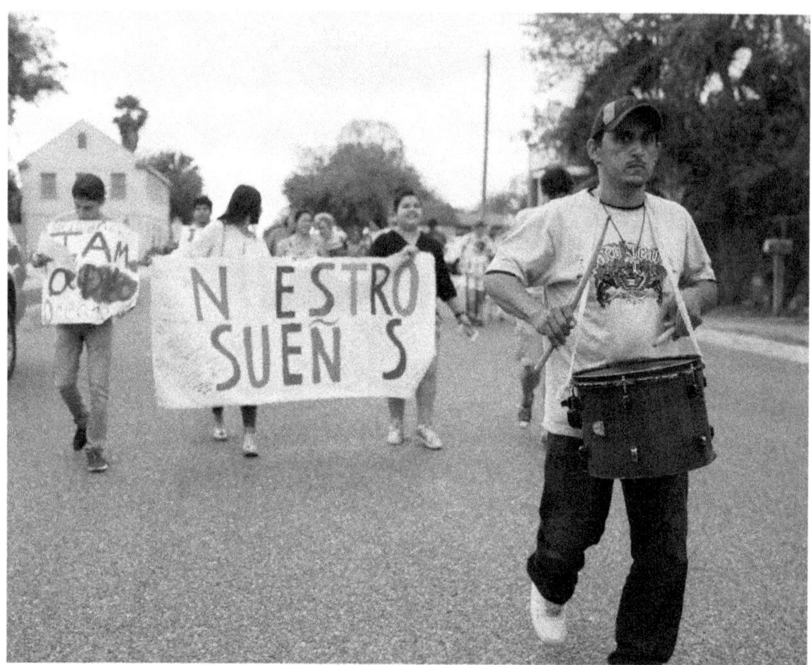

Las Imaginistas' first Dream Parade, 2018. Participants attended dreaming workshops prior to the event and made signage for their visions of a future, more equitable, decolonized city of Brownsville, Texas. The project led to the development of numerous community-initiated plans for a more equitable future, including a suite of legislative proposals to support low-income microvendors, which as of this writing were in the final stages of review by the Brownsville City Commission. Photo by Veronica Cardenas. Courtesy of Las Imaginistas (www.lasimaginistas.com).

their communities, the great social movements that galvanized the country around first African American and then other groups' civil rights, the war in Vietnam, and the nuclear threat set the performance ecosystem since the mid-1960s spinning. And while the term itself, *socially engaged performance,* is imperfect—performance by definition is conceived with at least one actor and one spectator and usually well more, so how can it not be socially engaged?—this working definition has served as a guide point:

> Socially engaged performance involves expressive behavior that is overtly positioned both inside and outside of art contexts. It is dis-

tinguished by expansive ideas of (1) who makes it: artists involving others in their projects for what they know or are part of rather than only for their art skills per se; (2) why it is being made: taking place for reasons related to participants' social conditions, celebrations, or struggles rather than strictly to realize an individual artist's vision; (3) what is made: using artistic tools to shape something that may or may not look like a conventional performance product (e.g., a play or dance composition) in response to a communal desire; and (4) whom it is for: an active relationship to its desired public/community, usually happening at a place that a broad range of people will feel comfortable attending, whether or not it is in a specially designated performance space.

Meet the Writers

We begin with Jan as our narrator:

Jan: My grandparents were Eastern European Jews who fled pogroms and sought assimilation in the United States. I grew up in a white neighborhood of Reading, Pennsylvania, because the region's Pennsylvania Dutch was close enough to my people's Yiddish to conduct business. I left home at age fifteen. Coming of age in the late-1960s and 1970s, I did experimental and street theater and facilitated workshops with people in a mind-blowing range of circumstances, including men in a maximum-security prison and teenagers in a psychiatric facility. My performance knowledge came from lived experience and formal study; in the early 1980s, I was part of the first class of the Department of Performance Studies at NYU. I have lived a hyphenated existence, in rural Pennsylvania and (urban) New York City, employed by universities and on-the-ground community-based cultural projects. Working as a socially engaged performer, then teacher, and then writer into the 1980s, 1990s, and early 2000s provided a prismatic perspective on the field.

I initially tried to write a book using my particular path as a through line and entry into this vast territory. It proved to be a bad idea, as my experience is such an infinitesimally small door into this diverse and massive subject. That's when my friend Dana Edell suggested I conduct interviews with people in the field. I'd been around a long time and Dana was sure that a lot of artists would allow me to interview them. And they did. So I began.

My mental tagline was fifty-five artists in fifty-five years. (We eventually interviewed sixty-seven people, had substantial email exchanges with another half a dozen, and extended the book's purview to May 2021, so fifty-five and a half years.) Through the direct accounts of people who were involved, I hoped to come up with a big picture (though certainly not conclusive; a book, not an encyclopedia) of what has constituted U.S. socially engaged performance over these years, with attention to values in the field and how dynamics that are commonplace today came to be as they are. I was interested in how the field has changed and how it has stayed the same. The conversational mode of diverse theater and performance people captures the excitement of learning that is generated from what bell hooks describes as "our interest in one another, in hearing one another's voices, in recognizing one another's presence" (hooks 1994, 8), and would, I believed, expand available sources of field knowledge.

Having begun the interviews in February 2020, I found myself, a few weeks later, in conversation with performance makers also responding to the pandemic, the quarantine, and, over the months that followed, the spotlight on exacerbated police violence against people of color. As I had witnessed in the 1960s, times of crisis exact a terrible toll, especially on people with the least to lose, but also inspire the greatest imaginings. And artists are always on those front lines.

Coauthoring with Rad

Around thirty interviews in, I realized that I could not write the book alone. I have been at a distance from the making of performance in recent years and did not know whom to approach particularly from the past ten years. And while married to a "Nuyorican" (someone born in New York City whose parents are from Puerto Rico), who has made me more sensitive to diverse cultures, and being the mother of twins, who have kept my feet on the ground, I am a white, middle-class, formally educated septuagenarian who carries the baggage and privilege of those identities. I sought an artist/thinker who could complement my effort, but from the perspective of a much younger generation, and grounded in different cultural markers. I found that in Rad Pereira.

I quickly appreciated Rad's nonhierarchical ways of relating to people of all ages and their openness to all who cross their path. (Authors' Note: Rad is the "their" of this sentence. We use gender-specific pronouns based on how people identify throughout this book.) Rad's mother is Brazilian and their father is a Russian Jew, which in Rad's case has led to a broad and intimate understanding of diversity, denying no part of their ancestry. Further, Rad's commitment to performance, policy, teaching, and social justice are aligned with the purposes of this book.

• • •

Rad: In my youth, I was often told I was too much, too many things, too big. As an entirely diasporic body and queer spirit, I came to know that my many paths in life and art would be multidimensional, complex, and at times confusing. Strict definitions and delineations of artistic mediums could not contain me; my interests ranged from performance to decolonization/re-indigenization to urban planning to healing and system change.

I am of Pindorama, Abya Yala (currently known as Brazil), a mixed-race descendant of African diasporic, Indigenous Brazilian, and Ashkenazi Jewish refugees. When my family and I immigrated to Turtle Island (the country currently called the United States) in 1997, I found camaraderie with the Jamaican and Haitian cafeteria ladies in Seminole and Miccosukee land (Plantation, Florida), whose stories and laughter reminded me of my aunties, and with the rabbis who endlessly debated me at Hebrew school.

As I grew, my mentors became my first Black acting teacher, who introduced me to liberation work, and the radical elder Communist man I worked with in the mailroom in high school. They celebrated and informed all my contradictions and interests, my queerness, my brownness, my mixedness, my unnameable wisdoms and curiosities, by asking questions, encouraging my spirit to go deeper, and flaming the fires of my boldness to have the courage to disagree and say no.

My mother is a radical community organizer. She has always invited me to question my perceived reality, as well as the systems that uphold it, which are often exploitative. She encouraged me to stick with the other "underdogs," stand up for ourselves, and fight to make our own ways. My father instilled in me the ability to make friends with anyone through charm, laughter, and the resourcefulness to find what I needed anywhere in the world. The interpersonal and systemic power dynamics between my parents were a microcosm for the ways the world works, who has access to what and why, who has power where, and how power is kept or shared. Being raised between cultures, between countries, between worlds allowed me a quantum view of the realities around me and provided the prism through which I perceive the interplay between society and art.

I was desperate to start acting professionally when we moved to this country, and I tried as hard as I could to bend and contort myself to fit into the status quo in an industry that wanted people in the shape of the categories they deemed valuable. The traumatic spiritual and psychological consequences led me to grow disillusioned with the industry by the time I was a freshman in college in Lenapehoking (specifically in so-called New York City). My dreams of Broadway and Hollywood shattered in front of me and slid down into the gutters of this place that has embraced my transformation.

My worldview was radicalized as I learned more about queerness, intergenerational exchange, Indigenous wisdom, dual power, decolonial existence, healing, antipsychology, Third Cinema, Black womanism, Third World/trans feminism, abolition, land stewardship, care, and tenderness through devised theater, cocreation processes, performance art, political theater, nonviolent direct action, immersive/participatory performance, and multimedia experiences. I started figuring out how to weave together my politics and values with my art and the way I move through the world.

When I met Jan in 2016, I felt the possibility of a life dedicated to interweaving ethics, education, politics, equity, and art. Jan was amazing in the way she could talk to all different types of people and synthesize analysis that could transform systems. Jan has helped me to understand my value by encouraging me to bring together all my different passions. She told me about this book and I was committed to supporting it in any way I could.

I perceived a lack of connection between artists and community leaders doing this work—from urban planners to architects to journalists to dancers—those who are looking for ways to use the arts toward self-determination to build, heal, deepen, and/or keep their communities alive and thriving through upholding values of sovereignty, justice, and joy. This seemed to result in an *invisibility of possibility* to enhance their efforts through coalition and collaboration. Socially engaged art, to me, is a way to walk as we dream our way through many of our current social issues: alienation, isolation, privatization, and dehumanization by corporate globalization, which often manifest through destructive systems, behaviors, and catastrophes in our world. It both saddened and emboldened me to hear my theater students, various LGBTQIA2+ youth, and fellow professional artists complain about their career prospects, the solitary life that pursuing it might bring, the lack of financial security, and their inability to articulate the beautiful value they brought to the world. Socially engaged theater and performance makers deserve to be valued for our transformative impact, power, community-created knowledge, and potential to empower our communities to articulate and enact a caring, nurturing world.

• • •

We are both fluid in how we integrate our knowledge and practice, and have foregrounded a range of interviewees addressing a range of topics from multiple perspectives. We invite you to go with the flow and feel it with your entire body, not just your mind. We imagined a kind of implicit dialogue on the page between the interviewees and ourselves. The interviewees lead and we reflect on key ideas. We looked to position ourselves nonprescriptively; nonetheless, we did not aspire to neutrality. We advocate for the integration of one's values in one's work, values that vary but share certain principles, such as "try to do no harm," "cultivate brave spaces," "embrace people in a range of circumstances," and "recognize the value of multiple aesthetic systems," which we also sought to do in our writing of this book. In an effort to be trustworthy guides, we have peppered the text with stories from our own experience, revealing shortsightedness at some moments, and rising to the occasion at others.

We intended for the first-person accounts of the interviewees to provide accessible inroads to our subject. In keeping with this choice, the pronouns *I* and *we* in this book refer to Jan and Rad; we have not written in the third person as distant scholars. Moreover, we do not always agree. Generationally, Jan has become cynical of the sweeping language of care and the too often unsubstantiated profession of high values, having seen it used in so many self-serving ways (e.g., advertisements proclaiming you have a friend in such and such a multicorporation.) For Rad, such language must be reclaimed and embodied.

In seeking to address a broad readership, parts of the book will be of greater interest and, conversely, possibly off-putting to some readers while very important to include for others. Some of the social movements that our interviewees discussed were violent and hurtful to whole groups of people; some readers may not want to go there, while others may encounter bits of history that they are avid to pursue. We ask readers to understand why we have included such a range of material and urge them to find their way through it as their intuitions guide them.

The Artists We Interviewed

While our working definition of socially engaged performance provided a basis for whom to approach for interviews, we still faced a wonderfully deep pool with too many people to draw from. To further focus our choices, we sought diversity in terms of the following:

- ***When*** in the period between 1965 and 2020 someone had done their work, and in relationship to what major currents of that time
- ***How*** they contextualized their practice, be it with specific communities, formally or informally, and/or institutions like regional theater, civic agencies, collaboratives like ensemble theater, or social movements

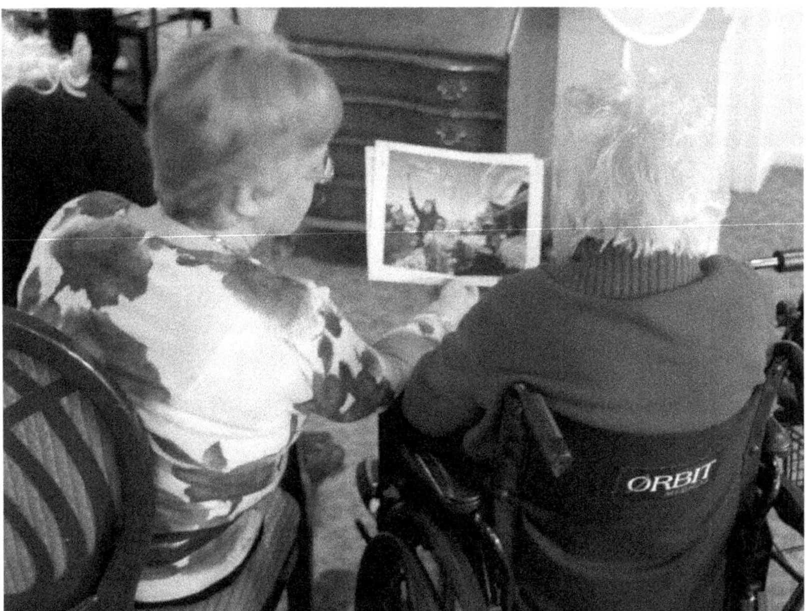

A TimeSlips certified facilitator shares an image prompt with an elder during a TimeSlips creative engagement session. Courtesy of TimeSlips. Copyright 2021. (The photo was taken in 2016.)

- ***Who*** the artists are in terms of their self-defined race, gender, sexuality, politics, dis/ability, cultural, geographical, and aesthetic grounding
- ***Where*** they work as an expression of their values and mission
- ***Why*** they do art that expands conventional parameters

Some of the interviewees are well known because of their national work and their published writing; others practice in very localized contexts, beyond which they are not known, but they are not less insightful for that. In fact, it is important in a field like this to celebrate those who work without national attention, especially since the arts and a Western hero culture put so much stock in being well known. This is a field that needs people committed to their local stomping ground; we are honored to have spoken with so many people whose local work is a beacon. And in order to include artists whom we did not know, Jan invited readers of HowlRound, a digital commons for theater and performance makers, to respond to a questionnaire, whose findings have also been included here. We spoke largely with artists who initiate or coinitiate projects, but we did not interview other participants, as integral as they are, because of time and space limitations. We've included brief bios of everyone we interviewed (see About the Contributors). The quotes themselves have been lightly edited for clarity. All interviews were carried out by Jan or Rad between February 2020 and April 2021. In the interest of text flow, we do not include citation information when we quote the interviewees.

Through Lines

The book's dominant through lines arose from the questions the interviewees most pursued. Then the insightful Lanxing Fu and Liz Lerman, who, like the two of us, are some forty years apart in age, read a draft of the entire manuscript. Liz commented, "Is this book about everything?" That response captured the challenge of taking on such a substantial body of work and chunk of time. We then reread the interviews, paying attention to the threads that seemed most evocative to interviewees, and became more deliberate about foregrounding the following lines of thought:

1. Meeting the Moment

Socially engaged artists make and remake processes all the time to meet their contexts, the people the work is for and with, the particular circumstances of those people at specific phases of their lives (such as the example of TimeSlips, described in the caption above), the times, and the artists' and communities' goals. There is not one way to make art; it is emergent and responsive to the moment. We try to capture this fluidity and also to address the challenges related to there seldom being enough money, time, or public understanding of what they are doing as art.

When something works, there's a tendency to want to institutionalize it, but the power may actually be in meeting the moment. Theater and performance makers are particularly well equipped to recognize this dynamic, being versed in adaptability, presence, and spontaneity. Relatedly, the contextual specificity of much socially engaged art means releasing oneself from hierarchical thinking that puts universality first no matter what. That same specificity means that artists learn to balance their purpose and the community's needs and desires.

2. Prioritizing Usefulness in Performance Making

We contextualize this book in a long tradition of usefulness as a natural component of art. We do not see the notions of *art* and *usefulness* as opposing. Whether to impart a people's history, celebrate or grieve at significant moments in a community's life, or simply to bring about regeneration after a busy workweek, art has long integrated usefulness as part of its purview, and can be at the same time formally rigorous and community-minded. Rather, we recognize usefulness along a continuum, present in a given art project to a lesser or greater degree.

By *usefulness,* we mean doing something concrete and of value in the context of its intended community. Creator of Theatre of the Oppressed Augusto Boal's idea of metaxis is helpful here: a space where the image of reality is the reality of the image; art with real-world consequences, at once symbolic and efficacious.

Usefulness brings up the idea of the political. We see the political as part of all art, in how a given project is situated publicly. A performance may express no overt ideology and still be political in as much as it is made available to and created by a particular group of people, who undertook some process to make decisions, received resources or not on some basis, and is evaluated by some criteria.

3. Diversity: Its Joys, Discontents, and Promise

We approach diversity as a process including, for example, who are considered artists, how they are educated and supported, how work is made, what content is deemed valuable and how it is brought to bear, how audiences are welcome and which ones, and whether or not intergenerational and intercultural exchange are encouraged and why. The expressive cultures of diverse people are as varied as their experiences necessarily are, given that equity has not characterized U.S. life. While at this time, whole sectors of public life are out of reach for whole groups of people, most can participate in the culture of the groups with which they identify. Arts and cultural experiences related to one's identity provide a way for even the most socially marginalized people to recognize, celebrate, heal, and organize themselves. They can self-identify rather than be pigeonholed from the outside.

Terms of identification change. As the ways we relate to one another evolve and our understanding of the differences and similarities in our experiences deepens, so, too, do terms adapt to our expanding consciousness. For example, the terms *people of color, minorities, marginalized people, historically excluded, system-oppressed, colonized people,* and more recently *BIPOC* (Black, Indigenous, and people of color) entered the common vocabulary as a way to recognize racial diversity beyond a Black/white binary. More recently, the term *global majority* has been favored by some as a way to decenter whiteness, but it leaves out First Nations people. Cherokee community cultural worker and theater maker Delanna Studi notes that she sees more inclusion of Native voices since the advent of the term *BIPOC,* because if the *I* in BIPOC is not represented, the term cannot be used (Studi in conversation with Pereira, May 19, 2021). In this book, we use the term *BIPOC* when it is appropriate and try to be clear when talking about specific racial, ethnic, and/or cultural experiences.

We are also interested in diverse *practices,* and recognize that they are not viewed equally by most of those controlling material resources for arts and culture in the United States. So when artists whose work aligns with mainstream criteria draw from lesser-viewed cultural practices, it may be intended as a compliment but is in fact appropriation. It's a way of saying, "We want to take parts of your art and use it in ways *we* deem worthwhile." On the other hand, all the art that has ever been created is a vast cultural commons. When does drawing on forms of expression from other cultures bespeak appropriation and when respect?

Diversity is also expressed in the various broad generational tendencies of socially engaged performance. These include the oppositional energy of the 1960s–mid 1970s counterculture, cultural identity-based solo work of the 1980s, dialogue-driven work of the 1980s and 1990s, cross-sector collaborations of the first two decades of the twenty-first century, and the explosion of digital performance and sense of racial reckoning in the context of the pandemic of 2020. Some formats cut across these decades, such as the continuity of plays and dance compositions (albeit within a range of aesthetic frameworks) at one end of the spectrum and using artists' tools and capacities in initiatives that are about process, not product, on the other. Diversity is also apparent in the contexts we write about, from community-based to ensembles to regional theater to cross-sector civic collaborations.

Diversity is a main ingredient of evolution. As the Earth leaves the Anthropocene and enters the Ecocene—a move from the current geological age, during which human activity has been the dominant influence on climate and the environment, to an ecologically sustainable era necessary for the planet's survival—we need to care for and about the diversity of all forms of life and our relationship with them (Dougherty 2020). We are interested in how this idea translates into performance making.

Key Terms Running Through the Book

Within these three through lines, a number of terms frequently recur. In addition to *usefulness, the political,* and *BIPOC,* discussed above, they include *theater, performance, art, culture, aesthetics, and ethics/values.* People inherit words and ideas differently, creating a fluidity of meaning specific to their respective experiences. We will try to hold several meanings of these key terms, including some that are contradictory.

By *theater,* we mean a consciously expressive enactment by at least one person as intentionally viewed by at least one other person. Theater tends be a collaborative form drawing on text and movement at the very least; *performance* is a larger frame, also including dance, the live making of music for at least one listener, as well as the enormous territory of expressive behavior, such as ritual enactments, a salesperson trying to convince a client to buy something, how we present ourselves in public situations, and so much more that, like theater, performance is an entire field of study.

Art, encompassing performance as well as other forms, such as visual and written expression, pertains to how and on what basis work expressive of an individual or a group is shaped (process) and what is made for various people to witness (product) in the realm of feeling and the senses. *Culture* is a whole realm of meaning making, including art and extending into areas like the specific food, clothing, and ways of behavior by which groups of people identify themselves.

We began with the idea of *aesthetics* as fixed criteria of how artists reach the public through the senses; *an*aesthetics as a *numbing* of the senses is a reminder of this slippery word's sensory root. The artists in this book present visions and versions of aesthetics that leave fixed criteria behind in order to meet the moment, find their art's usefulness, and draw from the cultural springs most meaningful to their circumstances. Bertolt Brecht is a classic example of a theater theorist who developed a political/politicized aesthetics to fit his goals (Willett 1957); theater makers who are at once active organizers, such as those who were involved in ACT UP, the AIDS Coalition to Unleash Power, exemplify aestheticizing politics.

Lumbee philosopher Bryan Brayboy's formulation of aesthetics as "*what a people* see as the beautiful, good, and true" (Brayboy 2021) became our touchstone for the idea of aesthetics. In some cultures, aesthetic experiences are associated with people of a particular education and of a particular class, whereas in others, aesthetics are completely braided with usefulness and meaning for the entire community. Brayboy's culturally specific articulation of aesthetics became a key component of the book's diversity thread.

Simon Blackburn understands *ethics* as a "climate of ideas about how to live. It determines what we find acceptable or unacceptable, admirable or contemptible. . . . It gives us . . . our standards of behaviour" (Blackburn 2001, 1). This explanation of ethics is aligned with Brayboy's concept of aesthetics in that both are community-specific.

Our sense of ethics involves both individual expression in how a person lives their values and a culturally accepted code of guidelines designating right from wrong. We see capitalism in the context of ethics in the United States—an imperative to make money, leading to practices that clash with how many individual artists view right and wrong, such as the

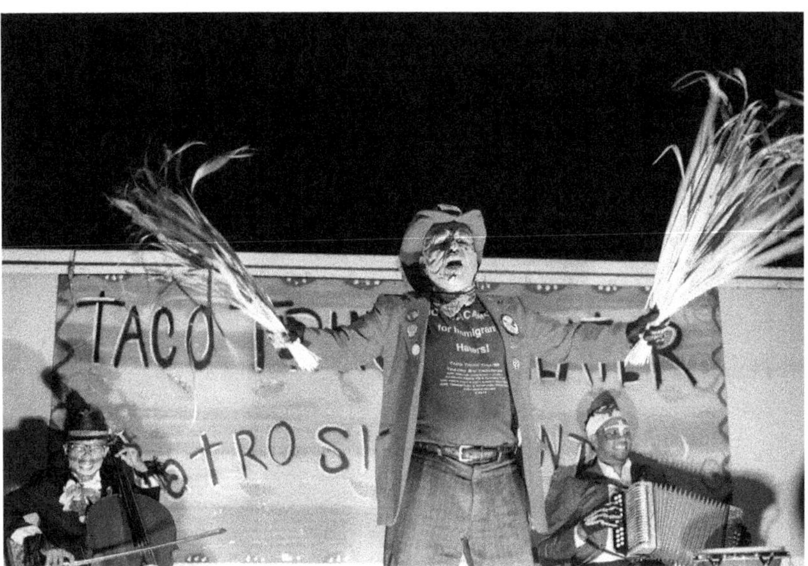

Taco Truck Theater Ensemble performing at the Contemporary Arts Center, New Orleans, 2019. Left to right: Spirit McIntyre, José Torres-Tama (lead performance artist and poet), and Fermin Ceballos. The Taco Truck Theater was an inventive dinner theater on wheels ensemble performance that addressed anti-immigrant hysteria and drew a parallel between the struggles of Latine people dehumanized as "illegal aliens" and the historical challenges of unarmed African Americans killed by white police officers. Photo by Cfreedom Photography. Copyright José Torres-Tama & ArteFuturo Productions (https://torrestama.com/taco-truck-theater.html).

inevitably of competition and overly monolithic criteria for excellence. Moreover, as "interpretative artists," actors often lack agency to create work that expresses their own values, and are expected to serve producers, playwrights, and directors. Many of our interviewees emphasized the importance of aligning their values with their creative expression and gave it as a reason that they were drawn to socially engaged art. We've included a few notable occasions over the past fifty-five years when behaviors considered simply the way things are were revealed to be ethically flawed.

The Book's Organization

The book is organized thematically. The interviews led us to this choice, as we heard how artists from different generations have dealt with similar issues. We found these recurring issues more engaging than a straightforward chronology. The thematic structure signals that the book is in no way all-encompassing but, rather, delves into selected issues that have remained relevant to socially engaged artists over these fifty-five years.

We sequenced the chapters as follows, within three parts:

PART I: (Re)Grounding is about where socially engaged performance makers are coming from in three senses—historically, philosophically, and pedagogically.

> **Chapter 1: Legacies** is a compilation of individually significant markers from the history of socially engaged performance, from the perspective of artists in the United States whom we spoke with who have lived it; the tellingly diverse historical influences that have inspired and set a direction for the work they have done at some time in the past fifty-five years.
>
> **Chapter 2: Commitments** underlies what all the performance makers in this book share: the equal pull to art making *and* engagement with particular communities beyond the immediate experience of the performance. Many of the artists we spoke with have often felt perceived as either art makers or social activists, as if they could not be both.
>
> **Chapter 3: Education** is about how socially engaged performance makers have learned what they needed in order to do their work, and the obstacles they have faced. It emphasizes underlying values and the dialectic between formal and informal modes of learning.

PART II: (Re)Mapping Community focuses on two clusters of challenges that come with the territory of U.S. socially engaged performance since the mid-1960s.

> **Chapter 4: Changing Notions of Who "We" Are** traces changing attitudes between 1965 and 2020 about what socially engaged performers may make and with whom because of their race, circumstances, class, gender/sexuality, and other identity grounders. It reflects on choices that performance makers have made around identity over these years.
>
> **Chapter 5: Community-Centric Civic Collaborations** explores the unfolding of creative placemaking/placekeeping—artists embedded in

community-development initiatives collaborating with public agencies and the people they impact—particularly from 2010 to 2020. Featured are examples of municipal-artist collaborations and the particular challenge of devising art projects with the police.

PART III: (Re)Generativity consists of two chapters about how the past and present recounted in this book lead to an aspirational future.

Chapter 6: A (Re)Generative Life in Art asks how lives equally committed to art and social justice find not just support but also renewal. Springboarding from a 2003 Urban Institute report and its 2016 reaffirmation by the NEA about six elements that sustain the artist's life, this chapter emphasizes regenerativity and aspiration within and beyond the current social and political framework.

Chapter 7: The Year Was 2020 traces theater and performance makers' responses to building pressure beginning in March 2020 with the quarantine, the threat of COVID-19, more visibility of police violence toward Black people, and efforts to find ways to meet this moment. The focus is a range of initiatives and in many cases a new sense of their work as part of the reckoning that many theater and performance makers have engaged in during this most tumultuous of years.

* * *

One of our hopes is that through this book, more socially engaged theater and performance people speak themselves into the archive, filling gaps in a field that is itself often marginalized in mainstream theater accounts.

PART I
(Re)Grounding

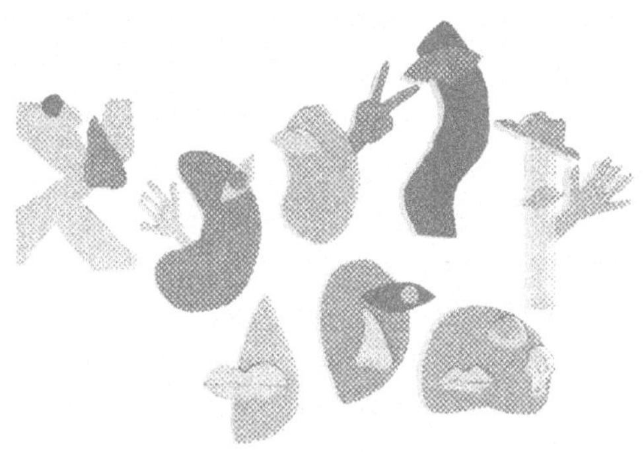

1 Legacies

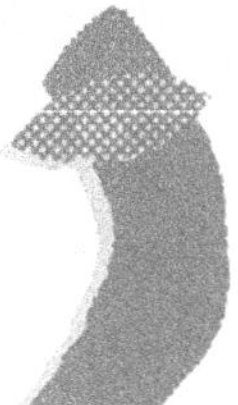

Overview

Our interviewees were Black, Native American, Asian diasporic, African American, white, LGBTQIA2+ (lesbian, gay, queer, trans, intersex, asexual, two spirit, and more), heterosexual, disabled and able-bodied, immigrant, Jewish, Muslim, and more. One of the first questions we asked them regarded socially engaged theater and performance from the past that has had the most impact on them. Their responses revealed a multiplicity of influences, not one unified narrative. They cited personally meaningful artistic practices and movements aligned with their sense of themselves and, often, that had been inclusive of and meaningful to their ancestors.

It was crucial for many interviewees to see their cultural or racial lineage represented in performances from the past. Nearly every artist of color with whom we spoke cited the importance to them of the Harlem Renaissance (the Harlem-centered cultural and artistic movement from the end of World War I through the mid-1930s [Lewis 1994]) and the Black Arts movement (a group of politically engaged Black poets, artists, theater makers, musicians, and writers between 1965 and 1975 who emerged out of the Black Power movement [Neal 1968]).

For artists situated in small towns or rural expanses, it was critical to recognize culture outside large cities. The value of regionally based expression and the notion of grassroots arts that grow out of the place they are situated, as articulated in the 1940s by Robert Gard (Gard 1999) and others, was raised up and remains a source of meaning.

Some interviewees found aesthetic inspiration in practices that were not from their personal heritage or even fully in tune with their politics. For example, a number of artists were smitten by scale, as in the early-twentieth-century U.S. pageantry movement, engaging scores of longtime residents and new arrivals in the enactment of a town's history. They were nonetheless critical of a dominant idea of that movement—that immigrants leave behind their ancestral cultures to assimilate into a national identity, expressed in some instances by literally changing from traditional wear to American clothes before a performance's end (Mehler 2010).

Some interviewees who favor the production of plays equally or more than process-oriented activities, such as participatory drama workshops, were heartened by the Group Theatre, a collective based in New York City and formed in 1931 by Harold Clurman, Cheryl Crawford, and Lee Strasberg. The Group Theatre straddled a commitment to especially new dramatic literature *and* support for people struggling, of which there were many, its being the Great Depression. Artists influenced by the Group Theatre also tended to recognize the ensemble theater movement in the United States in more recent years as bedrock for their own work (https://howlround.com/what-we-talk-about-when-we-talk-about-ensemble-theatre), which has often begun with the production of plays and expanded through engagement with a local community that they have gotten to know by living there.

Some artists we spoke with moved to the United States from elsewhere and were inspired by practices from their homeland. Meena Natarajan and Dipankar Mukherjee, codirectors of the Pangea World Theater, located in Minneapolis, had been part of the robust street theater of their native India, and were influenced by leading figures there, including Badal Sircar and Safdar Hashmi. Other artists found inspiration in companies they originally saw on tour and in some cases went on to collaborate with, such as Kathy Randels vis-à-vis Dah Teatar from the former Yugoslavia. Still others studied international theater makers, including the Polish theorist and director Jerzy Grotowski, and did work in that spirit. And partly due to the rise of Performance Studies in the 1980s, some recognized a broader swath of expressive activity as performance, whether they encountered it at home or abroad, such as Native American and African American rituals, that they may have hitherto thought of as anthropology or ethnography.

Other recurrent sources of inspiration were ensembles born of social movements. El Teatro Campesino was created in 1965 by Luis Valdez in conjunction with California farmworkers struggling for Chicano rights; the Free Southern Theater was founded in 1963 by John O'Neal, Doris Derby, and Gilbert Moses as an artistic wing to African American civil rights. More recently, Occupy Wall Street and Black Lives Matter have been sources of inspiration. Another activist thread has been theater makers focused on participatory *processes,* such as Augusto Boal and Theatre of the Oppressed, a set of techniques he first elaborated in the 1970s in Brazil, which remain a creative means for participants to become active subjects seeking solutions to social injustices they face.

For some who grew up in the 1950s and 1960s, the intense theatricality all around in response to civil rights, the war in Vietnam, and other pressing concerns manifested what performance can do in everyday life, for better or for worse. Jan recalls:

> One day when I was seven or eight years old, I was jumping on my parents' bed, in their room on the top floor of our house in Reading, Pennsylvania. Looking out the window, I saw my neighbor Al Salette's yard, seemingly on fire; just two doors down, a cross was burning in his yard. I finally got someone to explain that Al Salette had been part of demonstrations to integrate the lunch counter at the five-and-ten downtown. I later came to understand acts like the cross burning as public performances, intended for audiences. They were deliberately staged in public to be seen. Their concrete impact did not disqualify

> them from being performances; performance did not need to be only symbolic but could also have a direct impact.

Artist-activist Ricardo Gamboa grew up on the South Side of Chicago in a Mexican American family in the 1990s. Gamboa was an activist since their adolescence and close friends with the activist children of assassinated Chicago community activist Rudy Lozano. They describe the Black Panthers, a Black political organization founded in 1966 to challenge brutality against the African American community, in a way that parallels the cross burning as performance, albeit to radically different ends:

> The Black Panthers were arguably doing arts activism when they dressed up [in black berets and black leather jackets] and were inspired by Amiri Baraka and Black Aesthetic theater. There was costume: Their new type of uniform signaled their militancy. There were props—the guns, the Constitution—they would carry around. There were high theatrics.

Such performances are intentional threats, the cross burnings warning spectators of the power of the Klan and other white supremacists to attack at will, and the Black Panthers warning of repercussions if violence against the Black community persisted. Importantly, the Panthers also carried out their mission to ensure the survival of African Americans and other marginalized people through a Free Breakfast for School Children Program that fed thousands of hungry kids, as well as a popular education series that raised consciousness and awareness. The image of the panther was chosen because it is an animal that does not attack first but if attacked will respond in kind.

Boal cited Spanish Golden Age playwright Lope de Vega (1562–1635) as stating that all that drama requires is a platform, two actors, and a passion. In the context of the civil rights movement, the cross burning fits this description. A suburban yard became a platform to voice a very strong opinion; de Vega's requisite two actors were the one who lit the cross and the one who saw it burn; and the passion was clear. The cross burning attested to how widespread drama is: how ubiquitous its potential platforms, the range of who might be the actors, and what might be the passion. Such dramas do not need to be contained in a theater building and indeed can be far more powerful because of that. The makers of such performances express the perspective of a cultural group. And at the time Jan thought she was growing up in an environment with almost no performance, because she understood performance to necessarily take the form of plays written by individual playwrights and presented in theater buildings.

The sense of performance spilling out of buildings and into the social sphere manifested differently but not less powerfully for theater director and professor Bob Leonard. He was inspired by Shakespeare's relationship to the city of London, which he describes as follows:

> [a] transparency of civic revelation, writing at the birthing of the British Empire and revealing the arrival of the middle class and the shifting of power from the landed aristocracy to the developing capitalist market power base. He had to have been in the middle of all that, not concocting it from some backstage office, and had to be astute enough to hear it. It's odd to think I went to Johnson City, Tennessee, out of a drive to be in the middle of people who are struggling and working and loving and hurting and alive in our time in order to be worth anything. But that seemed, to me, critically important.

So while historical markers vary widely, the impulse to anchor one's professional aspirations to something personally and culturally meaningful is evident in the legacies to which the artists we interviewed are drawn. As the authors of *Theatre Histories* assert, "There are no value-free histories; it is always a matter of what values, and whose, inform a particular historical work" (Zarrilli et al. 2006, xviii). What follows are specific influences at the intersection of personal and cultural identities. There's a lot of information; we invite you to swim in its expansiveness rather than try to tether to every detail. We try to provide an experience for the emotions and the intellect.

A Selected Chronology of Socially Engaged Theater and Performance

The Long Tradition

> **Rad:** At our first interview for the book, Jan asked me where I drew inspiration. I told her that in my youth I thought modern history was like a flower in a vase with shallow roots, commodified. As my perspective deepened, the vase shattered, and the flower proved to have ancient endless roots, blowing open my understanding and forming part of my general radicalization as a human. When I got to New York City in 2006 for college, I wanted a Broadway career and then realized that those artists wanted to be flowers in a vase. Not for me. I want to be part of a huge tree.
>
> Since then, I've been most nourished in understanding how Indigenous communities, my own ancestors included, have used art for thousands of years. It wasn't about pedestalizing one person's genius; it was collective storytelling and story keeping for survival. So many ancient civilizations, which are kept alive through Indigenous people, did not disassociate the philosophical, spiritual, and material realms from art or life. In Abya Yala (Latin America), there's also no protest without artists; they are some of the biggest activists, and don't disentangle themselves from their communities. To even have to call something "community-based art" is fucked-up. What is the purpose of art at all?

Carlton Turner, Black artist and organizer, whose current work integrates the arts and agriculture, understands art and culture as a form of ritual, making us recognizable to others and to ourselves:

> Art has been around as long as human consciousness. Culture is how we recognize a people—by their rituals, dances, and songs, as they began to be in relationship to a place in a more intimate way, through the seasons, farming, their own specific foods, the solstices, making places of celebration, using visual art, all to locate themselves as a community.

Turner recognizes commonality between cultural anthropology and community-based performance, both grounded in the collective expressivity of everyday life. Cultural anthropologists and ethnographers study how people who share a common cultural system organize, shape the physical and social world around them, and are, in turn, shaped by those ideas, behaviors, and physical environments. Culture, according to anthropologist Clifford Geertz, is "a system of inherited conceptions expressed in symbolic forms by means of which men [*sic*] communicate, perpetuate, and develop their knowledge about and attitudes toward life" (Geertz 1973, 89). Culture teases out meaning in the world and makes the world understandable.

Recognition of performance's ancient roots deeply embedded in many communities weaves through this book. Gloria Miguel, a performer from the Kuna/Rappahannock Nations, noted that she had no historical influences for socially engaged performance because to her, it always existed; she was born into such a worldview about performance. Her family sang, danced, and told stories, just as their parents and generations preceding them had. Coya Paz, founder of the Teatro Luna in Chicago, recounts, "We started making work without understanding that we were actually tapping into a long legacy of people gathering in a circle to share stories to try to shift how certain populations are represented." Relatedly, community-based theater director Kathie deNobriga speaks of the influence of folklorists who wrote down such stories: "Zora Neale Hurston, Paul Green, people who really listened to other people's voices—that's a very strong foundation" for her own very place-based work.

Also running through this book is the age-old interplay of art and politics, well put by Andrew Boyd and Dave Mitchell in their book *Beautiful Trouble*:

> Blending of art and politics is nothing new. Tactical pranks go back at least as far as the Trojan Horse. Jesus of Nazareth, overturning the tables of the money changers, mastered the craft of political theater 2,000 years before Greenpeace. Fools, clowns, and carnivals have always played a subversive role, while art, culture and creative protest

> tactics have for centuries served as fuel and foundation for successful social movements. (Boyd and Mitchell 2016, 1)

We now peruse legacies that our interviewees evoked from the past one hundred–plus years.

Settlement Houses, 1886–Present

Culture can be a deeply grounding continuity in people's lives when they go through extreme external changes. During the waves of immigration to the United States in the late nineteenth century, immigrant cultures were often preserved at settlement houses, beginning with the University Settlement House in New York City in 1886. They were established in poor neighborhoods in big cities across the country both for cultural sustenance and to make educational and social services available to newcomers to these shores. Theater historian Todd London elaborates:

> Everything in the American theater since the late nineteenth century that's not Broadway entertainment or European import actually began in the settlement houses. They created a culture out of other cultures and allowed people to hold on to their ethnic identities even as they butted up against people with other ethnic and national identities. Between Hull House in Chicago, Henry Street on [New York's] Lower East Side, and others, settlement houses are key to the foundations for art theater in America. It was through those spaces that even modern European drama came to this country.

Settlement houses not only helped maintain nationally specific artistic and cultural traditions but also provided places and contexts for people to share these legacies (Jackson 2011).

The Little Theatre Movement, 1912–1925

Influenced by the independent theaters of late-nineteenth-century Europe, seeking social and aesthetic exploration more than material gains, amateur theaters were forming all across the United States, in search of not financial profit and commercial success but artistic and social expression. Known as the Little Theatre Movement, and like the Independent Theatre Movement in Europe, these theatrical companies and the productions they undertook represented an aesthetic break from melodrama in favor of realism, often reflecting on social issues, and characterized by experimentation. These theaters provided a home for a community of artists of various racial and national identities, also making a place for women, possible because they were not professionalized.

The Harlem Renaissance, c. 1918–1937

The Harlem Renaissance was created by African American artists who constituted a critical mass in what was the Black neighborhood of Harlem in uptown New York City. Linked to the civil rights establishment, its purpose, according to historian David Levering Lewis, was to improve race relations, given a backlash against Black people because of their economic advances in the war (Lewis 1994, xv). W. E. B. Du Bois, one of the movement's leaders, believed that recognition of a people's art and their humanity went hand in hand (Lewis, 1994, xvi). Asked about historical markers that influenced them, African American artists Linda Parris-Bailey, Toya Lillard, Ron Bechet, and Carlton Turner all cited the Harlem Renaissance. As Turner puts it:

> I try to understand what was happening in the Harlem Renaissance, in indigenous movements that found ways to operate regardless of what was happening on the larger front regarding race. From those movements I get another side of history that we didn't learn in school that should be helping to contextualize our movements and how we think about our current work.

And yet, of those we spoke with, only Parris-Bailey, who attended an HBCU—historically black college or university—learned about the Harlem Renaissance in school.

The Federal Theatre Project and the Group Theatre, the 1930s

With the Great Depression of the 1930s came a number of progressive initiatives on the part of the federal government to put people back to work in their professions. The Federal Theatre Project (1935–1939), a federation of regional theaters creating work for its particular constituents, did just that for theater artists. Surprisingly for its time, it was directed by a woman, Hallie Flanagan. Naming it as an important influence, Todd London remarks, "Of course. That notion of theater centers developing their own audiences and artists."

Parris-Bailey was most struck by the Federal Theatre Project's relationship to government:

> The Works Progress Administration and Federal Theatre Project were not among my artistic influences but spoke to me as the relationship of art to government and what was possible, making me kind of fearless. Studying the huge figures of the 1930s, the efforts around the country, you knew that what you were doing was possible and was not new.

Carlton Turner avowed, "Eras like the 1930s and 1960s—I don't think about much because Blackness wasn't valued. Those constructs aren't valuable to me." Theater historian Charlotte Canning also critiqued the FTP: "While there is much to say about the FTP as a precedent, it also has a troubling history of racism and exclusion. It was also a top-down model despite seeming very grassroots" (Charlotte Canning in an email to Cohen-Cruz, May 7, 2020).

Groundwater Arts contrasted government support for the arts in the 1930s in the context of the New Deal with its own vision of a Green New Theatre after 2020 as part of an ongoing, systemic power shift beyond a crisis such as the Depression. Its concern is the basis upon which any arts initiative is built, declaring that attention be paid to the foundation: "What we need is decolonization and abolition."

Kathie deNobriga emphasizes the value of the FTP thirty years later:

> If the Federal Theatre Project hadn't been allowed to flourish, things would have been very different, I think, in the 1960s. The FTP was

> seen as dangerous and subversive. The Living Newspaper, the story and song collections, [these] were too robust. It would be interesting to talk to the people who fomented the counterculture of the 1960s and see if the Works Progress Administration [including the FTP] had planted some seeds. There was a lot of interest in the 1930s as a historical movement among my peers.

Jan remarked to deNobriga that their mutual friend Carlton Turner saw the FTP as caring little about people of color, to which she responded:

> Maybe the FTP was predominantly white, but I'd then look to the collection of Slave Narratives that the Federal Writers' Project did [at the same time]. I feel pretty sure he would care about that. It was part of the same impulse of turning to people as source material and experts in their own lives.

For Arlene Goldbard, already a cultural worker in the early 1960s, the sense of the FTP torch passing on to her and her colleagues was palpable: "As a young person in the 1970s, I convened the San Francisco Art Workers' Coalition. All these WPA vets of the 1930s and 1940s were still alive there, and we were dying to talk to them."

For director Bill Rauch, the FTP was important *after* he and a cohort of artists had made the Cornerstone Theater Company together:

> I hadn't heard of the Federal Theatre Project and Hallie Flanagan till a couple years into Cornerstone Theater, and it blew my mind. The historical context we eventually learned allowed us tools to position ourselves. There was a power in knowing that history; but we started Cornerstone because the professional avenues available to us weren't interesting. Only 2 percent of the American people went to the theater regularly. That we could have successful careers and wake up one day and realize that we had failed to perform for 98 percent of our fellow citizens—we wanted a way for that not to be the case.

The Group Theatre (1931–1941) was one of the first serious ensemble companies in U.S. history and made an impact on any number of contemporary artists involved in regional theater. Historian and writer

Todd London remarks, "The Group Theatre [performing socially conscious plays on Broadway] corrected the mistaken idea that socially engaged theater is somehow separate from mainstream theater." One of the Group Theatre's best-known works was Clifford Odets's *Waiting for Lefty*, in support of striking taxicab drivers.

Grassroots Theater, the 1940s

Another robust era of theater history largely ignored in mainstream arts circles, the grassroots arts movement of the 1940s brought recognition to making theater about subjects close at hand, wherever one was. It did not buy into the myth that art flourished only in cities, as Todd London explains:

> The regional arts movement, specifically play making, started in the Dakotas and moved to North Carolina with Professor Koch, in the late teens/twenties, even as there was an avant-garde community forming in Greenwich Village in the teens. The regional voices idea was carried out through Robert Gard into the 1940s.

For deNobriga, grassroots theater was intensely personal:

> I and many of my small-town buddies looked to Robert Gard as a person making art in a rural location often described as having no culture and making work that reflected the concerns of people who were living in that place. The Gard Foundation has tons of information: There's a radio clip that in the first thirty seconds cites the "lure of local stories." In Wisconsin, Gard's chief areas of activity were in the theater arts and creative writing, also collecting and publishing the folklore of the state. He later established the area of Arts Development in the College of Agriculture under University Extension and remained a specialist in the arts in smaller communities and rural areas.

Glimmerings of Accessibility, Resistance, and Individual Voice, the late 1940s–1950s

While community theater is often looked at as simply the amateur remounting of Broadway shows around the United States, it was considerably more significant to the people who participated in it, including Jan:

> I grew up in a small Pennsylvania town that, as in much of the country, was home to a community theater. While it was a tremendous source of meaning for me to be in productions there, it was also clearly positioned as less than professional theater venues. Playing Millie in a production of *Picnic* was the epitome of my community theater experience. The line that stays with me most is "Someday I'm going to get on that train and go to New York." It captured my feeling that being in plays was about being different, and like Millie, the girl who would get away, to New York, where they did real theater. It took years for me to learn that I already was part of "real" theater; that community theater was part of a great tradition. Theater history was not just the story of well-known professional playwrights, actors, directors, and the like, but of all people who found meaning in the stories they told, enacted, sang, and danced.

In the same era, the United States was in the thrall of paranoia about a supposed Communist threat. Goldbard refers to that time: "The WPA was followed by the big discontinuity of the McCarthy era of the 1950s and silence, silence, silence." Todd London begs to differ, citing the immense bravery of some of the playwrights of that era:

> Arthur Miller was not silenced, nor Lillian Hellman, nor at the end of that time Lorraine Hansberry or James Baldwin. Maybe they were speaking solo because it took another decade before people figured out how communities speak.

The 1950s was also a time of the beatniks, characterized by very unique individual artistic voices, and the surfacing of a counterculture, not to be cowed by mainstream norms. Many interviewees cited the Living Theatre, "the mother of us all," founded in 1947 and dedicated to free and courageous speech and action around a range of social issues and continuing to this day. All of these dynamics—community accessibility, resistance to anticommunism, and the seeds of a cultural alternative to the mainstream—contributed to what came next.

The Overtly Political Theater of the 1960s and 1970s

By the 1960s, the flourishing of local expressivity characterized by Robert Gard and grassroots theater in the 1940s had largely split into two directions: a professional regional theater network and an amateur community theater, reproducing plays that had thrived on Broadway. Neither continued grassroots theater's emphasis on local culture. Regional theater, often with resident actors, designers, and directors, presented contemporary theater deemed nationally significant all around the country in professional productions that were considered all the more valuable for being close to the original. Community theaters became the venue for amateur theater lovers to remount shows that had flourished often ten or twenty years earlier.

But there was another, vital context for theater on the rise. The political movements that characterized the 1960s and 1970s were frequently bolstered by artistic wings. The level of emotion was palpable, often reflecting contradictions that demanded counternarratives to set the record straight. Soldiers of color had already sacrificed their lives in two world wars, and were serving yet again, this time in Vietnam. Coming back to second-class citizenship in the United States was less tenable than ever. The U.S. standard of living was rising, so more people had time beyond subsisting to strive for quality of life. The American Dream was showing its raggedy edges. And we were hearing about and seeing television footage of freedom movements across the world as more and more people fought their colonial oppressors.

Parris-Bailey spoke of the resurgence of the powerful cultural movement known as Black Arts. Black southern artists were a part of that, for some through the Southern Black Cultural Alliance and specifically, as Parris-Bailey recounts, through engagement with John O'Neal and the

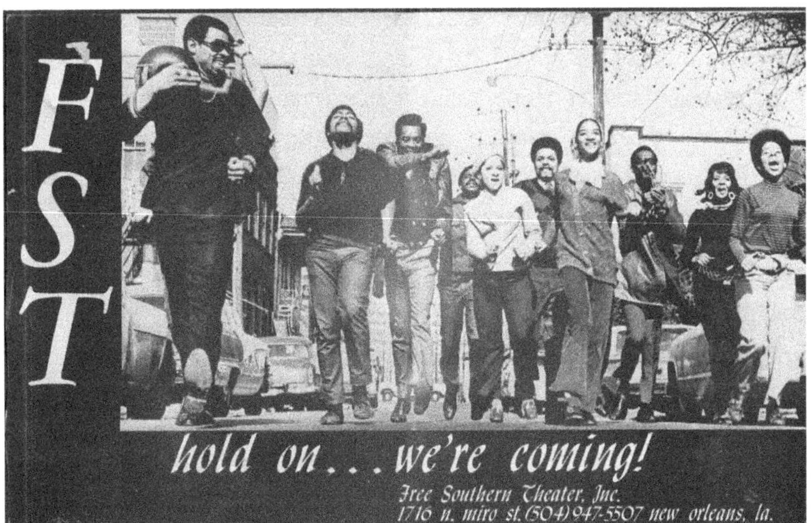

FST: hold on . . . we're coming! *Courtesy of the Amistad Research Center and Junebug Productions. Photographer unknown.*

Free Southern Theater (FST). Reading *The Free Southern Theater, by the Free Southern Theater: A Documentary of the South's Radical Black Theater, with Journals, Letters, Poetry Essays, and a Play Written by Those Who Built It* (1969) when it was published put her "on the path":

> I had been a student activist in New York since junior high school, working as a tutor in a storefront program, and made my first visit to the Black Panther headquarters in the late 1960s. I discovered I wanted to be a playwright right about then. When I read the FST story, I said, "Oh! This is how it fits together!" An aha moment for me. Because I was able to link to this southern movement. If there had not been that Black Arts southern movement, there would not have been a ROOTS, or it would have been a white organization. The southern Black cultural movement and John O'Neal, that's prehistory, and does not get enough attention.

Young theater makers of this generation have also been inspired by O'Neal and the Free Southern Theater. Carolina Dỗ, a Viet theater maker with the Sống Collective, explains:

> I love Junebug and the folks at Free Southern Theater. And the story circle process, because that's where it starts. It's like how we build the space, so that people will come into it and have the agency to tell and to hear their own stories. Because for the past forty, fifty, or sixty or so years, the Vietnamese community here in America, that's been pushed aside. We've consumed other people's cultures without putting importance on our own.

Black performer and youth leader Toya Lillard, coming of age a generation later, also speaks to the importance of Black Arts:

> I love the Black Arts movement acknowledging issues like gender—there was no term for intersectionality at the time. I can really place myself in the Black Arts movement. The civil rights struggle had already been fought and quote, unquote won; the Black Arts movement was the artistic arm of the Black Power movement.

While Arlene Goldbard is a writer and visual artist, her experience applying her skills to the activist context she lived through in those days is also relevant to performers:

> During the war in Vietnam, recently graduated from high school, I became a draft counselor. Because I'd always been drawing and painting, I did the posters. I got involved in organizing for Vietnam Summer. The women's movement was happening, Haight-Ashbury, everything was skyrocketing. In 1971, I got a job at the Neighborhood Arts Program (NAP), founded in 1967, as a designer and printer for their flyers. They were providing tiny grants—for example, for poetry readings—and all the flyers were printed on a mimeograph machine. We attempted to start a union, the Graphic Artist Guild. All these things put me in touch with community-based artists, like the Mime Troupe and muralists from Galería de la Raza.
>
> In the mid-1970s, people were organizing against the official bicentennial commemoration of the American Revolution, which focused on events that made people feel excluded in terms of what was America. I was part of organizing against these things for the Art

Workers' Coalition. The publication *Arts Biweekly* came out of that. I was part of "mimeograph journalism" about the cultural policy and issues of the day.

Funding opportunities for a more inclusive theater ecosystem were also cropping up, as deNobriga recounts:

I'm thinking about the rise of funding for community-based work at the National Endowment for the Arts level. A lot of that was built on the backs of people doing culturally specific work—African Americans or Latinos, Hispanics, looking at what was being put on stages and celebrated, not in the mainstream. It was clear to people like Luis Valdez of El Teatro Campesino and the Free Southern Theater that what they were doing had value for the people it was made for.

At what point do you say, "Not only does this work have value for this 'minority' but for a broader audience. It shines a light on the human condition"? I don't think that really happened until the counterculture wars later in the 1960s with African-American, Latine, and women's voices. I think the Robert Gards and the Paul Greens and others made a little drop in the ocean, but they didn't build a movement—I should say movements—the way people did in the 1960s.

Free street theater also flourished in the 1960s and 1970s. Coya Paz differentiates between grassroots street theaters and those founded from the top down:

The Free Street Theater started with a state grant. The first named founder worked at the Goodman [a major Chicago institutional theater]. The city was, "Oh, we're having racial tension in our city. Let's start some free street theater." They had bought this truck and tried to do free Shakespeare in the parks and no one wanted to see it in 1967, so they gave us all that stuff. Then they're, "Recycle and start this power-to-the-people-like theater." I'm so happy that it happened. The impulse at the beginning was very liberal. Free Street became more radical as time went on.

Community, 1980s–1990s

Activist theater in the 1980s and 1990s was characterized by artists working within their own communities on their own issues, as national movements faltered. In *Local Acts: Community-Based Performance in the United States* (2005), Jan marks the beginning of the new wave of socially engaged theater with the New Orleans jazz funeral that John O'Neal, cofounder of the Free Southern Theater, convened to mark the end of the civil rights era as well as the end of the FST, created to accompany it:

> [It was] conjoined with a three-day conference entitled "A Valediction without Mourning: The Role of the Arts for Social Change." O'Neal thus marked the death of the company at the same time as he affirmed the continuity of activist theater. . . . Just as a jazz funeral communicates the ongoing life of the departed's spirit, O'Neal communicated that . . . the FST's . . . spirit lived on in other activist companies working in their own communities. (Cohen-Cruz 2005, 61)

The regional theater movement was also a return to the local, but largely to decentralize theater beyond major U.S. cities. Todd London points out their difference:

> The idea of working in community in the period from the mid-1980s on has really become the mainstream of American theater thought. Regional theaters were intended to be locally grounded and resident, but partly because of the financial structures and needs, they were unable to detach from the Broadway and European repertory model and got mired in a kind of institutionalism that forced them to be more mainstream and less local, less regional.

There were many differences among theaters that sought to express their communities. As cultural activist Caron Atlas emphasizes:

> You can't sum up this history into one connected line. There's the Alliance for Cultural Democracy and Black Arts and hip-hop. They are multiple and not overlapping. I feel lucky that I went to Tenaz conferences [Teatro Nacional de Aztlán, the national organization of

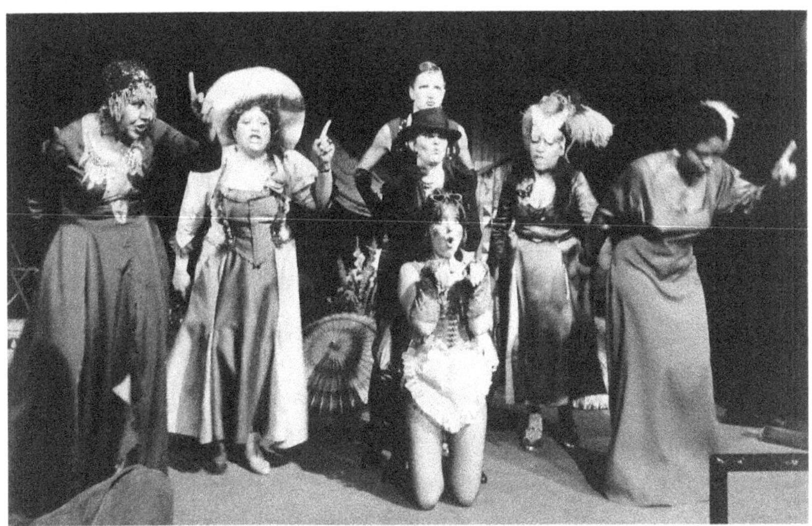

An Evening of Disgusting Songs and Pukey Images. *Production photo. Left to right: Muriel Miguel, Lisa Mayo, Peggy Shaw (at rear), Lois Weaver (in front), Pam Verge (kneeling), Gloria Miguel, Naja Bey. Performed at Theater for the New City in New York City in 1979. Courtesy of Muriel Miguel, Spiderwoman Theater.*

> Chicano theaters] and experienced a lot in Latine arts, which have their own rich traditions.

Muriel Miguel founded Spiderwoman Theater in 1976, initially with other Native American women, including her two sisters, Gloria Miguel and Lisa Mayo. But only the three of them had theater training, so she opened the company up to several additional women with training. Lois Weaver was among them; in 1980, she, along with Peggy Shaw and Deb Margolin, went on to create the troupe Split Britches, which became an icon of feminist theater. Weaver describes Spiderwoman and Muriel Miguel in particular as her foundational source:

> We built Split Britches on what we learned in Spiderwoman. Muriel Miguel has been a massive mentor. I learned from her to trust fantasy as a source. That links to [our attraction to] popular culture, so what you have always wanted to be or do onstage was always the first question.

Interestingly, Miguel had been a member of the Open Theater, which had had an enormous influence on Weaver in the 1970s, when she trained with Open Theater alums:

> Joe Chaikin and the Open Theater opened the whole world to me. I learned from them that (1) I could make my own work; (2) that I could rely on impulse; (3) it could be abstract and multilayered and didn't have to be a narrative.

Weaver also acknowledges the impact of the Wooster Group:

> It's not the kind of work we wanted to make. But that really subtle, deep consideration of culture, even popular culture. *Route 1 & 9* was very seminal for me, the controversial way that they dealt with difficult subjects, like race [juxtaposing white actors appearing in blackface—that is, minstrelsy—with other troubling forms of U.S. popular entertainment]. I thought, Yeah, I want to do this in my own camp sort of way.

Dozens of people we interviewed pointed to the influence of the rigorously experimental Wooster Group.

Wooster Group director Elizabeth LeCompte was previously a member of The Performance Group, founded by Richard Schechner, who is also one of the founders of Performance Studies, an interdisciplinary field of scholarship with a major influence on the work described in these pages. Performance Studies is notable for the breadth of the art and culture that it examines. While demonstrations and marches occurred all through history, they were not generally recognized as part of the same field as theater until the new discipline named it as such.

The field is difficult to define, as it is in constant flux; nonetheless, it is useful to consider John MacAloon's formulation of cultural performance as "occasions in which as a culture or society we reflect upon and define ourselves, dramatize our collective myths and histories, present ourselves with alternatives, and eventually change in some ways while remaining the same in others" (MacAloon 1984, 1). Through this lens, we can see demonstrations as spectacles of civil disobedience, carefully crafted for impact on their audiences. Jan attributes the experience of studying in the new Department of Performance Studies at NYU beginning in the early 1980s as providing *her with* a framework that allowed her to include under one umbrella what had seemed before to be an impossibly eclectic range of influences.

Racialization, Radicalization, and Diversity After September 11, 2001

Lebanese American artist Andrea Assaf vividly describes the impact that 9/11 had on her and many MENASA (Middle East, North Africa, South Asia) people, artists or not:

> Nine-eleven was a real shift in my experience of my racial identity as an Arab American. Quite drastically, night and day, from September 10 to 11. Those of us of Arab or Mideastern identity went from being this cosmopolitan enigma that could be a lot of things in the multiculturalism of New York City to public enemy suspects. In the 1980s and 1990s, most people didn't know where Lebanon was on the map—maybe they would have in the 1970s because of the political climate. Yes, there had been the First Gulf War, but it wasn't a thing on people's minds until after 9/11. That was when I was starting to create my own work as an artist, and it has indelibly influenced what I've created over the past twenty years.

Assaf explains that it was not just that others saw her differently, but that she felt compelled to explore that part of her identity, becoming "obsessively interested in questions of war and peace whether working with refugee communities or war veterans or making my own work about being Arab American after 9/11."

Also around the turn of the twenty-first century, a number of our interviewees were impacted by steps in the funding world toward more consideration of what began to be known as JEDIAB—justice, equity, diversity, inclusion, accessibility, and belonging. Although often criticized as tokenism, some funding efforts went deeper. Numerous interviewees praised the Future Aesthetics program, funded by the Ford Foundation from 2002 to 2014 and led by Roberta Uno, for its contribution to a more inclusive art ecosystem in the United States. It put money into the hands of artist-innovators of various cultural backgrounds, arguing that as the country became more diverse, the art created by the changing demographics was vital to our national culture. The Future Aesthetics initiative, recognizing innovation beyond a white aesthetic, opened new avenues, particularly for emerging young artists of color, explored cutting-edge aesthetics that went hand in hand with demographic change, and "remade narratives around past, present, and future intersections of art and social justice" (Chang et al. 2015). It was also an antidote to the practice of appropriation by some white artists who saw the expressions of other cultures as something they could mine and profit from.

Future Aesthetics "was animated by a belief that changing demographics had shifted the narrative of American identity, thus promoting new strategies for community inclusion while simultaneously catalyzing new art forms" (Chang et al. 2015). Grants to networks of arts institutions, organizations, and individuals committed to this new work supported BIPOC artists whose work came to define and influence the next generation. For example, Future Aesthetics funded the Hip-Hop Artist/Activist Fellowship at ROOTS and the National Performance Network (NPN). The inclusion of hip-hop artists was a turning point in ROOTS' effort to be a racially diverse organization. MK Wegmann, who cowrote the grant with Lisa Mount, elaborates:

> It provided that bump for both a generational shift and growing BIPOC participation that was intentional. . . . Every year we [the ROOTS Executive Committee] would all sit there and say, "What can we do to increase BIPOC artists at ROOTS?" The Hip-Hop Fellowship provided that critical mass that changed everything.

Seed Lynn, part of the first cohort of hip-hop artists in 2004, acknowledges the initiative's importance to his own development:

> Getting introduced to ROOTS and being embraced and connected to people, institutions, opportunities, because, remember, the hip-hop fellows went to the annual meetings at ROOTS and NPN . . . They funded our work. So, that made me think, Oh! Every path is not through New York like I thought! That's bullet number one. And doing work that is really centered and rooted in storytelling and listening,

> that's bullet number two. That's how I identify now, in my work with my company, Storyographers. I'm a cultural worker. I'm a listener.

Creative Placemaking, Creative Placekeeping, 2010–2020

Many people have been inspired by the integration of the arts into societal infrastructure, which, in a 2010 white paper by Ann Markusen and Anne Gadwa, was called "creative placemaking." Nonetheless, describing the role of the arts and culture in community development, the term evoked ambivalence because the notion of community economic development has often been code for gentrification: development for whose benefit? An incisive critique by the now cultural manager of Oakland, Roberto Bedoya, led to fruitful conversations about curbing these dangers and revising the language to *placekeeping.* Under Jamie Bennett's leadership, ArtPlace America, a ten-year funding initiative for creative placemaking projects, gave more thought to how the arts could be an economic engine without leading to gentrification, through reinvestment in communities that center their agency and participation.

What Does This Account Say About Now?

The Historical Influences Juxtaposed

These legacies tell a story of artists' aspirations to enact their values through performance processes. They call upon us to hold, honor, and respect multiple perspectives at once.

The histories of the people we interviewed bore witness to their very existence.

Everyone needs to see their story, *themselves,* reflected in history. What good is an account of history that leaves some of us out? Yet many historians have assumed they were talking for "everyone" when, in fact, many people who have been under- or misrepresented claim other people, incidents, or interpretations as core elements of their story. We need to get over the cultural hierarchy that places one group's artistic influences above another's.

Choreographer Liz Lerman alludes to this when citing the Russian avant-garde and Dada as important influences personally but goes on to say:

> I understand that these histories were put in my path to mine for my own use and I never had to consider if they reflected my race, or the experience of my various cultural identities. There were plenty of other artistic influences happening at that time, but these were not placed in the same light, at least not in my education, including, for example, the Harlem Renaissance.

What's unacceptable is how much more documented and resourced white cultural figures are than equally creative people and movements from diverse cultures.

Acknowledging the contributions of other cultures is not just important to the people who identify with that source. New Orleans–based theater maker Nick Slie comments on how much he has learned from how a similar history is experienced by different groups of people:

> I was talking with [Black artists] Daniel Alexander Jones and Sharon Bridgforth about the Black avant-garde. It seems to always precede the white avant-garde—jazz, the Black poets. I see a desire in the Black avant-garde to interrupt coherence, which can be a great tool of oppression. I often see a white avant-garde slingshot out into this expansive world, only to point its finger back at itself: "Aren'tcha impressed by what we know?" I see the Black avant-garde have this same explosion outward to point to something wider: "Look at all of us; look at the we."

Slie's reflections bring to mind the all-too-human impulse to be flattered if we are deemed special and unique, and in the process leaving others, just as special and unique, in the shadows. Commonly referred to as "exceptionalism," this has led to the situation many cultural workers find themselves in today, one that puts the onus on individual artists to make change, leaving out the cultural communities in which they are embedded.

Everything new is old; Carlton Turner says innovation is an act of remembrance. The references that our interviewees cite bespeak a through line—to be connected through time to the life of our culture. Cultural policy thinker Erik Takeshita spoke of how the persistence of community building that strives to be inclusive in the history of art was actually used against our field because of other forces:

> You can go back to the WPA, the Harlem Renaissance, the community theater movement, the settlement houses . . . the incredibly long history of art building community. The Russians and the Soviets did such a great job of using art to build community that during the Cold War, we in the United States had to do everything opposite of the Soviet Union. So the United States used art to advance capitalism. It had to be about individual genius, the theatrical value of the piece of art, the aesthetic thing. We worked very hard to decouple art from community. We always had artists involved in social movements; that continued. But we didn't elevate, encourage, or support such artists. The art schools were, "Oh, you have to respond to your own muse," which is wonderful and it's great for artists to play roles of provocateur and critic and these other things art can do, but the fulcrum kind of shifted in one direction.

Takeshita's remarks suggest that we need to pay more attention to global politics in understanding the de facto art policy of a given era; that our field is often a pawn in a much larger game.

Hearing a diverse cohort of artists speak from personal experience attests to the fact that no one cultural group can fully tell the history of socially engaged art. And that's good. There is not a coherent, unified narrative, because not all people have been allowed to choose or have chosen the same circumstances in which to live and thrive. We long for the day we can share in one another's cultural legacies without risk of appropriating them—that is, not properly acknowledging and honoring the source of a culturally specific practice or tradition, or getting permission to draw on it, or looking for how the people at the source can benefit. We've endeavored to honor this fundamental principle by including people from cultural contexts who have not typically been invited to join in shaping the historical narrative. We move with respect by attributing words and the development of ideas to those responsible.

Personal Reflections

The interviews caused us to think about our own historical influences differently, as Jan notes:

> The past speaks to us differently over time. As a child, I dreamed of a theater of common ground that could bring people together across our many differences. That required a context that valued theater itself, and so I marveled that shopkeepers were paid to close their stores so they could attend the plays performed at the annual Dionysian festivals in ancient Greece, so important was that discourse to civic life. A theater of common ground also meant that many people participated in it, so I was excited to learn about the mumming tradition that took place during the twelve days of Christmas in much of Europe, harkening back to the Middle Ages. Groups of friends or family members would mask up and go from neighbor to neighbor, performing in exchange for food and drink. A theater of common ground would be both broadly accessible and aesthetically captivating, so the Bread and Puppet Theater awed me with its vision of a theater as fundamental to our well-being as bread and as magical as puppets. Indeed, director Peter Schumann and the company baked and gave out sourdough slices at all their shows: communion without religious imperatives.
>
> I now see the contradictions in these still-compelling examples. Those who attended theater in ancient Greece, as is widely known, were free men. Mumming was tied to Christian holidays, so I don't know where that would have left me as a Jew. While Schumann was wildly creative, he controlled nearly everything that troupe did, from the top down. And all of these examples reveal my ignorance, as a child, of equally compelling performance beyond the West. Even the notion of common ground is complicated by the fact that our experiences are shaped by unequal opportunities and different cultural traditions, not all of which are equally documented, disseminated,

and appreciated beyond their own communities. And to whom is the ground that I am calling common available, and how did the inhabitants come to be there?

Now, instead of seeking a theater of common ground, I seek examples of theaters that are usefully knit into what their communities need, performance projects that meet the moment. Writing about socially engaged theater and performance of the past fifty-five years at a time when live theatrical gatherings with a sizable number of attendees have been suspended due to the pandemic, I'm drawn to historical examples of how limitations give birth to theatrical innovations. In the military-controlled Argentina of the 1980s, Augusto Boal was unable to make protest theater without landing back in prison, so he turned to invisible theater, staging public enactments that observers did not know were staged. Performing artists in 2020 created digital experiences of this most live of mediums. For all that's been at least temporarily lost, many artists speak of new audiences they've gained because of streaming their work.

Also influenced by the great diversity of our interviewees' performance influences, Rad recalls images that have etched themselves into their consciousness since childhood:

> I remember the dirty, athletic clowns performing at traffic lights for money back in Pindorama, Abya Yala, where I was born and spent my first eight years of life. They were rigorous with their craft and joyful in spirit. I sensed layers of political commentary to their performances that I could feel but not yet understand in their fullness: necessary layers of allegory and metaphor that protected them from the authoritarian aftershocks of the recently ended dictatorship, the oncoming monsoon of neoliberalism rained down on us from the North and the East, the deep-seated systemic and internalized racism, class disputes, and the violence of the hyperspeed emergence of a middle class.

I is social, part of the multiple *we*, trackable in history, a word whose relationship to *story* becomes, we hope, concrete in this telling. To the degree that people's lives have been so forcibly different, so are and will remain our histories and the artifacts we make about them. Art and culture can be seen as a diagnostic—what is the gap between how a people sees itself and how others see them? Who gets to decide who a people is? History has provided endless examples of art modeling the way people of various cultural traditions want to be, the future they wish to live in, and the aspirations and values they seek to embody through their praxis.

2 Commitments

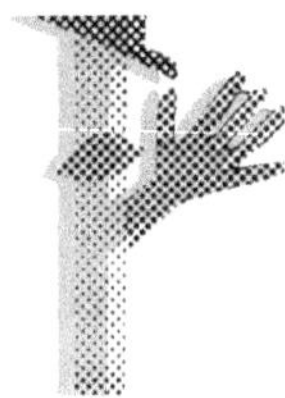

It was Lisa Mount's theory that divisions got set when the National Endowment for the Arts changed their guidelines and you had to pick either artistic excellence or artistic merit. We systemically and formally made divisions that you were either artistically rigorous or community-minded but not both.

—Mark Valdez, former director, Network of Ensemble Theaters

If I am not for myself, who will be for me? But if I am only for myself, what am I? If not now, when?

—Rabbi Hillel, *Pirkei Avot (Ethics of the Fathers)* 1:14

Many of the artists we spoke with are uneasy with performance that is centered only on themselves. Just as unacceptable to them is abandoning personal exploration to focus only on community well-being. We focus here on theater makers who are committed to both personal expressivity and community-mindedness, not forsaking artistic rigor, and explore why at times it has been difficult to embrace both. We also include reflections on ethics, which are a core component of this question.

The Changing Status of Conjoining Artistic and Social Commitments

In the great rivers of history, many performance makers have had no problem engaging with their communities both symbolically *and* concretely around a social issue; indeed, in the long tradition, art is embedded in the life of its community. In more recent years, however, artists have sometimes been expected to either spend all their professional time and energy developing their individual artistic vision or focus only on contributing concretely to the social life of a particular community with art as a means. In an interesting nuance, it's been fine to be an aesthetically rigorous *political* artist if addressing political content within the four walls of a theater.

But art and community are another matter. The very word *community* throws up associations with amateurism and do-goodism. It's inconceivable to some that professional, trained artists would choose to work with a community; they must be bad artists. How could someone develop an artistic palette in a community setting? They must be do-gooders, a pejorative term for largely well-meaning but naïve humanitarians or social reformers, often referring to women who, on a voluntary basis, help people in need. Mark Valdez, former director of the Network of Ensemble Theaters (NET), notes that the feeling of having to choose between commitment to aesthetics or to a community's social needs and aspirations is one of the tensions that has dogged the contemporary ensemble theater movement. In what follows, we track changing views about holding these dual commitments.

The impulse to challenge the status quo in terms of both art *and* social life, form *and* content, was intertwined in the Living Theatre, founded in 1947. Its members describe themselves as "molded by Abstract Expressionism x Jazz x Beat Culture x Rock n Roll x Punk x HipHop x General Strikes for Peace. From the front lines of creativity and free speech all the way beyond the borders, vanguards and limits of the 21st century" (www.livingtheatre.org).

Over the next two decades, companies formed that likewise participated in a sociopolitical moment through art. The Free Southern Theater, founded in 1963 by Doris Derby, Gilbert Moses, and John O'Neal in Mississippi, and El Teatro Campesino, founded in 1965 by Luis Valdez and a cohort of farmworkers in California, were cultural and artistic wings of liberation movements for African Americans and Chicanos, respectively. These companies did not choose between art and politics; they stretched form as they expanded content and made art that directly challenged power relationships in the workplace, in union meetings, and through concrete political initiatives like boycotts.

The interplay between social movements of the 1960s and 1970s and their artistic wings was generative. For example, the Free Southern Theater integrated story circles into their practice; cofounder John O'Neal adapted the technique from a civil rights organization, the Student Nonviolent Coordinating Committee. Story circles have been a foundational way to open participation in creative expression to community members, before, during, and after performances (Davis 2019). Story circles are ubiquitous now—in professional training, play building, with audiences as follow-ups to shows, and in self-standing community contexts.

Another robust cultural strategy to engage a community is integrating popular components with political content and goals. The *actos* of El Teatro Campesino were a popular Mexican form of short skits that the company created and performed on flatbed trucks and in union halls. Their *corridos,* based on Mexican folk ballads, affirmed and heartened struggling farmworkers. The San Francisco Mime Troupe, also addressing social issues since the 1960s, is grounded in a contemporary version of commedia dell'arte. The Mime Troupe has played with popular forms, including melodrama, vaudeville, and musical theater, to draw diverse audiences in parks and other public places through its broadly appealing physicality and humor. The Bread and Puppet Theater has drawn large audiences to its haunting, quirky, beautiful, and at times funky puppets of all sizes, from figures that are several stories high to dancing potatoes on the ends of forks, with the large-scale end of the spectrum making possible their frequent participation in outdoor events like demonstrations and parades focused on issues from the war in Vietnam to nuclear proliferation to climate change.

The economic circumstances of the United States in the 1960s and 1970s made it easier for young artists to be part of theaters with overtly social justice values. As white flight increased in urban areas, artists there had more space and time to make art because rent was so cheap and squatting was a tenable possibility. Even in New York City, apartments were relatively affordable in what were then considered edgy parts of the city (read: not attractive to real estate developers), like the East Village. Artists did not have to be palatable to donors and institutions in order to make a living to pay their rent; together, they could gather what they needed to survive, which granted them autonomy. But there was a degree of uncertainty. Urbanization and suburbanization came in waves, making space or taking it as the economy dictated, and leaving artists to adapt in its wake.

By the late 1970s, the great social movements of the 1960s and 1970s had peaked. In 1975, the Vietnam War ended; the Voting Rights Act and other legislation, though far from conclusive, took the national spotlight off civil rights; and the growth of the United Farm Workers provided a more traditional political conduit for social action. Partly because of new funding guidelines, as Mark Valdez articulates in this chapter's epigraph, many theater makers felt they had to choose between focusing on art or on community. Ensemble companies were squeezed between identities as regional theaters—which aspired to a market-driven professionalism and institutionality that downplayed controversial politics in order to be palatable to more people—and community-based theaters, which by and large did not compete for the same funding and were free to identify themselves more holistically.

Some artists continued to hold both aesthetic and sociopolitical commitments. Alternate ROOTS (Regional Organization of Theaters South), founded in 1976 at the Highlander Center in New Market, Tennessee, was developed to meet the needs of politically progressive southern artists who create art by/for/about/within communities of place, tradition, affiliation, and spirit. ROOTS quickly established itself as a thought leader in the field of community-based arts and the only regional collective of artists committed to social and economic justice (www. alternateroots.org). ROOTS members have not only helped one another develop artistically through workshops and the sharing of works in progress but have also furthered one another's personal, social, and political growth through

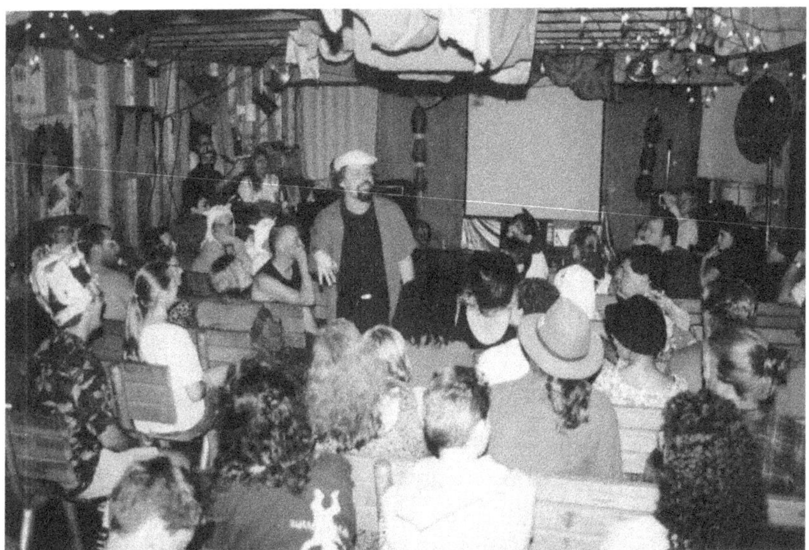

Café Bizzoso, the late-night performance venue at annual ROOTS' Week gatherings, circa 1990s. Here, Normando Ismay, aka Papa Bizzoso, tells a story about family members in difficult and ridiculous situations that they escape with wit and humor. The audience could become family members by confessing to having the Bizzoso gene and adopting a new name. Mary Lufftosa had brought sheep-wool wigs, which people wore, and good acts received thunderous bleating from the audience. Photographer unknown. Courtesy of Normando Ismay.

such initiatives as "dismantling racism" workshops integrated into all ROOTS annual meetings. Nonetheless, some artists still perceived a split. Liz Lerman describes pushing for more art when she was at Alternate ROOTS gatherings in the 1980s and 1990s, and for more community involvement when she was at mainstream art convenings. For her, both have always been essential, as she beautifully captures in her 2011 book, *Hiking the Horizontal.*

Andrea Assaf, who describes herself as "a child of ROOTS through and through," articulates why art is inherently political for those with marginalized identities:

> I feel like it's such a mark of privilege to have them not be interrelated. I don't know how to be an artist of color, queer, and a woman and not have the social and political issues of the world come into my work, whether it's an interruption or intervention or a thing that must

> be talked about. It's the old "The personal is political" feminist slogan. One of my favorite poems is Adrienne Rich's "What Kind of Times Are These," where she writes that she wants to talk about politics but has to talk about trees "to have you listen at all." I feel there's always that stance.

Values-driven companies that integrate art and equity provide members with the ability to live according to their principles without risking their livelihoods. The Cornerstone Theater Company, for example, was cofounded in 1986 by Bill Rauch and Alison Carey with other recent Harvard graduates. They took to the road, making plays with local people in towns all across the United States. They were motivated, Rauch said, out of "curiosity about who actually lived in this country and a hunch we could be better artists if we made work responsive to people who didn't usually go to theater."

Many artists across the country continued to integrate theater making with other concerns that went beyond content to action. Lois Weaver describes being in Spiderwoman Theater as "landing in Heaven, in a sense that I could put together my politics and my theater making." In the early 1980s, Weaver and Peggy Shaw cofounded the WOW (Women's One World) Café Theatre, a community space grounded in feminist and lesbian aesthetics and concerns. It evidenced that "being political" can express itself in more ways than content, as Weaver points out:

> The structure of WOW was a political move and that's what I'm most proud of—that we set up a social/political structure for functioning collectively that continues on. Even today, there's no artistic director; there's no hierarchy. It's a cooperative. You have to put in work in order to get your work supported; it's run by biweekly meetings and a yearly retreat. It belongs to the people who show up and who run it. We always had this joke; we'd have a big fight about what color to paint the ceiling. And the truth was, it would be painted the color the person who was painting it chose. When someone would ask, "How do you get into WOW? Who's a member?" [we'd say,] "Well, whoever has the key." And everyone had keys. I'm as proud of the way we

> set up the functioning of that organization as I am of the work that's come out of it.

There is often the perception that people of the global majority (i.e., Black, brown, Asian, Indigenous, and other nonwhite people), LGBTQIA2+, and disabled artists are only interested in politics. Yet many individuals and companies defy such assumptions. Split Britches, initiated by Weaver, her partner, Peggy Shaw, and their heterosexual colleague Deb Margolin, has been an icon of lesbian and feminist theater. The company has put as much attention to the stage as an imaginative space as to it as a place to dispel stereotypes, which was more a by-product of just doing what they were doing. Weaver elaborates:

> That really started for us in Spiderwoman, where we just set out to tell our own stories and to do that through playing with stereotypes. We were never really consciously doing that, either; we just grabbed those things that gave us pleasure and we thought were funny and would like to explode into people's faces. We didn't start out to make feminist theater or lesbian theater. We started out to make theater as lesbians and feminists. We always wanted to make that the given and not the subject of the story.

In the late 1980s, developers began reinvesting in New York City's Times Square and other neglected areas in places across the country. A new wave of urbanization and institutionalization began to push more artists to the peripheries of cities and created the necessity for a different kind of lifestyle to sustain their capacity to be artists. In some cases, artists lost touch with their creative practices because they had no time or energy to give after long hours of working other jobs to sustain themselves. Artists who have developed the skills of knowing how to navigate grant and funding structures have been better able to carve out careers as working- or middle-class artists.

Yet another form of socially engaged theater rose to prominence in the 1980s: solo performance. It often drew from artists' experiences as part of marginalized groups and, like ensemble theater, nurtured the integration of their values in performance, allowing them control of their own content. It also recognized commonality in less obvious ways. Kathy Randels, for example, while still in college, created a solo performance that necessitated getting to know incarcerated women:

> It was about my relationship to anger, aggression, and violence, being a woman living in a patriarchy. It made me ask why I don't have the impulse to fight back or defend myself. I started looking at women who do and who have acted on that impulse.

Twenty-six years later, Randels is still connected to formerly incarcerated women through The Graduates, a company she cofounded with Ausettua AmorAmenkum of the Kumbuka African Drum & Dance Collective. And she continues to work with other people who love performance craft. She explains her criteria, saying a project must have "a purpose beyond just me, if it hits on a big need in the world. I don't want to relinquish either artistic experimentation or justice-driven work."

Changes in the arts funding policy in 1990 took power away from individual artists and companies that gave voice to radical and inclusive politics. A catalyst was the "NEA Four," solo artists Karen Finley, John Fleck, Holly Hughes, and Tim Miller, whose controversial focus on gender, sexuality, subjugation, and personal trauma led to a loss of their National Endowment for the Arts funding. They became a target of the U.S. "culture wars," which refers to polarized social forces around issues like abortion, guns, and homosexuality that raged again in the early 1990s. Congress amended the statute governing federal funding for the arts to include considerations of "general standards of decency and respect for the diverse beliefs of the American public." The four artists fought back in court, arguing that NEA funds could not be withheld for political reasons (http://newmuseum.org/pages/view/residence-1).

Other artists were making different kinds of political choices. In 1994, after a decade in Boston, the Double Edge Theatre relocated to rural Massachusetts. Director Stacy Klein explained that the members of the company wanted to be close to their community, whereas their only access in the city was through "programming or knocking door-to-door." This was in keeping with Double Edge's vision of Living Culture and Art Justice, which, Klein explains, means that "the people in a community around a theater or other cultural program should be part of the endeavor itself":

> Teachers, carpenters, plumbers, mosaic artists, artisans, contractors, excavators, real estate agents, gardeners, farmers—we needed all these people to develop the theater, and, in turn, they learned they needed us, not just economically but creatively. We are now employing kids who were five when they first came to us. Living Culture includes building our greening and environmental practices and sharing that with our audience.

Cornerstone and Double Edge are part of the revitalized ensemble theater movement that has embraced a holistic approach to being an artist, with an emphasis on nurturing both the individual and the group. They are an integral part of the physical community. Attention is paid to company members' artistic and personal growth. The group is defined not only as the ensemble but the greater community. This aligns them with values expressed by Navajo playwright and theater artist Rhiana Yazzie, which she contrasts with the mainstream:

> [U.S.] theater somewhat embodies the major white supremacy ethics of individualism and taking credit for the work of a collective. You have to be the top to be seen. . . . The strong individualism, which values this loudness and boldness, is not valued in Native communities.

Paying attention to only the formal qualities of an artwork—character development, arc of the story, visual choices—as shaped strictly by the artist, without attention to their relation to a social context, was described by several of our interviewees as a privilege. In contrast, numerous interviewees described their work as shaped by constantly having to fight for their communities' right to exist.

The rise in community-engaged performance sometimes led to a debilitating binary, whereby the work of artists concerned with social struggles facing their communities was derisively described as "PC"—politically correct, meaning coercively imposing leftist political views on others. Yet saying one is apolitical is itself a political stance, a politics of disengagement from public life. It contributes to an environment in which many BIPOC, LGBTQIA2+, poor, and disabled artists only get funding when their art is about their historical trauma. Numerous interviewees spoke of turning away from trauma-centered to healing-centered art as a means of envisioning a world that includes justice and joy for them.

Recentering Communities in the Performance Experience

> *Even when I was mayor of my little town, I kept thinking, This is just a secret play. I'm the director; no one even knows they're in a play. In a play, people want something, they have to do things to get it, there're conflicts and obstacles, and they have to work together. The residents of my town don't know they're in a show, but I know it, so how do we make the best outcome possible?*
>
> —Theater director, mayor, and arts consultant Kathie deNobriga

The interplay between attention to art and attention to community and social issues is a continuum, not only within the art world but also at different moments in an individual artist's work. DeNobriga notes that she has used some of the same skills as a theater director and as a small-town mayor, the latter role emphasizing community needs but still drawing on skills she honed as an artist, such as guiding people to work together, overcome obstacles, and obtain objectives. By the end of the twentieth century, in the spirit of an artist-mayor, performance attached to its community's needs was again becoming more recognized—in regional theater, activist contexts, and everyday life. We turn now to each of these contexts, which provide different opportunities and challenges to balancing these commitments.

Regional Theater

In the late 1990s, Todd London, then artistic director of New Dramatists, an organization devoted to playwrights, witnessed a shift in regional theaters as they began paying attention to how ensemble and community-based theaters connect artistically to the people in the places they are located:

> At first, I was still feeling the influence of a generation of experimental playwrights. There was an avant-gardness about it that emphasized formal experiment, overthrowing and breaking old structures, and the search for the new. Over the years, the culture placed an increasing emphasis on story: whose story gets told and how, who has the right to tell it, and that we are all storytellers, which you wouldn't have heard in the theater [institutions] in the late 1990s. It's a kind of cultural agreement that I don't think would have risen like that without the structure of story circles and going into communities and telling stories of communities rather than your own personal imaginative communities as you populate them yourself as a writer.

Whether or not initially concerned with social issues, actors in ensemble companies settle in places that they come to care about and engage in, an alternative to the system of auditioning production by production, making it difficult to put down roots anywhere. As company members focus on issues of concern to them, they build relationships with audiences and collaborators who care about the same things, whether or not they have been involved in art. Specialists in other fields don't so much need artists to uncover data about these issues as to find a compelling way to present them publicly. Nick Slie gave the example of scientist Mark Davis, responding to *Cry You One* (2013), a play about the Gulf of Mexico's disappearing wetlands, devised by New Orleans–based performance groups Mondo Bizarro and ArtSpot Productions, who advised, "Give me enough facts to stay with you but enough fantasy that I go for a ride."

The place-based nature of much ensemble theater leads to a particularity often absent in regional theater, which strives for resemblance to mainstream commercial theater. Mark Valdez elaborates:

> Really fascinating about NET's Microfest series [community engaged mini ensemble theater festivals in different parts of the United States] was my discovery that different regions of the country have different aesthetics. The work looks different in New Orleans than it does in Detroit, Honolulu, or Kentucky. We forget because regional theaters are all doing similar-style productions of the same plays. I can pop into Kansas City Rep, the Denver Center, Dallas Theater Center, the

> Alliance, or the Roundabout, and every production of Lynn Nottage's play *Sweat* pretty much looks the same.

In this interview excerpt with Jan, Valdez poignantly articulates the cost of general rather than specific local theaters:

> **MV:** [Institutionalized American theaters] separated themselves from their communities. As a field, we allied ourselves with wealthy individuals who value a "national" or commercial aesthetic, and it's come back to bite us in the rear. When we lost our connections to place and the problems, joys, and stories of our communities, we became irrelevant to them. Why would the city of L.A., where I live, for example, make an investment in theater—what are we doing for the community?
>
> **JCC:** Yes. They need to know what theaters do besides sell tickets, that artists can go into schools and teach literacy through art and know how to bring people together across differences so they can sit down in a room and have a conversation together without killing each other. That artists' skills can be deployed for social purposes and not only be recognizable as art objects.
>
> **MV:** When NET [the Network of Ensemble Theaters] did Microfests in a number of regions of the country, and worked with community groups as well as performed plays, a lot of NET members asked, "Why are we doing this?" I had a deep belief that we have more to offer our communities than the plays we produce. Until we can learn to talk about all the other things we do, nothing is going to change. For our survival, relevance, and the aesthetics—it makes the art more interesting, and the objects more textured, nuanced, and complex.

Todd London wrote in an essay about Bloomsburg Theatre Ensemble (BTE) that if the regional theater movement [that took off in the 1960s] was about *de*centralization, then BTE, twenty years later, represented a moment of *re*centralization: recentering our communities in our town squares, civic institutions, schools. That's where we are now, having to recenter ourselves, make ourselves matter.

Valdez points out that diversifying professional paths so the nonprofit sector is not all about regional theater has been difficult:

> I came up in the 1980s, in Texas, when a career in regional theater was the only visible option. You became a director, actor, or writer and went to a regional theater in a big city. Yet, instinctively as artists and community members, we push up against that. We know there are other ways; we may not always have them at hand, but we're searching for this other thing that isn't the regional theater, a different way to engage and make art. Those of us who gravitate to community and ensemble are in an in-between space. On one side, we're taught about regional theater as the model for a successful career, and on the other side is this interest in social change, social justice, and a desire for an alternative to a traditional theater career.

Many who work in nonprofit institutional theaters, ensemble companies, community-based contexts, cultural organizing, and activism share subsets of the core values, practices, and principles that were hitherto the domain of strictly grassroots theater. Interest in being in direct exchange with audiences and communities is growing. Playwrights are doing more story circles and directors are offering more talk-backs with community members participating as experts, not only audiences.

London identifies ensembles, including Junebug and Cornerstone, as the avant-garde in the 1980s and 1990s and the mainstream now:

> I think of them as the true cutting edge of the theater, even though they were working in quieter ways, not in the sense of calling attention to their innovations or making manifestos like the Futurists. Place-based companies like Appalshop's Roadside, Bloomsburg, Junebug, Cornerstone, Dell'Arte—how else to think of them other than avant-garde?
>
> The proof is that their values are what the institutional theaters are now trying to ape and glom onto. The Public Theater is always its own animal and [founder Joseph] Papp shared values with all of it, Broadway and avant-garde and community-based, but Public Works [a project that develops a performance of a classic each year with a large cast representing a great swath of New Yorkers], for example—major regional theaters are trying to replicate it because it is leading edge.
>
> It's not about Lear [deBessonet, Public Works founder], who is a really thoughtful and talented public artist; it's about how it sits in

> the institution and institutional theater. That thing that happens when some idea or body gets co-opted by an entity that doesn't share its values. Lear's goal is to be Percy MacKaye and have public parades everywhere or be Hallie Flanagan and make sure there's theater in every community across the country. But I don't know how you do that in the context of regional theater – franchising Public Works as if it were McDonald's or Subway. . . . There's just no way to live like an ensemble or a socially engaged or community-based practitioner within a regional theater.

The Public Theater proudly touts other institutional nonprofit theaters that have followed its lead and produced their own Public Works projects, including the Dallas Theater Center in collaboration with Southern Methodist University's Meadows School of the Arts, the Seattle Repertory Theatre, and the National Theatre in London. While it's typical for people and institutions to wait for someone with whom they identify to do something new themselves, the Public did not invent the broadly participatory heart of Public Works. To give just a few examples from the last fifty-five years, many of the great theaters that accompanied social movements in the 1960s and 1970s either began with people who made art as an avocation, not a vocation, like the farmworkers who started El Teatro Campesino, or integrated local people into their performances, like Bread and Puppet since the 1960s and Cornerstone Theater since the 1980s. There's a deep tradition of people not trained as artists making theater with people who are for reasons that are deeply important to both of them and their communities. While earlier examples did not make a distinction between artists and others, such as the Haudenosaunee, who told stories to get through long winters and to keep their histories alive (Dioganhdih Hall in conversation with Pereira, May 23, 2020).

The issue of values plays out in many ways. Arlene Goldbard cited mainstream artists and institutions adopting the *methods* of socially engaged art but not the *reasons* to deploy them. There's no doubt, for example, that when money became available for regional theaters to interact with their local communities, a number of them instituted outreach or education departments as part of their fund-raising plan whatever their respective theater's mission.

Likewise, François Matarasso, in his book *A Restless Art,* observes that dominant cultural institutions in the UK have integrated the idea of direct participation, that the audience not be passive, and that everyone has the right to make art. But, Matarasso argues, establishment participatory art does not typically, like community-based or community arts, align truly being heard in an art project with a desire to participate more in the body politic.

Michael Garcés, director of the Cornerstone Theater Company for the past sixteen years, describes the effort to get institutional nonprofit theaters to understand community engagement:

> Often when conventional theaters talk about engagement, it's really marketing in a different guise, which is problematic. I try to parse it for them: There's nothing wrong with marketing. I want people to come to our shows, too. You just have to be clear when you are doing marketing and when you're doing engagement. When there's fuzz between the two, there's a dissonance that people feel deeply and is problematic.

Garcés explains that, unlike authentic dialogue, marketing is a kind of dialogue where you have a very specific end in mind and you're trying to manipulate the conversation to that end. Theaters do it all the time: through publicity posters, trying to make a show look enticing, or manipulating the audience to feel certain things. He elaborates:

> The problem occurs when we are being disingenuous, when we are pretending to have an authentic interaction but we're really trying to manipulate people to a particular end. Engagement should be a conversation in which we, the initiators, are clear about our intentions and do not have an ulterior motive or predetermined outcome in mind.
>
> We know we want to make something, but we don't know what it will be. It could look like theater or not. It might be a civic project and not theater, and that's great. If the outcome is that we don't want to do something, that's fine. I try to maintain the principle that we

> don't know what the outcome will be in every aspect; whether we're engaging around what the script is, what the design is, what the play is, who's in the play, we want to be entering as transparently as possible and not manipulating a particular outcome.
>
> Our practice is truly trying to elevate engagement, community concerns, and outcomes alongside aesthetics; one can't dominate the other. Our job is to fill both of those to the max. Art ***is*** the social engagement; the social engagement ***is*** the art. They must be held together. Our work is most effective both aesthetically and in ways that speak to civic life and community building when both succeed equally and are uncompromised. We fall into a bind when we allow them to get into opposition and value one more than the other. If we have created something beautiful but haven't valued the engagement as much as we could have or we've done good engagement but the aesthetic isn't all that good, neither is particularly satisfying to me. That's when we don't succeed.

Garcés feels terrible when he is working in conventional theater and something hasn't succeeded aesthetically. At Cornerstone, when he feels they haven't completely succeeded aesthetically, "at least we've done all these other wonderful things," he says. "That's a gift, even though, as an artist, leader, and person, I don't ultimately feel happy when we haven't done both. The social engagement is better when the aesthetics are better, and vice versa."

Activist Contexts

Daniel Park, a labor rights organizer, theater maker, and recruiter for Philadelphia Asian Performing Artists (PAPA), also focuses on community engagement, but from an overtly activist perspective. His interactive theater company, Obvious Agency, takes audience engagement into audience action. Parks explains why:

> So much of our art has become co-opted, and then stagnated in that traditional model: "I am the artist, and I am producing. You're the audience; you are receiving." There is still this capitalistic model of producing

a product that then gets received. There's maybe an opportunity to learn, intellectually, and maybe emotionally understand something. But there's no engagement beyond that. Very rarely does that engagement turn into changed action.

My company is focused on interactive performances because we want to see people practice doing new behaviors. Not just telling them, "Hey, racism is bad," but saying, "What if you deliberately behaved differently and had a safe place to try that out? How would that change things for you? How does that change what you believe you're capable of in how you want to be living your life?"

Another activist context for the integration of aesthetics and social concerns is that of artists who may appear to leave performance to work politically but in fact take their practice into other venues. In the 1980s, in the face of the AIDS epidemic, a number of artists were drawn to ACT UP—the AIDS Coalition To Unleash Power. Take this exchange between Richard Elovich and Debra Levine; the former was an openly gay performance artist and the latter was just finishing grad school for an MFA in directing at Columbia when ACT UP was taking off in the late 1980s:

DL: I got a big-deal grant from Creative Time for ten thousand dollars to do a production in Anchorage and I wanted to do something around AIDS. I had a concept in mind, and then I went to an ACT UP meeting to do research, maybe partner with people. I listened to what was going on in the meeting and totally realized that what I was thinking about was not politically on point. I was an outsider who thought that I could do something about the issue. I gave back the money to Creative Time and I joined ACT UP.

[While the nature of Levine's art making changed, her skill set was equally valuable in an activist context, as her ACT UP colleague Richard Elovich underlines in this exchange.]

DL: One of my big actions with ACT UP was at Shea Stadium, a Mets-Astros game. ACT UP bought a block of like three hundred seats. We had put together banners that had slogans like "Don't balk at safe sex." It was kind of an educational demonstration, a spectacle—

RE: It was an interruption.

DL: Yeah, it was an intervention. There were nine days of issues that ACT UP was doing, and this was the day for women, and we were really talking about the fact that men had to be responsible for safe sex as much as women did.

RE: Magic Johnson hadn't come out yet. Or Rock Hudson, even, I think.

DL: If you buy a big block of tickets to a baseball game, they'll put your messages on the LED displays. And they did; you saw "Act up, fight back. Fight AIDS." We didn't disrupt the game. We did it during the seventh-inning stretch. It was a huge media event. I had produced site-specific work before with Creative Time. But this was the first time I took all the skills I had from the theater realm and shifted them into grassroots activism.

RE: What Deb's saying is really important. We were taking arts activism into venues where we wouldn't normally have had access by manifesting it as art. That baseball game was exactly that. . . . I remember when I technically stopped making performance art. But I never left it. AIDS activism overtook it. I took that skill set and my Creative Time money and I made a needle-exchange video. I took my Manhattan Theatre Club money and did *This Is Not a Soapbox,* in which we introduced civil disobedience training to the blue-haired subscription audience. They were all handling needles and we said at the end, "You all are guilty of a crime."

ACT UP inspired the work Daniel Park does now:

I think a lot about ACT UP's direct actions. I often feel disappointed in our contemporary movements because our direct actions look about the same almost all the time. We protest. Okay, sure. We rally. Okay, sure. We sign things and we call people, but these things happen and then they're relatively forgettable afterward. Content and form don't necessarily line up. I really appreciate that the work of ACT UP was all connected. They were doing die-ins because people were fucking dying, and they needed people to not just ignore that fact.

Park works to integrate his education and his skills in labor organizing into his work with PAPA:

> I tend to reference the farmworkers movement in California, the cannery movement in Alaska, the folks in the various labor movements in Hawaii. In all of these regions, different ethnic immigrant labor was brought in and then replaced and used as a wedge between other communities as they were trying to organize for labor rights. I focus on the intersection between racial and labor justice in the arts. Anytime I can, I point to labor movements that were being driven by folks of color, especially when they are cross-race, multicoalition, or cross-ethnicity.
>
> In the arts, so often our community distances itself from the idea of labor. We don't think about the arts as a legitimate economic sector. Then artists internalize that and distance themselves from the idea of capitalism without even really thinking about it much. They don't think about themselves as laborers, as people who deserve to have rights. They don't think about the fact that artists are used to working seven days a week and that intense hustle, and that there are people who died to make sure that we could have five-day weeks and all that good stuff.
>
> In my personal work, I think about that a lot and try to remind artists, "Hey, we are workers inside a capitalist system, and there are alternative ways to organize. We deserve to have rights."

Park has tried integrating artists in organizing groups:

> Often when artists get embedded in movement work, the opportunities are focused on the artists and what kind of products they're going to come up with at the end. We wanted to go the opposite route and ask what are the integral skills that artists uniquely have that they can bring to movement work. How are artists integral to these organizations? What can they bring that's important and valuable? How can the art that they make be inspired by their work with movement folks?

The long history of artists as activists and performance as part of the culture shift of social change can be seen more recently in the Occupy Wall Street and Black Lives Matter movements, where performers who integrate materialist explanations for social conflict in their art are integral. The approaches to protest performance in the 2000s have been wide and diverse, some innovative and some relying on tried-and-true methods. Most social movements begin with anger but are sustained through inspiration and possibility, with art one of the generators.

Sharee Clark, cofounder of Freedom Fighters in Wilkes-Barre, Pennsylvania, an expression of Black Lives Matter, describes a protest she attended in June 2020 along with five hundred others, an extraordinary number in that area, hosted by a group of middle and high school students. Seeing that some of the young people were overwhelmed by the response, she got on the bullhorn both to do a little crowd control and provide other support:

> I wanted them to know that people are going to stand with them in their endeavors. I began to think, What is this going to look like six months down the line? How are we going to keep the momentum? Right now we're in the wind of a trend. Everybody's emotions are high. What is needed to get lasting change? Letting people know that this is not a sprint, that it's definitely a marathon. In order to destroy systemic racism, it has to happen brick by brick. It's not something that can happen as a result of this protest. I wanted to remind people that the protest brings the attention that we need, but it doesn't bring the changes that we need. Eyes are on us right now, the entire world, because of these protests, but what do we do from here?
>
> The desire to see young people empowered is how the thought process for the organization started. Every two or three days, a different group was popping up with a protest. How awesome would it be if we all get together. We have fingers all over, but if we come together as a fist, we can give a mighty blow.

Clark and others got together to discuss strategy, asking, What if, rather than people simply taking turns on the mike at large, angry protests, they became more deliberate about what actually impacts people? Clark elaborates:

> The first thing that came up was music. People can relate to music and music can carry messages. We knew that music had to be a part of our protests. What happened then was kind of magical. We looked for different creative ways of expression where people could get the same angry message out but not be redundant. We found we had poets, and dancers, but it was all about justice, about equality, through all these varied expressions. We could have a protest for hours, and people were not ready to leave. . . . I believe it was the creativity. The young people found a voice that they may not have had prior to the protests, and they found a safe place to express in a form that's comfortable to them. We didn't put any limits on what style or what type of creativity they could use. We just encouraged people to express themselves through their form of creativity. For young people, that's freeing. It was a safe space, a no-judgment zone. It didn't have to be polished, because this is your feeling, expressing your thoughts. Young people got a lot more confident in what they possessed because they had someone to validate their importance and the importance of what they have freedom to create.

The Political in the Everyday

One's everyday community can become a platform for intertwined commitments, as performance artist, director, and writer Daniel Alexander Jones experienced in Austin. Cynthia Taylor-Edwards, active in the theater scene as a performer ("the go-to person to play the Black mother") and producer of her own community theater company, asked Jones to direct Shay Youngblood's *Shakin' the Mess Outta Misery* with a couple of young actors and women from her church, some of whom "maybe had only ever been in a play in grade school." Jones elaborates:

> This was East Austin, Black Austin; people have jobs and families. So I said. "We're rehearsing for six instead of one month, on a drop-in

basis." She said, "We can't afford space." I said, "We're gonna rehearse in my house, four days a week at seven P.M." I made vegetarian collard greens. They laughed. "Why would you do this?" Then they tasted it and the room fell quiet. Along with this was storytelling and them talking about their relationships with their mothers and their children, and what songs! The next afternoon, Miss Pearly, one of the women in the cast, knocked at my door with a big cardboard box of collards and she said, "We thought you could cook these for tonight."

That show may have been the best thing I ever directed. There was not an utterance or gesture that did not come from across time. They owned every part of it; it was aesthetically one of the finest things I've ever done because it was itself. It won awards, and the Austin community loved it. People would ask me, "How did you get them to . . ." Which brings me back to your question: "What do you call [this kind of art]?" I call it our work, making art, making theater. The purpose is supposed to be that you bring people together, tell stories, and have these experiences. The idea that it belongs only to a professional class—I get off that boat.

Kathie deNobriga, community-based theater director, socially engaged art consultant, and erstwhile small-town mayor, expands on the skills beyond those of conventional theater that have informed everything she's done:

Analysis of a contemporary situation and agreement of not only what needs to change but how. There's the dimension of the [participating] people, who come to the table with all their raggedy-assedness, their racism, ageism, ableism, timidity, fear, all that. So the ability to work with human beings where they are, not where you wish they could be but actually what they are capable of, both willing and able to do together as a socially cohesive group. That has a lot to say about self-awareness, engagement around conflict, compromise, all those things of working together. When you look around our country nowadays, people don't have that anymore. They aren't willing to come to an agreement about what the issue is. It's always "those people," and that's not very useful.

> One of the things—it's not just mechanics—as a planner that I find myself often voicing is "Who has the capacity to do this? We all agree we have to do this action, but who actually can do it? Who's got the capacity in terms of time, resources, and willingness to compromise?" I make my living as a strategic planner, and this is always an issue. It's about a level of self-awareness, too. If you pull out to a thirty-thousand-foot level, which I like to do, I think it's all related to how you create the conditions under which people do their best work together. I've found that to be true as a consultant helping people make strategic plans and as a community theater maker.

Ethics

Commitment to both aesthetic exploration and social challenges takes many forms but cannot help but put ethics front and center. That's because socially engaged performance is so much about developing relationships with people that go beyond professional contracts. Jan's brother, Randy Cohen, was the first writer of *The New York Times Magazine*'s weekly "Ethicist" column, which is in the form of letters from readers about ethical dilemmas to which "the Ethicist" responds. His touchstone for the idea of ethics is that it "concerns the effects of our actions on other people. There can be solitary sin: You can sit alone at home and covet your neighbor's ox. But ethics isn't ethics until there are other people involved" (Randy Cohen in an email to Cohen-Cruz, April 21, 2021).

The most social of arts, performance, involves relationships with other people all the time. The ethics of attribution involve acknowledging the source of not only a specific citation but also the people who helped shape one's ideas along the way. A simple example of ethical behavior in the context of performance is acknowledging the source of a given practice. Speaking about the use of story circles without acknowledging that the practice came into use in theater circles in the 1960s through the Free Southern Theater and John O'Neal, who'd learned it from the Student Nonviolent Coordinating Committee, Nick Slie of Mondo Bizarro in New Orleans notes:

> You run the risk of erasing especially Black people when you don't acknowledge these practices that come from these traditions. . . . John [O'Neal] was unwilling to codify things because it was for the people who didn't need that. I see Stephanie McKee [current director of Junebug] trying to protect that legacy and make it free to everyone. John taught us story circles. We don't publish it or put it on our website. We try to be really sensitive; if we're going to use it, we just want to check in if anyone from Junebug wants to cofacilitate with us, if there's money passing hands. That's a nuance there.

Toya Lillard, executive director of viBe Theater Experience, spoke about uneven power relationships when people with more clout want to "collaborate" with the young women of color she works with at viBe:

> **TL:** It's intent versus impact. There's a whole history of young people being told they're in community with certain folk, but they aren't; they are being told what to do. For the young women of viBe, it's about power.
>
> **JCC:** Uneven power in supposed collaborations.
>
> **TL:** Exactly. The lived experience of our young women of color is exploited. They don't have control over their narratives and they're really incredulous, and rightly so, of power structures that seem to be invitations into collaborations but are not. That is, heavy-handed adults come in and say, "Come write your own play, find your voice," and then this adult comes in at the end [and says,] "I'm gonna make it better," and they edit the whole thing, and the kid is like, "Wait a minute, that's not the piece that I wrote." Because we don't trust young people. The perfectionism attached to producing theater and if young people create something—it's not viable unless an adult comes in and makes it real theater. So there's a lack of trust when they're told they're collaborators. That's at the root of what creates barriers. And coming in with language that creates barriers. I learned this the hard way, by using language that creates barriers. They're not interested.

The facilitator has to be okay with a different aesthetic if the young people are 100 percent creators without professional adult theater artists guiding or directing.

The U.S. Department of Arts and Culture (USDAC), initiated by Arlene Goldbard and Adam Horowitz to manifest a federal department of arts and culture that does not actually exist but they wish did, advises artist/activists to pay attention to how they begin a project, because that's where they lay the foundation for what will continue (usdac.us/imaginings, their guide to creating community conversations using the arts). This can mean not just regarding a project but a career-long trajectory.

Rad experienced the importance of staying aligned with how a project begins in an experience early on in their career that leveraged funding in exchange for obedience:

> In 2013, I had just graduated from college and was full of ideas and passion for how to transform the theater world into a more equitable place. My collaborators and I were riding high from winning a handful of awards in the previous year for a show that held beautiful, intimate parts of our selves: hip-hop music, spoken-word poetry, dance, physical theater, magical realism, all told through the very Black, brown, and queer lens of our experiences.
>
> We were approached by a seemingly well-meaning white woman who proposed producing and investing in the show at her event space in midtown New York. She offered us free rehearsal space, performance space, marketing, choreographic support, and money. We took the bait and started building this production that featured six young Black and two white folks, and was creatively supported by five Black and brown folks. The red flags started popping up after a few weeks: the producer's unrealistic expectations, volatile communication, emotional harassment, use of the N-word, insisting we take responsibility for selling alcohol even though there was no liquor license, and a general lack of knowledge about theater protocols. We were so grateful to have the space and the resources that we grinned and bore it.

> The reality of the situation came clear when we opened the show and the police arrested her. We found out that the space was not a legal performance venue. We were accused of stealing money and running an illegal bottle club. After months of emotional abuse, dangerous working conditions, the threat of a lawsuit, and continued surveillance on our computers, we woke up to the realities of predatory people in the theater world. This woman was drawn to the cultural capital that comes with diversity, but she was not committed to the internal and systemic work needed to do this work with integrity and care. We hadn't realized that under her patronage we would not be able to embody the ethics of our play in the process we hoped to cultivate.
>
> That experience changed and traumatized me. I left the commercial theater world for a few years and immersed myself in political performance art and multimedia arts, while building my commitments to my ethics in a way that would allow me to sense the red flags and not compromise on values ever again.

Another ethical issue is reciprocity. Some artists see only what the power of grassroots arts can do for them. Goldbard calls this phenomenon "the artist as human paintbrush: 'I'm going to use you in my composition and get all the credit, all the everything,' and that's not so good." On the other end of the spectrum, some artists try to be too invisible, seeing their work as channeling community partners, rather than including space for themselves. Goldbard emphasizes the importance of artists being conscious about where they "position themselves on the continuum: The most common issue I've seen are lead artists with strong ideas of what the project should be and who unwittingly do damage to project participants by quashing their ideas and not giving them equal standing."

An artist's ability to balance multiple commitments is also about how overt they can be about their values, given what they need to do to survive. Artist Caroline Woolard looks at the intertwining of one's politics and one's art as a privilege. She gives the example of Laura Raicovich, director of the Queens Museum when Trump was elected in 2016, who sought to commit the institution to being anti-Trump. Raicovich was especially concerned that the community of immigrants around the museum would continue to feel safe there under the new administration. The board refused, claiming they were not "political" and could not make a statement like that. Raicovich had threatened to quit if the board did not make such a statement, so she did. But she recognized that her coworkers could not, by and large, take that stand because, unlike her, they did not have husbands with health insurance to keep their families safe; many simply needed the job. As Woolard recounts, they were "stuck in a place that's not aligned with their values because they need to eat."

Integrating Commitments to Art and Community Concerns

What follows are examples of integrating commitments to both art and community concerns from two ends of the spectrum—Carlton Turner, whose work leads with social justice, and Bill Rauch, whose work leads with aesthetics. Ethical concerns are central in both projects.

Carlton Turner: Leading with Social Justice

Carlton Turner's trajectory from a socially engaged performer to executive director of the regional organization Alternate ROOTS to national leader in the arts at the intersection of social justice to founder with his wife, Brandi, and lead artist of the hyperlocal Mississippi Center for Cultural Production (aka Sipp Culture) in Utica, Mississippi, is an example of how fully the arts may be integrated in a broader cultural frame committed to social justice purposes. Such framing also reflects people's personal journeys.

As an undergraduate, Turner received a scholarship from the athletic department at the University of Mississippi. He spent four years "feeling lost, seeing raw, uncut white privilege, studying literature and history written only by white writers who did not speak to my life and experience." He recalls writing poetry in the margins of his textbook. His brother Maurice, a jazz musician, who had also enrolled at UMISS to be with him, said, "You write; I make music. Let's do something." They went to a brother's house off campus, wrote music for two weeks, and quit school in 1996, just weeks before their graduation. They were, said Turner, "sick and tired;

it was sort of a protest." Their mother was upset because education was supposed to be key to liberation; how could they throw that opportunity away? They tried to explain that this was the 1990s, not the 1960s (though they have since gotten their degrees).

That was the beginning of their company, M.U.G.A.B.E.E.—Men Under Guidance Acting Before Early Extinction, which blends jazz, hip-hop, spoken-word poetry, and soul music with nontraditional storytelling. Turner explains the name:

> [It]comes from the idea that when we were growing up, Black men were considered an endangered species. It was a time of the drug wars and gang wars and all the things that were continuing to dismantle [the] progress of Black men. Much like what we've seen with Trayvon Martin and Jordan Davis, [Black men] have been seen as a threat to the community. We wanted to bring about some positive music and art that could project a different type of Black male presence, especially coming out of a southern culture.

In 1998, the Turner brothers found an artistic home at Southern Vibes, a Jackson, Mississippi, poetry club run by local Black artists. Carolyn Morris, a member of Alternate ROOTS and later its director, came up to them after a show and asked if they knew the organization:

> And soon we were connected to like-minded individuals and companies as committed to social justice as to art. The ROOTS community asked, "How can the work we do as artists serve a different outcome for our community and people?" I got my Ph.D. in institutional racism at UMISS and my Ph.D. in community cultural organizing at Alternate ROOTS.

After serving in a number of staff positions at ROOTS, Turner became executive director in 2009. The organization flourished with his very value-driven and collaborative leadership style. He left in 2018 "to focus on investing more in my local community through the Mississippi Center for Cultural Production . . . the culmination of a longtime dream to bring my passion, learning, and network to support the people in my small town of Utica, Mississippi, through arts, agriculture, and

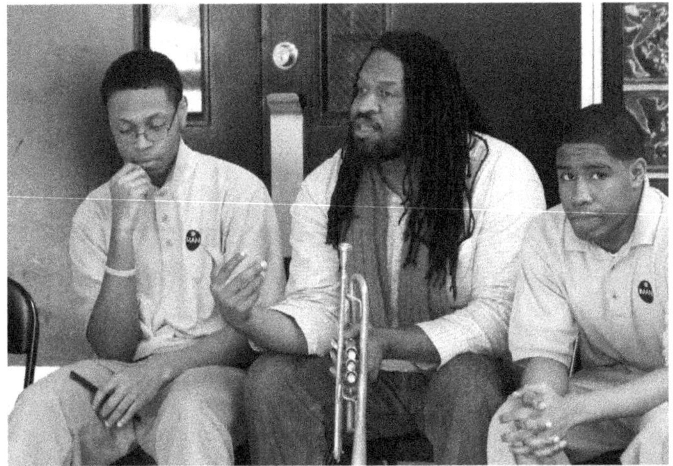

Story circle with musician Maurice Turner and students from Imani Christian Academy in Pittsburgh, Pennsylvania, as part of UPRISE: Raising Black Men Project with the August Wilson Center. Photo by Carlton Turner. Copyright Turner World Around Productions. Courtesy of Turner World Around Productions.

community development." Turner describes Sipp Culture as "working to shift our community mode from consumption to production: growing and sharing food, documenting our culture in digital and analog media, and telling our stories through movement, theater, and sound. It means producing the culture we want reflected in the stories, food, systems, communities, and the art we create."

Sipp's community is grounded in the aesthetics of Black, southern, rural culture bearers, which characterizes the art it facilitates. "Their imprint can be found on every community throughout the nation in the architecture, songs, spiritual practices, the movement of bodies, and in the language of freedom":

> We understand the integral connection between the artist voice and community health and wellness of our rural space. We know that the stories told, who gets to tell them, and where they are told are central to the shaping of policy and ultimately inform the quality of life in our community. Our health and wellness are negatively impacted when the only stories representative of our experiences are told from the subjectivity of the observer. To that end, Sipp Culture works to develop the imagination and enhance the creativity of our

> community (near and far) through critical dialogue driven by arts and cultural exchange. We recognize the importance of counternarratives in shaping the critical discourse of a community and we recognize our work, as holders of space for story, requires us to uplift as many of those stories as possible in order to shape and reshape public policy.

Sipp's mission is to support and organize people moving toward more self-sufficiency, using art, culture, and agriculture as fulcrums. To that end, Sipp launched the Rural Performance/ Production Lab to assist and nurture rural artists during the creation of new and original works in the areas of performance, including movement, image, and sound. The impetus is so artists do not have to go elsewhere to make their work; that with a support network, they can make art in their home communities. Sipp staff believe that such artists have much to contribute to their localities, both materially and nonmaterially. They strive to cultivate a culture of imagination and possibilities and manifestation of dreams:

> We don't want to control what happens to Utica; we want people to have the tools to manifest what's important to them. Young people don't know what they are eating in food and in culture. Part of our work is helping people understand their relationship to food, not by "training" them but, rather, believing if they have information, they make choices which may or may not be in their best interests. Now it's not knowing they are being poisoned.
>
> The aesthetic is listening, recognizing that what we have is a set of skills and relationships and if we hold on to them for ourselves, that's criminal and extractive. If we share them with a community as resources, they create something bigger and longer- lasting. It's about collaboration, partnership, transformation. We want to see what happens in this community if we spend twenty years living these principles, testing ROOTS' hypotheses, like its Resources for Social Change, in a concentrated community. There are fewer than 1,000 people in town, and 4,500 in this zip code. Can we have a culture shift?

Sustaining a cultural institution in a small, financially under-resourced town depends on making the case for national importance and drawing national funding. Given his high profile from the ROOTS years, as evidenced in the many awards and grants he has received and the national boards on which he sits, Turner can make that case and powerful people listen. This is not only a fund-raising strategy; Sipp's rural arts initiative is national in scope, allowing artists from around the country to share strategies and problem-solve together. This nourishes both Sipp and rural theaters nationally. Working locally, regionally, and nationally, Turner expands a democratic vision of arts and culture.

Bill Rauch: Aesthetic Concerns, Social Justice Values

Director Bill Rauch, playwright Alison Carey, and a cohort of founding members of the Cornerstone Theater Company met at Harvard. Upon graduation in 1986, they spent five years in hyperlocal rural contexts—small towns across the United States—adapting classics with people in response to issues they were contending with. "Cornerstone still works in hyperlocal contexts, or certainly did in our early years in L.A., where we often worked with neighborhoods," Bill explains.

"I'm completely different because of the Cornerstone experience," avows Rauch. "The Cornerstone work is a lot about overcoming fear of the other and not staying in our separate camps. You can only know yourself by getting to know people who are different from you. We started working within communities and became about bridges between communities."

Rauch then took the reins at the Oregon Shakespeare Festival, a move he made "in the hopes that we could foreground values of equity, diversity, and inclusion and do more aesthetically radical work at a large-budget institution with a long history." His commitment to marginalized writers, directors, and actors is evidenced in the jump in the number of actors of color from 20 percent to over 70 percent before he left.

Rauch changed the format of the Green Show, OSF's free outdoor summer festival of short performances on the courtyard stage, which had featured Renaissance music and dance, then modern dance. He made it community-based and professional, a venue for rotating performances by local, regional, and international artists. Thus did Rauch apply values honed in local contexts to the regional theater world, bringing more attention to the local.

In 2019, Rauch was named inaugural artistic director of the Perelman Performing Arts Center at the World Trade Center, a location that, he explains, has experienced "successive waves of trauma: from Dutch colonizers massacring Lenape to making the African burial grounds outside city limits, through waves of immigrants, to the architect of the Twin Towers articulating a vision of world peace when it opened in the early seventies, and then the trauma of 9/11."

Rauch believes there's much promise in what that place could be, and he will try to create work that "has an impact, brings people together, cuts across performing arts disciplines, connects people across cultural differences, and brings people from all walks of life into the building."

Rauch provides this example:

> We hope to present and produce work not only across disciplines but also across methodologies. We might premiere an opera that celebrates a specific cultural community, an original community-engaged dance piece with local immigrant and first-generation youth from that same community, and a music group from that same culture's country of origin. Were all three pieces to be performed in our building at the same time, the transformational energy and exchanges could be quite astonishing.

In a way, Rauch has come full circle, foregrounding diverse cultures and local expressions as he did in the early days of Cornerstone. By remaining true to its founding principles, the Perelman Center can avoid the trap of becoming ever more driven by the market, which compromises so many large institutions over time.

We appreciate that some performance makers lead with the art, some lead with a social or political concern, and some are constrained by their circumstances from doing all they wish on either end of the spectrum. We have no interest in dictating what artists do. We delight in the array of forms performance takes and the expansiveness of its contexts. We do, however, advocate for underlying values that assure the work will benefit all the participants.

3 Education

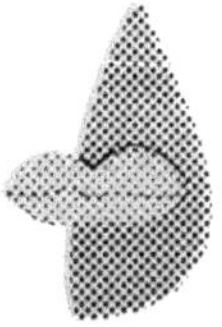

Knowledge systems permeate our daily lives as teachers and learners, individuals [and] parts of communities. Fundamentally, knowledge systems exist in order to maintain, bolster, enliven, and perpetuate a group. A community.

—Lumbee philosopher Bryan Brayboy

In the above quote, Brayboy grounds knowledge systems in cultural specificity. In what follows, we share what we heard from interviewees who come from different cultures and communities about their own education as socially engaged performance makers. We begin with underlying principles that are relevant beyond specific communities.

Paulo Freire's conception of education for liberation and freedom was affirmed by many of our interviewees. Liberation is the process of becoming free from a critical or difficult situation involving outside control, even if internalized. Freedom means the right to live one's life as one sees fit, making one's own decisions and expressing one's opinion without fear of censorship or retribution. In contrast to Freire's ideal, mainstream K-12 educational models in the United States still rely on Industrial Age pedagogy that prepares people to become market tools of industry. It is a model based in rote learning, memorization, and what Freire called the "banking model," conceiving of the student as an empty vessel that an all-knowing teacher fills with the knowledge necessary to carry out a particular task, such as take tests, operate machinery, or be part of a chorus line, an approach that can be found in any field, including performance.

Freire developed his pedagogy working in Brazil with those he referred to as "the oppressed." In the absence of conventional educational resources, he focused on what people could learn in dialogic exchange with others in the same situation. The artists we spoke with also embrace dialogue as a component of an education that creates liberated, free-thinking artists, proactive in their lives and communities. Imagination, the capacity to conceive of an alternative, and in this case to strive for it, plays an important role in such an education. What conditions support and what inhibit the free-flowing imagination? Cultural activist Terry Marshall of Intelligent Mischief says, "We are in an imagination battle," because not only is it nearly impossible for people who are busy surviving to have the capacity to access their imagination or to dream but also because of the ways in which the behaviors of oppressive systems have infiltrated our minds (http://adriennemareebrown.net/tag/terry-marshall).

Education's etymology supports the idea that people already have knowledge inside them, which is *educed,* or called forth, through a learning process. This idea aligns with Freire's notion of education for freedom, connecting with and listening to an internal voice. That struggling people have historically seen education as a path to a better life aligns it with the notion of liberation.

However, training suggests that there is one way to do something, which the student must learn and then follow. Choreographer Liz Lerman's contribution to socially engaged performance includes integrating people of all ages, as well as including dancers whose bodies did not fit into the professional norms of the times. In fact, Lerman was purposeful in making the body a canvas for radical change. She finds it instructive to notice which populations are said to be "trained" in preparation for their work and which are described as "educated" (Liz Lerman in a phone conversation with Cohen-Cruz, December 1, 2020). Police are trained; so are low-level staff; and so are actors and dancers. Training suggests learning a set way to do something, from the outside, that can be passed on whole cloth. It evokes Freire's "banking method" in contrast to education for liberation and freedom.

We turn now to our interviewees. Recurrent themes include underlying values that dictate why one approach to education is favored over another; what kind of education is needed to fulfill commitments to both self-expression and community; what cultural traditions and practices are centered and which are marginalized in training and educational programs; and how informal as well as formal experiences have provided aesthetic and moral grounding.

Underlying Values and Accompanying Challenges

The concept of hegemony—the often-unconscious way that the views of those in control become the norm—helps us understand how art practices that clearly privilege particular cultural practices can be considered neutral. In U.S. theater programs, students are often instructed to first strip down, learn to work with the skills that constitute that particular art form (voice, movement, acting; line, gesture, composition, etc.), and then to apply them to working situations. But there are value judgments about performers' very bodies; not a few young women, especially in dance, have been told that they must lose weight while still students, or that they are not perceived as "leading role material" according to Euro-American norms of coloration, facial features, and hair texture.

The experience of Lanxing Fu, who is Chinese American, reflects how value-laden assumptions about what lead characters must look like pervade much U.S. performance and training:

> When I was cast in major roles, the dramaturgy of the entire show was changed to accommodate the abnormality of seeing my body onstage in a story it didn't belong in. I once had a voice coach train me in a Mandarin accent so my voice could match my appearance for the part and explain my presence in the time period.

There are also norms regarding professionalism that take for granted the excavation of our emotional and spiritual selves for the sake of making art. Far from neutral, such experiences can be traumatic, healing, revelatory, or a myriad of other possibilities. Cultural critic Arlene Goldbard elaborates:

> It's about moral contract versus legal contract. To whom are you accountable? People do a lot of damage when they have the wrong answer to that question. There's a lot of transgression around intimacy and coercion, given that so much of community-based art is with very vulnerable people—like incest survivors or incarcerated persons. A lot of people don't offer the necessary level of protection and don't know how to deal with dynamics of coercion: "I told my story, so now you really need to tell yours. . . ." People who are coerced into unprotected intimacy might feel terrible afterward. A lot of projects need more help in holding confidentiality.

Performances created with people in nonprofessional contexts often draw directly on their experiences. Deep issues arise during this process; we carry our experience within our bodies, and storytelling triggers emotional memories. We cannot expect people to open up, pour out their souls, and go on about their day. It can be a very sacred and spiritual experience to explore our inner worlds; not everyone has the tools to do so safely, closing themselves back up before they go back out into the world.

As Goldbard recounts, sometimes when people are asked to share sensitive experiences in art training or making, emotional distress is considered collateral damage; anything is acceptable in the service of art. There may even be a bias against the concern about emotional damage: The question "Are you doing therapy or theater?" arises with some frequency. But as Goldbard suggests, the teacher or facilitator is first and foremost responsible to the students/participants. When thought *is* given to the ethics of the work, to community well-being as an inviolable principle, education either goes beyond art as conventionally understood—in this case, including elements of therapy—or artists partner with people with relevant expertise.

Integrating healing can be as simple as a check-in at the beginning of a workshop or rehearsal and a check-out at the end, communicating care for the participants. It could look take the form of writing a shared list of community agreements that the participants cocreate as to best uphold their agency. Or healing might play a fundamental role in one's practice. Liz Lerman has described healing as an ancient component of performance itself:

> In my book *Hiking the Horizontal,* I wrote, "People danced and that is how they healed their children. They danced as a way to prepare for war." They understood they needed embodiment, imagination, projection into the future; in addition to the repetition—you do it every day or once a year, whatever the discipline of time—time was part of it; it's persistent. I compare that experience to when my mom died. I was a perfectly trained human being—classical ballet, a degree in modern dance forms, but none of that served me when she died.

Explaining that her mother's death led her to work with older people, Lerman continued:

> Any number of artists have asked me about what I was doing in that senior center for ten years. Because they are trying to figure out [bringing art to] a prison system or this or that. I realized one of the underlying dynamic magnets to the work I was doing then was healing.

Rad describes their own well-being in the context of conjoining community organizing and art making:

> During my college years in Lenapehoking (NYC), post-9/11, post–Occupy Wall Street, pre–Black Lives Matter, I was slowly radicalized by the realities of living on occupied Turtle Island. I had experienced these realities firsthand for much of my life, but they had gone unexamined. My formal and informal education gave me language, tools, and consciousness to fight and heal to liberate myself from the trauma of existing in these oppressive systems. I began to understand the foundations of the systemic and institutional injustices my loved ones and I continually experience. I was seeking answers to big questions, medicine for my woes, and solidarity; I found these and more in the way community organizers and art makers move through the world together.

> In my first devising project, we celebrated the twentieth anniversary of the fall of the Berlin Wall with the twentieth birthdays of myself and my classmates. We shared stories about our youth and coming of age to find a parallel emotional journey to what the lead up to, moment of, and aftereffects of tearing down the wall must have felt like to German youth. After another senseless murder of a Black teenager, [this time] in Ferguson, Missouri, we made a participatory ritual about the intersection of climate change and the policing of Black and brown bodies that invited and sort of forced the audience to deal with the internalized oppressions by embodying the central pillars of the prison-industrial complex and environmental racism.
>
> After returning from my homeland and feeling a rootlessness mixed with realization of my family's attempted assimilation into whiteness, I made a liberatory Decolonization Rave with a dozen other artists of the global majority, to recognize and heal our collective and individual inherited trauma. I found fulfillment, validation, and wholeness in the work I was learning how to make with my communities. I began to feel what a life centered around cultural activities rooted in collective responsibility could do for our emotional, spiritual, and physical well-being.
>
> This was in stark contrast to the way I was trained, which was to be an eager and willing empty vessel that I could sometimes fill with my own imagination but mostly with the imaginations of the director and the playwright. I was expected to lay myself bare, trauma on command, heart open. But no care was given to emotional well-being or mental health. We were taught how to open ourselves up but not how to close ourselves up or to set healthy boundaries and standards. Most actors I know who were trained in Eurocentric programs are emotional intimacy junkies because of this.

There are healing techniques that come from specialized training such as trauma-informed practice (van der Kolk 2015). But artists do not need to become therapists to integrate healing, as Lerman avows:

> I rejected the term *dance therapy* in reference to my work but still respect the field, even though my natural allies were going into dance

therapy and thereby giving up their aesthetic forms, accepting the medical definitions, practically going to med school. In order to get a foothold in the health-care world, it would be easier now, and I was saying no to that, there's another thing. I feel the healing power internally as part of dance.

Another value of socially engaged art is appreciating aesthetic diversity, which is reflected in the kind of education made available, the kind of art that gets made, and its relationship to a community or audience. Rihana Yazzie speaks to the sense of worth that comes with acknowledgment of specific communities:

> [One of] theater's powers is building self-esteem. The U.S. government has assaulted the self-esteem of Native people, which is why you see suicide rates so high. . . . If you're a Native person in the audience watching Native people onstage, it's healing, because we never get to see ourselves reflected back in any kind of media.

Lumbee philosopher Bryan Brayboy embeds cultural specificity in an understanding of aesthetics in the context of Indigenous knowledge systems:

> I have taken up [aesthetics] to articulate our ways of valuing and our value systems[,] as how we come to think of what is good, true, right, and beautiful. We might ask: What do we value? What is good, true, right, and beautiful? Values undergird everything within knowledge systems. They guide decisions and actions. (Brayboy 2021)

Lerman explains how this concept of aesthetics has been important to her:

> **LL:** We know aesthetics from the Greeks as the "good, beautiful, and true," but Bryan adds "what a people see as." Okay, downtown New York dancers are "a people." I drew nourishment and information from their aesthetics—postmodernism—but never totally accepted it because the values that lived through its systems seemed so strange. And this is still true. Whereas irony is king, I believe in sincerity. And so on. These are not oppositional, but in my work irony is a tool, not the end product.

> **JCC:** How has Brayboy's definition of aesthetics been relevant to your work?
>
> **LL:** It was a driving force at the Dance Exchange. We were a people, an ensemble, and we worked really hard at understanding what we believed was good—what we were willing to spend our time on. Beautiful—I think beauty is a really important part of all this. It helps you sustain your relationship to dark things and hard times, and it balances the accompanying grief and anger that go with this. *Beauty* is a big term; it's quite relational—if I put this color next to this color, this object next to this object, this dancer next to this music—it has its own momentum. And truth—most of us are busy trying to understand the multiple truths that exist. The problem is a person like Trump, who muddies the water by twisting the idea of multiple truths—there are good people on both sides—when really, he is purposely lying to advance his agenda. Then the idea of multiple truths is disastrous.
>
> **JCC:** And there's a difference between multiple truths and calling lies "truth"! But say more about aesthetics.
>
> **LL:** Aesthetics is the work of being in the world. It's problematic; it's like you want to flip it. . . . Let me tell you this story. I was on a panel for a major grant. And every time an artist who is working in community came up, one or two of the panelists would say, "Let's look at the ethics." Finally, I pounded the table and said, "Are you not looking at the ethics of every other artist on this list? What's happening here? I refuse to have the discussion unless you do that." That's what I mean.

This suggests seeking the ethical in any aesthetics as in any life.

The challenge to situate an art program in an appropriate aesthetic is not just an issue for students but also for institutions as a whole. As arts and culture researcher Maria Rosario Jackson and her coauthors articulated:

> Universities and art schools [are] . . . influenced by standards from away. . . . [M]ajor art schools and universities often do not teach the art forms connected to the heritage or traditions specific to their

community or region. Rather, most arts schools have curricula that are governed primarily by New York and Western European paradigms. (Maria Rosario Jackson et al. 2003, 19)

Education can either support or undermine artists trying to square what they believe is worth doing— for example, the "good and the true"— with their art, be it socially engaged or any other. If a training program has been shaped by aesthetics with which a student does not feel aligned, how do they do their best work?

The good, the true, and the beautiful are also circumstance-specific. Disability artist and activist Kevin Gotkin speaks about an aesthetics that creates access in his work to people with disabilities. He gives the example of Cheryl Finnegan, who makes beautiful benches with text that reads "This exhibition has asked me to stand for too long. Sit down if you agree." Gotkin elaborates: "You sit down as a way of engaging in this thing your body has been told not to acknowledge in the presence of art." Such art creates something often missing in aesthetic spaces—"the freedom to do what you need and to disrupt forms of etiquette. Access in disability art combines art and justice and is innovative in the way it resists engrained models of what art is and should look like."

Theater artist and scholar Cristal Chanelle Truscott has critiqued the absence in most theater training programs in U.S. higher education of not only multiple cultural approaches but also the concomitant cultural values embedded in them. In her own experience as an undergraduate at a PWI (predominantly white institution), "instead of approaching performance with the fullness of their creative and expressive archive," she saw actors whose creative inclinations had been censored and their particularities erased "because they were convinced that they needed to read 'neutral.'" Truscott responded to the limits of theater training that she encountered by developing SoulWork, created out of African American performance traditions and aesthetics, explaining:

The term *soul* is understood in African American cultural expression to describe an esoteric, aesthetic occurrence that moves someone "spiritually," in the sense that it cannot be explained through words.

> Rather, soul can only truly be understood intrinsically, through feeling, emotion, embodiment, and expression. Dictionary definitions typically cite four main characteristics of soul: (a) the spiritual or unique/individual immaterial part of a human being; (b) a person's moral and emotional nature, the ability to feel empathy; (c) a quality of feeling deep emotion and arousing it in others, especially as revealed in an artistic performance, particularly soul music; and (d) all of the above as understood, created, and practiced by African Americans as an essential element of Black cultural expression. (Truscott and Gabriel 2017)

Truscott is interested in the aesthetics that come out of every culture, and asks this question:

> How wide can we open our arms and how much can we offer artists to know themselves and find ways of understanding their body and their voice? Every culture has traditions of training, of arts and cultural practice, and of community engagement that could be of service; particularly because we're in this country that has access to so many identities and ancestries and lineages, university training spaces around methodologies need to look different than they do.

At the extreme other end of being grounded in one's own cultural traditions while appreciating others is being uprooted from one's culture, as with the U.S. government's treatment of Native Americans. The Civilization Fund Act of 1819, for example, was purportedly to infuse this country's Indigenous people with "good moral character" and vocational skills. The law tasked Christian missions and the federal government with teaching young Native Americans subjects from reading to math, eventually leading to a network of boarding schools designed to carry out this charge. The act was, in effect, an effort to stamp out America's original culture and replace it with one that Europeans had imported to the continent. Over time, countless Native American children were taken from their families and homelands and placed in faraway boarding schools, a process that was often traumatic and degrading.

Ronee Penoi, a Laguna Pueblo/Cherokee/Polish theater artist with Groundwater Arts, reflects:

> My great-grandfather, who went to Carlisle Indian School, was code switching before those words were used. I have to look back and listen hard to understand where I come from precolonization. Something was taken away that I'm trying to find again. There's a very personal line of stories that wanted to be told in my immediate family, and I'm connecting that to a larger story.

Both Indigenous peoples in the U.S. and enslaved Africans were forbidden from practicing anything that related to their own cultures and heritage, but they kept much alive through storytelling, which many Indigenous communities use to record their experiences. These stories were retold in secret, and were a way to honor their ancestors' experiences (https://theconversation.com/how-african-american-folklore-saved-the-cultural-memory-and-history-of-slaves-98427). Such a pattern, and form of genocide, can be found in colonial situations all around the globe; enslaved people were forbidden from reading and practicing their cultural traditions, as well. To assert one's cultural voice is aligned with expressing one's political autonomy. As Dipankar Mukherjee puts it, "My artistic aesthetic is my politics, and my politics is justice."

Hierarchical thinking undermines the capacity to be centered in one's aesthetic. Education and training are tinged with expectations based on class. Not only is formal, post-secondary school education—for example, "higher education"—often raised up over vocational *training* but it's assumed that nearly all private institutions are better than the majority of state schools. Both these assumptions and the idea that college by itself will best prepare everyone for what they want to do in life are deeply flawed.

In the West, the intellect has long been considered a more solid indicator of knowledge than the corporal or emotional, which are often artists' strengths. The theory of multiple intelligences, attributed to Harvard developmental psychologist Howard Gardner in 1983 but recognized in practice well before then, posits eight modalities of human intelligence: visual-spatial, verbal-linguistic, musical-rhythmic, logical-mathematical, interpersonal, intrapersonal, naturalistic, and bodily-kinesthetic (Gardner 1983).

Yet in practice these modes of intelligence are not given equal weight. Caroline Woolard, solidarity economy artist and professor, talks about the role of the artist and the valuing of different knowledge systems:

> From the beginning of their path in this world, artists are often people who resist colonial monocultures of knowledge, like an emphasis on written language, on English, on test taking. I think artists like us are people who say, "No, there are other kinds of knowledge. . . . I know that there's embodied knowledge, and visual knowledge. There's this felt sense that I am going to follow. Even though my teachers and the institutions around me are telling me that it's not valuable." That stubborn love of other forms of knowledge leads us eventually into a radical awakening about structures that don't serve us because we've had to say, "No matter what, even if you think I'm going to be a starving artist forever, or you think this knowledge doesn't matter, or I have bad grades, or I don't register in any of the areas that you think matter, I'm going to do it anyway. I'm going to be great at it." And that is a beginning of radicalization.

We turn now to how artists are educated in both informal and formal settings.

Informal and Formal Educational Contexts

Performance techniques and values are passed on through both informal and formal means. We refer to informal learning as intellectual, creative, spiritual, and emotional development that impacts one's work and takes place by osmosis, experience, and over time, often in the context of some other activity, such as a recreational program or participation in a church choir or through a profound relationship with a person who helps set one on one's path. By formal learning, we mean deliberate study of something within a concentrated time frame. Both are necessary and valuable educational modes, although informal learning has tended to be less acknowledged, recognized, and valued than its formal counterpoint.

Informal learning includes such modes as how culture bearers and in some cases one's family and extended community provide a young person with experiences of aesthetic traditions, what one absorbs from the culture in which one is embedded, and experiences traveling, existing, and working in the world. Formal education includes classes and programs offered in universities, conservatories, artists' studios, and as part of many companies' ongoing work.

What follows is a look at a range of learning contexts to suit the needs of a range of students and artists. From methodologies developed over time by specific companies, tailor-made to their needs, to practices that evolved comprehensively over time to meet the needs of various communities, such education responds to people's different learning styles as well as life circumstances.

Informal Learning

Performance artist Daniel Alexander Jones's arts education began as a child at home:

> I feel like I was trained from birth. My parents met at a Girls Club of America branch in Springfield, Massachusetts, that my mother's mother ran. She had worked as a sewing teacher in one. My father grew up in the Boys Club. They were an interracial couple at a time that wasn't happening and a lot of that was because of the club. I grew up with these community workers. They were all teaching all the time, even though that was not formal. My earliest memories are being in that club and learning a tremendous amount about how what you do impacts other people. That's my foundation. You are not here by yourself. You can be cute and you can want your toy, but boom. It set a way of thinking that afterward would either help me be congruent with institutions or alienate me from them. I came up mostly in public schools when there was art there. We weren't poor, but we didn't have extra money. The school gave us supplies and space to do stuff. So it didn't feel that art was elite, but that it was something everyone did.

Mentorship is another component of training. Young artists may learn as much about life as about art from their mentors. Jones continues:

> My real education was an embodied apprenticeship, working with Robbie McCauley and Laurie Carlos, and staying with Laurie for a while. It was that old school you gonna do the laundry, do the dishes, go to the grocery store, hear people talk shit on the phone.

Jones found the ethos of taking the whole person in hand in the Black theater world to which he gravitated:

> My first proper professional gig was with the Penumbra Theatre [Company] in St. Paul. It was tied to a Black theater world context; I was very fortunate to get my feet under me as a young artist where I was learning from watching people who were expert in what they did and also had the ethos to say, "Come here, boy; this is how you do this. Do you have a bank account? Did you go grocery shopping?" So they took care of the person, and that made all the difference to me. As part of that, I've taken for granted that community work is always part of it, not a separate identity I claim. Always watching them take a look at people—I remember being in rehearsal and Rebecca [Rice] just looking at someone in the corner of the room working, and later I found out she knew there was a domestic violence situation and she could clock it just by observing, and she did an intervention right then. And it was all part of the work together.

Jones is speaking not just to how everything a person is creates his or her artistic potential but to how everything a person is must be nurtured in the process of becoming an artist.

Informal education also includes the people and events one learns about along the way, outside of school. Carlton Turner avowed that learning about social justice pioneer Fanny Lou Hamer "shaped my work as surely as did the artistic influences." Other interviewees evoked Muhammad, social realism novelist John Steinbeck, post–World War II Jewish humorists, behavioral scientists, shamanists, the labor movement, suffragettes, and people who participated in the lunch counter sit-ins of the civil rights era. Writer, director, and performer Marty Pottenger appreciates the role of humor in working toward social change. She cites South African satirist Pieter-Dirk Uys performing as Evita Bezuidenhout, his invented white Afrikaner socialite and self-proclaimed political activist. Uys was wildly popular during the entrenchment of apartheid: Mandela watched his performances in prison as white Afrikaners were watching them from their homes. Also named was protest as a model of performance throughout history.

Performance makers also pass on skills to community people they work with. We refer to such learning as informal because it is often framed in a recreational context, or as a special offering for people not pursuing a performance career. It often involves a trained theater maker sharing skills to facilitate expression that is unique to a specific community. An example is Ricardo Gamboa, who began a theater program with young people, most of whom were between the ages of twelve and fourteen, in Chicago. In their third summer together, youth violence and gangs were in the headlines. The youth noticed those asked to provide authoritative perspectives on that violence were not young Chicagoans themselves. So they made a play about Chicago youth violence from their perspective. Gamboa elaborates:

> It wasn't "Just tell your sad story of growing up as a person of color on the South Side that lost somebody." They were like, "We think these stories are important to get out, but we don't want it to just be that." We did structural analysis of violence, and then they ended up critiquing Rahm Emanuel and the closing of over fifty schools and mental health clinics on the South Side and West Side of Chicago. We did physical theater training and research, including site visits with different public health people who talked about violence as a public health issue.

As with Gamboa's group, theater workshops have historically brought in people new to art making. Frequently in the time period this book addresses, actors and ensembles have facilitated workshops at places without their own arts programs, in inner-city neighborhoods, prisons, senior centers, psychiatric hospitals, and other institutions, often in the spirit of exchange, of wanting to know people in other circumstances through making art with them. One impetus for theater people committed to social change, points out Arlene Goldbard, was "to transmit arts-related skills while helping to develop critical thinking and establish a clear link between the two capabilities, thought leading to action." In the past decade, theater techniques have especially expanded to people served by community development and municipal agencies.

Also important to mention is Susan Perlstein, who founded and directed Elders Share the Arts (ESTA) from 1979 to 2003 and then expanded the work through the National Center for Creative Aging (2001–2007). Recognizing how much the arts enriches the lives of the elderly, she has developed opportunities for people over fifty-five to participate in arts workshops in organizations that serve older adults and at other community sites, and has prepared teaching artists to work with older adults.

Informal learning can also be spaces of *un*-learning, to which Rad bears witness:

> In my blood and my bones I found as much of an education as I did in all the classes and camps and workshops put together. I don't remember who told me that too much school as an artist can "whip your grandmama's song out of you." I don't think this is a blanket statement, but I believe it to be true for me and many other racialized and colonized people. I have already fought and healed through many generations of white supremacist, patriarchal social conditioning; I didn't need any more from an institution of "higher learning." My internal work has been undoing and unraveling this conditioning with its survival mechanisms, and finding my grandmama's songs by attuning my ears to the wind, to pulse with the land and the roots of the trees that surround us. By rewiring my individualistic conditioning into collective joy, discernment, and foresight. I've kept many of the technical performance tools I learned in my training but shed that which did not serve healing and well-being.

Formal Education

The Theater Workshop

While arts programs often focus on what students need to enter an already established professional ecosystem, it is also a means to change or expand that landscape. There's a great tradition of theater laboratories, often instigated by directors looking to make a different kind of theater than they inherited and needing people with the orientation and skills to do so. In the latter nineteenth century, for example, Stanislavsky's laboratory midwifed the shift from melodrama to realism first in Russia and then in much of the Western world, including the United States. Anton Chekhov supplied a new kind of play; Stanislavsky developed acting techniques so his actors could realize them.

The Group Theatre of the 1930s, building on Stanislavsky's work, featured classes with Lee Strasberg in the service of the new American plays that the company was producing. In the 1950s, that work morphed into the Actors Studio, a workshop for professional actors to hone their craft, bringing techniques of realism to actors bound for the stage and screen. Director Elia Kazan described the work there as transforming acting from a magical gift one either had or did not to something that could be developed (London 2013, 450).

In the 1960s, again in response to a desire to make a new theater, directors, including Joseph Chaikin, developed techniques to more fully realize the work of a new generation of playwrights, including Jean-Claude van Itallie, in a spirit of collaboration that characterized the counterculture of that time. In this case, the playwright followed the actors—van Itallie's method featured watching Chaikin's Open Theater actors develop a theme and creating a script out of what he saw.

Theater director and playwright Linda Parris-Bailey articulates that for Carpetbag Theatre, extending their craft is ongoing, not something that happened only before their professional life began:

> There are so many influences on our practice. Our time at Highlander Center—I worked there eight years with Jane Sapp and Guy and Candy

> [Carawan]. When everybody was engaged in Boal practices. These influences are part of how we see ourselves as an organization and an ensemble. There's not ONE influence; we can't teach A Technique. We can define it like Jo Carson did—as "revealing, reclaiming, reframing"—but it was derived from so many practices that are rooted in the idea of collective knowledge, of people, the root of our work. Ideas of popular education are woven throughout in terms of how we engage with community, the stories we derive from our community engagement. We are lifelong learners.
>
> Whenever a practice seems to suit our goal of telling stories that strengthen our communities, the individuals, that make us know that we are strong and valuable, capable, not in a Pollyanna sense but in terms of power, those are the stories that we want to share and give back to our communities. I find a kind of commonality in our field with this practice, a way of digging stories out. We have used everything at our command to do that. We're also engaged in digital storytelling, very important for us, making a way for our community to speak for itself.

Parris-Bailey describes a model of learning that is not linear, with the end point being entering the profession, but is iterative within one's entire artistic life.

Ensembles That Provide Student Training

A number of contemporary theater companies not only continue to train together but offer learning programs (often an important source of revenue for them) with distinct aesthetics. Dell'Arte International's Professional Training Program focuses on physical practices, vocal and movement improvisation, and the study of mask, clown, melodrama, and commedia dell'arte. The SITI Company, whose director, Anne Bogart, built on Mary Overlie's Viewpoints, puts that approach in dialogue with the Suzuki Method. Sojourn Theatre offers a summer institute through its umbrella organization, Center for Performance and Civic Practice (CPCP), "recommended for anyone working in community development, public health, local government, housing, transit, planning *and* the artists/designers/culture makers/heritage holders with whom you are collaborating on public good projects" (www.thecpcp.org). Urban Bush Women's Summer Leadership Institute is "an annual 10-day intensive" that UBW founder Jawole Zollar calls "'front line social justice workers,' by connecting dance professionals and community-based artists in a learning experience that leverages the arts as a vehicle for social activism and civic engagement" (www.urbanbushwomen.org).

Double Edge Theatre in rural Massachusetts embraces a rigorous physical practice, which the members of the cooperative continue to practice as a company and with students. Ensemble member and co-artistic director Carlos Uriona describes it in this excerpt from an interview with Jan:

> **CU:** We train silently, for the most part, all together, for two hours at a time. It's like our ritual; it's in those moments that we dissolve somehow the moments when we get stubborn and stuck, thinking that the emotion will not flow—but then it does flow. The same when we're working on the land together. That allows us to be very resilient with ideas and perceptions.
>
> **JCC:** What do you do silently together in the training space?
>
> **CU:** It starts without improvisation or theme. We try to work with physical resistance. That's how anyone can do it. You do yours; you're not going to do the same as the twenty-three-year-old who is climbing a rope. I run; I have arthritis; there are always all kinds of conditions. This tradition started long ago and continued with Meyerhold and Grotowski—that you can bring more spontaneity to your work as an actor instead of controlling the emotion through the text, [that] you let the emotion come through. Then you adjust the text to that emotion.
>
> **JCC:** Did company members bring their various training orientations and backgrounds to Double Edge as building blocks?
>
> **CU:** [Director] Stacy [Klein] developed the training with the ensemble. It is based on the actors' autonomy and is quite influenced by who's here, their backgrounds and different skills. I brought, for instance, my interest in outdoor spectacle, deriving from my background in Argentina. Stacy and, later, Matthew [Glassman] brought their Jewish traditions as part of the process and creative content.

JCC: What do you mean by the psychophysical phenomenon in your training?

CU: An example is how the twelve of us trained together yesterday, keeping twenty feet apart, covering about a third of an acre. Beautiful, inviting. We were running, keeping distance but having the vibe and the feeling—what does it feel to connect this way? That's already a psycho situation that puts you in a different position. We go into the training with disagreements and agreements and attractions—the whole spectrum of ourselves. When you're working out, you release endorphins and chemicals. We're trained to accept the assembly line, an industrial model of behavior, in all our relationships. It's in order to accept something that is not natural. We need to rewire ourselves. When we're activating our bodies, we're activating chemicals, and that helps us think differently. After training, I go to a similar meeting as I was at before and now it's completely different. The positions are less narrow and stuck.

• • •

There are many young people (and all ages) who want to work. We try to teach that art and survival go hand and hand, especially in order to own your own work. This can be cutting firewood, picking vegetables, cleaning the compost. . . . I do that and I have forty years of theater experience. Not everyone has the capacity, as we are so far removed from collective ownership and survival. These are actually good jobs, meditative. Like the old East Asian monastery, you would do those things to free the mind. The psychophysical humbles you to do the kind of job that is not supposed to be for you. Then you go back to your computer and write the two lines of verse you wanted to write, inspired by the fecal matter of the cows.

College and University Programs

In the 1970s, U.S. college and university theater programs were, by and large, geared to the profession as it was. They featured theater history and dramatic literature, and all that went into realizing a play. While some schools invited experimental directors to teach special workshops or a few classes, those of us looking for a broader notion of performance—not necessarily centered in a play, in a theater building, with professionals, and for strictly aesthetic and entertainment purposes—sought theater workshops outside of higher ed.

More options opened up in the latter years of the twentieth century. Much of the English-speaking world was embracing *applied theater*, a new term bringing together old and new practices emphasizing the participatory use of theater techniques, taking place other than on stages in theater buildings and accessed by other means than paying the price of admission. Applied theater has thrived in the UK, with theorist/practitioner/professors like Helen Nicholson and James Thompson. Closely related to U.S. community-based theater, which has a long history, the ideas and practices animating applied theater have increasingly been taught in U.S. higher education, as well.

But such programs are the exception. Rad reflects on the norm:

> When we moved to Turtle Island, in 1997, on unceded, occupied Miccosukee and Seminole land (South Florida), there were lots of big huge movie theaters in brand-new strip malls, the fantasy of faraway Broadway, not much good television, occasional cultural dance performances, and free live-music concerts in parks. The only pathway I saw for a life as a performer was in one of those mediums, so I dedicated myself to being a workhorse, to find a footpath as a working middle-class artist, an opportunity rarely to be found in my homeland. I devoted thousands of hours to meticulously learning the Eurocentric techniques and methods I was told would bring me individual success on Broadway or [in] cinema.
>
> Sure, there were beautiful moments of collective ebullience after months of hard work preparing a theater show, but mostly it was each person for [himself or herself], carving out a training and work ethic toward one of those elusive commercial industries. I got scholarships to summer camps where I could learn and dedicate myself to my craft, and then applied to twelve college theater programs, all in the hopes of becoming a performance machine, like the people I saw in

> the YouTube videos I spent hours watching and copying. If my body was like the slender, athletic bodies I saw sweating and dancing up a storm eight times a week, if my voice was precise, high-larynxed, and spotless, I could be up there singing with them. If my acting was specific and clean, with a touch of unbridled raw passion, I, too, could make it into the ranks of who I was taught were the most prolific storytellers of our time. So I went to musical theater college to learn how to be a performance machine.

In 2009, Goldbard, Jan, and a team of researchers wrote a report for the Curriculum Project, based on a sampling of arts training programs across the United States and a set of interviews with teachers and art makers to identify a good education in community cultural development, another term for community-based arts and culture. They hypothesized three necessary components: (1) practices that have already been part of the craft, like developing one's range of voice and movement, to which were added specialized skills, such as facilitating group creation, leading story circles, and aligning art with organizing; (2) a theoretical and historical education so as to be sensitive to the ethics of broadly participatory work, and to a range of issues that come with the territory, such as dismantling racism and other social inequities; (3) hands-on mini internships—for example, doing the work in communities with more experienced people (www.curriculum project.net).

While the first and third components can easily be part of performance workshops, colleges and universities offer a great range of courses that could contribute to component number two, delving into other disciplines that deepen a student's theoretical and historical education. Be it gerontology or education, race theory or therapeutic studies, the potential for a holistic education is strong at such institutions, but tricky nonetheless, given that other departments may not have sufficient space for students who are not majors, or may require prerequisites, or may not easily integrate such subjects with the arts, given the fact that not all students in a class will focus on that.

Lanxing Fu is codirector of the Superhero Clubhouse, grounded in bridge building across disciplines toward climate resilience. Fu's interdisciplinary training at Virginia Tech set her on her path. She studied theater with Bob Leonard and humanities, science, and environment with Eileen Crist, who put together courses offered from departments across the university that were relevant to the contemporary environmental crisis, to create that program. Fu elaborates:

> I was really inspired by her work. The degree was eye-opening. It was wonderful to look how all the different areas are interconnected and realize that I was studying theater, which is so compatible with the complexity of all these other things I was learning. It had potential for building relationships between people and ideas that I felt were necessary to confront some of what I was learning about in a bigger sense.

Some college arts programs lay the groundwork for deep thinking and expansive practice without extending to other disciplines. Performer Nick Slie of the New Orleans–based company Mondo Bizarro describes Louisiana State University's Department of Performance Studies as just such fertile ground, exposing him to big ideas—he recalls learning early on about performance art through RoseLee Goldberg's books—and being encouraged to take on meaningful content, which he experienced his first semester performing in an adaptation of Ralph Ellison's *Invisible Man.*

In contrast, other artists describe their experience in higher education as impervious to what they cared about most. As Meggan Gomez, former director of the Theatre of the Oppressed NYC puts it, "I'd have to give up a lot of autonomy and agency to live that life, too many things I wanted to say." A number of artists remarked that the life for which art programs in universities prepared them seemed too egotistical, star-struck, and alienated from their real concerns. Most theater programs are discriminatory at their root because they teach only a Eurocentric tradition of theater and performance, leaving out huge swaths of history and training that pertain to the cultural traditions of BIPOC students. Inspired by the great uprising in support of Black Lives Matter and a long tradition of student revolts, many students are now utilizing transformative justice principles to challenge that status quo.

Rad recounts that current students and alumni at Pace University, for example, claim that their education was not delivered as promised;

that they were sold a utopia of diversity in which they would receive the highest quality of innovative training but were met with years of emotional abuse, discrimination, and slander. The program displayed pictures and videos of one of the most diverse programs in the country, saying students of color could thrive and train among their peers in nontraditional ways that really suited their needs. Students reported white teachers using the N word, doing impressions of how they should "act more Black," and repeatedly excluding students of color from playing leading roles or having opportunities to perform at all. Faculty would portray certain students of color who spoke out as difficult and unemployable when casting directors, directors, and agents would come asking about them for potential professional opportunities. These current students and alumni created a comprehensive movement called See Our Truths, whose members initiated various accountability processes and also filed a lawsuit against the university (www.instagram.com/seeourtruths/).

Daniel Alexander Jones describes his own experience of being categorically excluded from consideration for major roles at college because of race and gender, variations on which I heard from numerous artists of color:

> I got a partial scholarship to [a small, predominantly white private college] and that was the worst culture shock. I was sent to be a drama major and it was still white racist patriarchs running that program. They straight out told me at the end of my first year that I would never be cast in a leading role because of both race and, I think, gender expression. And to consider doing something else. Even though I thought I was probably the best actor in that cohort. It devastated me. That was the first time I came into direct contact with institutional racism and those hierarchies. Not only was I told "No, you're not right" but also "No, there will not be any way for you to succeed."
>
> So I left for a semester and went to Emerson College briefly, and thank God, the people there said go back and fight. And I did go back and became an Africana Studies major and met a wonderful professor in Africana Studies who specialized in Black drama and African literature. I felt rescued and brought onto my path through working with

her. When she heard my story, she said, "Yeah, that's how they are. But how are you gonna be? What are you gonna do? I'll give you the tools you need," and she did. I found a way to be a drama major in that program. I went to Brown for grad school and that's where people were open to training me, I got more liquidity. So number one is my upbringing and number two is my journey through institutions.

In the higher ed context, sometimes there is a tension between socially engaged and mainstream art. Jan recounts:

> For a three-year period while a professor at NYU, I codirected an AmeriCorps project—a federally supported public service initiative during the Clinton administration that provided participants with some tuition funding and modest stipends—with ten Tisch School of the Arts students. While often finding the community-based art experiences they did through AmeriCorps highly meaningful, students in this project and related courses almost invariably felt torn between pursuing the kind of art they'd previously aspired to, that higher ed tends to promote, by and large focusing on individual and financial success, and the public-oriented vision of these other experiences. Some of their other teachers were often the biggest detriment to their pursuit of this direction, wanting them to spend their time on "real" theater.
>
> Students often felt they had to choose. Some would have a meaningful experience in socially engaged art that then would be siloed away, given their institution's main professional concerns. For example, one day I was chatting with a film student who'd had a terrific week-long experience with a small cadre of NYU arts students at Appalshop, a community arts organization in Whitesburg, Kentucky. Once back at NYU, he was again ensconced in a film school with mainstream values emphasizing success in terms of fame and fortune. We got on the subject of marriage. He said he wanted to marry someone fabulous. I asked him what that meant. "Someone who does something amazing—makes extraordinary films, travels to some out-of-the-way place, and finds a great story, brings it to the world's attention," he replied quickly.

This emphasis on "the world's" approval was familiar. Rather than focusing on the people whose "great story" it was, this student emphasized mining a commodity to bring back to "the world." The foregrounding of individual success, measured by money or fame, is out of sync with community-based work, where mainstream recognition and fortune are not only an unlikely but also an unfitting measure of success. Many artists are repeatedly told that these measures of success by capitalism's standards are a pinnacle to aim toward, but one can't measure fulfillment and the medicine of stories through money, fame, or recognition. Moreover, how can institutions rationalize the cost of an education if the career that follows is not highly lucrative—even though only a small percentage of arts students go on to make their living in the field at all?

The narrow notion of what an arts education entails, which we have encountered at many institutions, makes it difficult for new material to be brought into the classroom. For example, the racism embedded in U.S. culture encompasses socially engaged artists as well, but the siloed nature of much higher education is an obstacle to including such study in arts departments. Keryl McCord, founder of Equity Quotient, is among those offering dismantling-racism workshops, which she takes to a range of venues, including college classrooms in the arts.

> The core of our work is a learning lab around dismantling racism. It's not about equity, diversity, and inclusion. Because the lack of equity, the lack of diversity, and the exclusivity in the field are the results and outcomes of policies and practices and rules in the way the field was built. So we don't want to talk about EDI; if we want EDI, we're going to have to deal with dismantling racism and other systems of oppression.

McCord's presentation about race and racism goes back to the 1400s and the doctrines of discovery. The "original sin" in the United States, she avows, "was not slavery, but the theft of land and the genocide of the Indigenous people. Without the land, there was no need for labor." The presentation traces racism up through Jim Crow and the present, including "the systematic structural rules, laws, and policies that in the last seventy years excluded Black and brown people—like how Black and brown people were ineligible for Social Security [in] 1935, because it excluded domestics and agricultural workers."

With that common understanding of how the United States got to its present state regarding racism, McCord then focuses very specifically with the group she is working with on how to dismantle racism.

> We use a lot of arts practices—TO/Boal exercises, like Colombian Hypnosis. We use the continuum of change of how you become a multicultural, antiracist organization. We have two-day and one-day workshops on how we got from then to here. We then spend time on the question: We know what we want to liberate ourselves from; what do we want to liberate ourselves to? That's what the focus then needs to be; that's the conversation this country is having right now: What do we want this country to be like? In the workshop/training, through a facilitated process, participants come together and decide where they want their university or department or organization to be on this continuum, which they identify, from where they are now. We ask them the steps they need to take and what's standing in their way, because you don't need anyone's permission to become more equitable and inclusive.

Alongside racism there's also sexism. Nick Slie points out a bias against women who have been leaders in the field:

> Why is Hallie Flanagan never taught in theater school? She was a hero; she held everyone's container. She believed in the traditional work, in the radical—the house had to be big enough to fit everyone. MK Wegmann is like that. The naked wild dancers are as important as the Free Southern Theater. She asks, why are we arguing in a limited container? We're just not serving everyone.

Jill Dolan's groundbreaking book, *The Feminist Spectator as Critic* (1988), articulates how even the assumed *spectator* for the bulk of dramatic literature has been a man.

A significant intervention to a fixed idea of what is important to learn—a canon—is hiring teachers with different perspectives on what is important. Coya Paz, for example, teaches the history of dramatic literature at a university, and includes Bertolt Brecht, who is credited as a major, if not *the* major, theater theorist of the twentieth century. Yet she realized that though he was greatly influenced by Chinese performance tradition, including Chinese opera, she was not asked to teach that material in the earlier theater history sequence.

> Why not? Why do we introduce this retroactively when we get to the 1940s? It's nonsensical that I didn't teach it as part of performance in the 1400s [laughs]. We have been revising this, but only recently when I thought, Wait a second. Brecht is important because he effectively borrowed from a millennial-long tradition elsewhere. How do we get our students thinking about those things?

Nancy Cantor, currently chancellor of Rutgers University-Newark, refers to colleges and universities as anchor institutions, well positioned to contribute to their geographic communities. As such, they play not only formal but also informal roles in learning. For example, Native American performer Gloria Miguel of Spiderwoman Theater describes workshops that the company did with people on reservations. When they were leaving, they frequently sought people at local universities who could continue such work.

Sometimes colleges and universities partner with local arts companies to provide ongoing arts education. In Philadelphia, Pig Iron, in partnership with the University of the Arts, offers an MFA & Certificate in Devised Performance. Building on an internship program, Touchstone Theatre in Bethlehem, Pennsylvania, initiated an MFA program in Performance Creation with Moravian University. (Full disclosure: Jan teaches there.)

Theater and performance maker Leslie Ishii Peters recalls her own MFA program at the American Conservatory Theater and how that inadvertently influenced her development of a curriculum based in liberation theory:

> Training at the American Conservatory Theater (ACT) absolutely whitewashed me. At the time we were working on accents and dialect, and of course they want[ed] to teach "received pronunciation," the British version of "speaking well." I'm like, "Look, I'm Asian. I need to make

sure I learn Asian accents." "Oh, no, Leslie. You need to learn the RP first. Learn the Irish accent first, then Scottish." I'm like, "Well, there are Asians in the UK. Many of them are Indian and Chinese. Maybe I should learn an Indian or South Asian, and a Chinese accent." "No, Leslie. First, learn . . ." and I was like, "Uh." It was relentless.

I learned the International Phonetic Alphabet, which, by the way, I want to go on record [as]saying, back in the day when they taught the International Phonetic Alphabet so you could break down the sounds and be able to learn where to place them in your mouth and how to take on a dialect or an accent, the American theater did not teach the entire International Phonetic Alphabet. On the diagram with the symbols, they only included the sounds that were in our American Standard English dialect, which was our American dialect indicator of how well you speak. It was based on how well you could make those sounds. If you spoke with this dialect, you were considered a good actor. There was a hierarchy, of course, and the unconscious perpetuation of white supremacy culture and continued colonization. When I learned that there were more symbols to the International Phonetic Alphabet, I was pissed. I was pissed. This was such implicit bias toward white standards of English that was meant to exclude and dehumanize those who did not "speak well" and those who spoke with non-U.S. or non-British English accents.

Then I went to East West Players, now the longest-running professional theater of color, and introduced myself shortly after I arrived in L.A. and met Nobu McCarthy. She was the artistic director at that point. Because I had training, she said, "You will teach." I'm like, Uh-oh, she's my elder. I began to create my own approach to acting and voice technique through my learnings of liberation theory, from my mentor Yuri Kochiyama, who fought in coalition with the Black Panther Party during the Black Power movement. Yuri was a key leader who started the Asian liberation movement in coalition with the Black Power movement. I thought, We have to heal and we have to be able to have empowerment to tell our stories for our liberation. While I was at ACT and living in San Francisco, I would also go to Glide Memorial Church, where Reverend Cecil Williams and his wife, Janice Mirikitani,

> poet laureate of San Francisco, would preach liberation theology. I later worked with Janice and recorded documentary footage of both her and Yuri regarding their life's work and their activism, which was greatly informed by their being survivors of the World War II U.S. concentration camps.
>
> Yuri taught me to "learn the liberation movements and you will learn what oppressed peoples are fighting for, what they are demanding. Then you'll know how to be in solidarity." As my colleague Carmen Morgan, at artEquity, says, "Get an analysis." Meaning, understand how all of these oppressions have worked and how they've wreaked havoc on all of these peoples, these communities, and how the oppressions continue to replicate themselves. Study this so you learn to recognize it. I continued to study all of this, and at the time I realized I wanted to make a curriculum that comes from liberation theory. Now I do that work to decolonize our bodies, minds, and spirits. We have to be able to release the habitual tensions, the internal structures formed from internalizing systemic settler colonialism and white supremacy culture that is structural racism and oppression. We must breathe and reestablish our own rhythm, reclaim our own self-determination. I don't teach Shakespeare first. I teach self-determination and support the artists to come from that place grounded in who they are, their identities, and their own lived experience and/or their own legacy that they carry.

Some programs are created as part of universities but not departments. They therefore benefit from university resources but can be more fluid. The Hemispheric Institute, which focuses on politically engaged culture and performance, and was created by NYU professor Diana Taylor with Latin American colleagues, offers EmergeNYC, "an incubator for emerging artists working at the intersection of performance and politics" (https://hemisphericinstitute.org/ en/emergenyc.html). Artist/activist Ricardo Gamboa describes why being part of it was so important to them: "The EmergeNYC program . . . gave me language, like, 'Oh, this is what I've been doing, arts activism.' And 'Oh, embodiment.' It exposed me to so much."

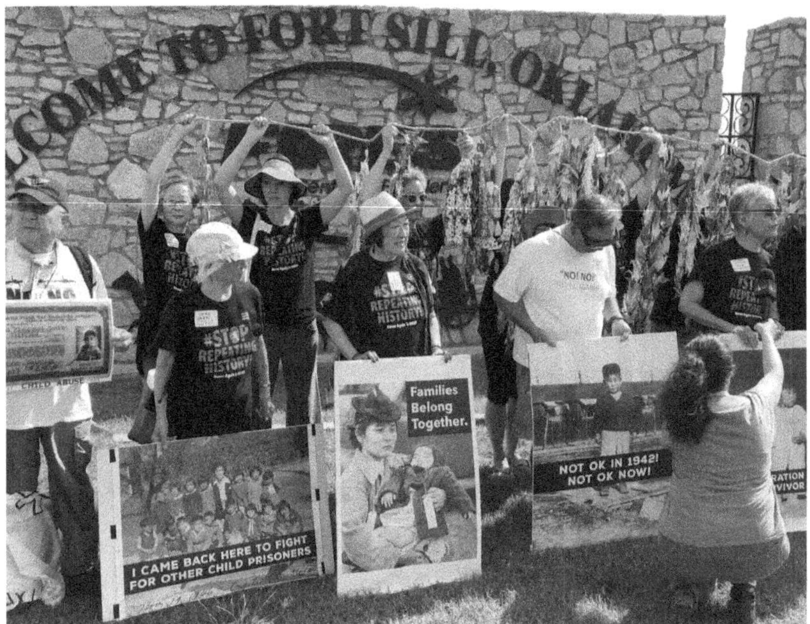

"Tsuru for Solidarity," a direct action that Japanese American social justice advocates perform as part of their efforts to end detention sites and support front-line immigrant, refugee, and Native communities. Photograph by and courtesy of John Ota.

What happens when students graduate and look for work? Some artists interested in social justice find much of their arts education insufficient or even irrelevant. Linda Parris-Bailey recounts studying Grotowski at SUNY-New Paltz and Stanislavsky at Howard University, but when the Carpetbag Theatre's Knoxville, Tennessee, audience/community consisted largely of disenfranchised people, their own stories were more meaningful to them than what she'd studied in school. How can training be in more of a conversation with the profession, to keep the former relevant and the latter energized?

A four-year undergraduate education is not for everyone. It wasn't for Jan, as she recounts:

> It took me ten years to get a BA because I was learning so much through other means. Graduating from high school a year early, I put off college and went to Israel, where a chance encounter led to

performing with the national theater, Habima. The idea that a Sabra—a homegrown Israeli—would begin to undress in public, which the role, the Saxon girl in *Becket,* required, was unacceptable. Because of the Six-Day War (1967), actors were leaving to do their national service, causing me to think concretely about joint allegiance to one's profession and one's country, and eventually about troubling Mideastern power politics, as well. Also influential was contact with an arts program for new immigrants, which the mother of a cast member had started, and which stretched my understanding of what the arts do in the world.

Back in the United States, another chance encounter led to employment with the Players' Theatre of Manchester, New Hampshire. Touring rural parts of the state brought me into contact with a range of people. At the Players' Theatre director's urging, I then studied corporal mime with Etienne Decroux in Paris. In addition to physical training and contact with students from many countries, I witnessed powerful street performances supporting student and worker rights, because Paris was in the midst of the social upheaval known as the Events of May (1968) throughout Europe. Theater's ability to broadcast anyone's voice was a new realization.

To relieve my parents' distress, I applied, late, to two colleges, hoping neither would accept me, but one did. I did a semester there and then went to Scotland for the winter field period, performing with a colleague from the mime studio in a community-based theater, and staying in Europe another year.

Coda: A Dialectical Approach to Performance Education

We heard in the interviews that each person learns best through his or her own combination of formal and informal learning, a dialectic between reflection and study at a bit of a distance and from firsthand experience in the world. Cristal Truscott embedded this understanding in SoulWork, which she began by tracing her own development as an expressive human being. It beautifully combines informal and formal learning.

> One of the key principles of SoulWork is the Cultural Conservatory, which begins by thinking of an individual's culture and upbringing as their first conservatory experience. . . . The things people were raised or born into that they did not create themselves before you could express the autonomy to say, "Oh, this is how I want to do it and actually this is my identity"— the things you learned and know that weren't explained to you but were taught to you through the communal spaces in which you were engaged as a human and particularly artistically.

Nourished through a deep connection with the Black church, Truscott learned to sing with her whole voice and heart because she was surrounded by people doing that.

> I didn't learn how to hear harmony by learning music theory. I learned it because of the way music lived in so many of the communal spaces I was immersed in, as a young person, from my home to my church to the playground, so when I came into an institutional space as a young artist, that was something I was already bringing—because I had learned in my communal spaces—I had the ear, this sensibility. I wasn't self-conscious about my voice, because of that Cultural Conservatory. SoulWork also has formal elements that are learned in studios like other methods but draw specifically from African American performance traditions.

While Jan resisted formal education in her late teens and twenties, she came to see the value of the combination of informal and formal.

> Eventually I finished my BA through a program called University Without Walls, in sync with my experiential learning style, enabling me to take some college courses and also get credit for "life experience." While I do not regret my lopsided attraction to informal learning, I recognize its weaknesses as well as its strengths.
>
> Pre-university, I received no theoretical basis for understanding the world around me and did not know how to understand the systemic nature of people's struggles. There was nothing vertical in my education, no deliberate building of one thing on another. On the other hand, I studied what compelled me.

> The power was in the combination of informal and informal learning. Becoming a teacher, I harvested how I learned for my students, who, as artists, were likely to learn corporally as well as intellectually. I instituted a "field work" component in my university classes, whereby students cofacilitated workshops with people in a range of circumstances, having learned so much myself through firsthand experience. I added collective reflection, followed up with reading and writing, which my own education lacked. I have since recommended field work, followed by formal reflection and further study, for any theater makers, believing we need to immerse ourselves in other people's lives to know them beyond stereotypes, but also need a larger context to reflect on and better understand it.

In academia, disability artist and activist Kevin Gotkin learned to think very broadly and expansively about liberatory forms of facilitation and pedagogy. But he also absorbed biases in such spaces, such as the notion that expertise is only derived through formal education: "The idea of booking someone to talk on a topic was a very elitist, higher ed idea, a model that I was just taking up." As soon as he began working in communities, he realized that everyone contains expertise in something. He learned a lot about facilitating by actually doing it out in the world: "even asking people to dream with you, to try and get out of the structures we live in—for them, the sense of a foreclosed future is a part of their experience as a disabled person—so dreaming is not just this simple process, but so we can imagine this other space."

We grow up absorbing the aesthetic ideas and practices with which we are surrounded, for better or worse. An artist who attends college may or may not have a good experience. Some people find their path apprenticing with a company; others learn as they go. Given how interdisciplinary most of the work of socially engaged performance is, that's a good thing, as Lanxing Fu explains:

> The main difference between being part of Superhero Clubhouse and a more conventional theater path is if you were lucky enough to study theater, you think it's about collecting skills to be able to assume the role you want in the theater—a writer, an actor/writer, et cetera—

> then apply for jobs. For me it's wearing so many more hats than I expected, and while doing it—I didn't know how to produce a festival or curate an application process—you have to learn in the moment, by doing badly and then doing again. So much of my time in my art making is not writing a play or making gestures; it's talking to people, gathering and organizing them, communicating. A huge part of what I do is connecting with people. I think that's true for anyone trying to make a life that does not follow a particular track.

Arts education is a lifelong endeavor because art is. Educating socially engaged artists can't just be about training in aesthetic techniques; it also is about knowledge illuminating the conditions in which, and the people with whom, artists work. Socially engaged artists usually work in a range of contexts, each calling for particular skills and knowledge, some of which are not even art per se, such as writing, organizing, and relating to people without assumptions. Different contexts speak to different histories, which also impact the work. Performance makers' ability to respond to specific times and places rather than simply enacting a set training again and again means one never stops learning, just as one never stops growing. The iterative relationship between experience and learning, practice and ideas, is another manifestation of Freirean dialectics, suggesting how knowledge grows in exchange with other people and in concrete situations.

Freirean pedagogy also brings us to Augusto Boal, Freire's Brazilian fellow countryman, whose system of community-based, expressive, self-activation is called Theatre of the Oppressed. Jan once asked Boal about his naming the system as an homage to Friere's ideas of proactivity and people with the seemingly fewest resources learning in dialogue with one another. Boal told her that while resonating strongly with Freire, he had initially called the system Theatre of Liberation; it was his book editor who insisted he change the name to Theatre of the Oppressed, believing it would be easier to market. It's rather astounding that the theatrical approach to becoming a proactive person, used frequently by people who are in no material way oppressed as well as by those who are, would have entered the world with a name emphasizing people's lack of agency rather than all of our great potential.

PART II
(Re)Mapping Community

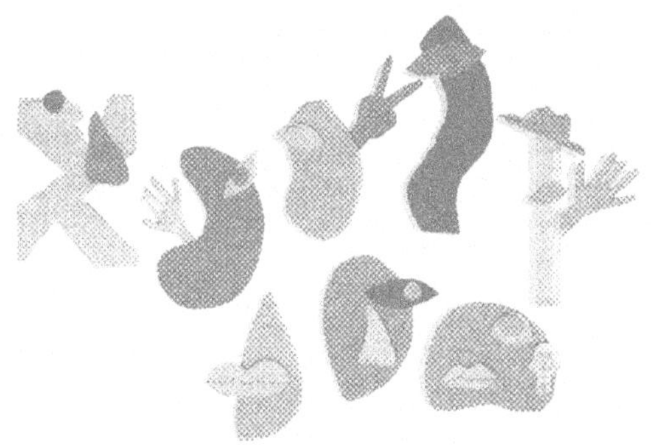

4 Changing Notions of Who "We" Are

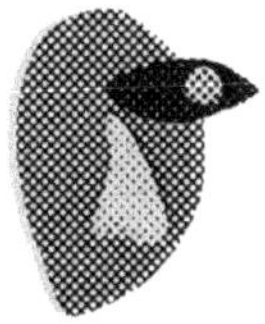

I don't see the point of doing theater if it's not with Native people who have lived experience of being Native, because at the end of the day for me, I believe the reason that we are doing theater as Native people is to recoup what we've lost.

—Rhiana Yazzie, director, New Native Theatre

My ideal world is less oriented around identity politics and more around affinities with acknowledgment of the multitudes each person contains.

—Lanxing Fu, codirector, Superhero Clubhouse

While rooted in experience and socially shaped by relationships, identities are historical constructs that exist and develop across real time and space, subject to revision and change, and are not the expression of fixed selves. While we avow that there is no such thing as race, that we are all some racial and cultural mix impossible to fully sort out, that gender is behavior and sexuality is fluid, we also recognize and affirm that these identity grounders impact us tremendously while the systems of white supremacy, colonialism, and capitalism still exist. In this chapter, performers reflect on choices they have made around identity over these fifty-five years.

A History Marked by Segregation

Seeing, Not Seeing; Being Seen, Not Being Seen

While the founding documents of the United States avow commitment to plurality, diverse artists' experiences suggest that this ideal is more aspirational than realized. For example, Gloria Miguel of Spiderwoman Theater is of a Kuna/Rappahannock family that arrived in a largely Italian Brooklyn neighborhood in the 1930s. While she says she did not experience anyone directly trying to suppress her culture, she explains why:

> They didn't believe there *was* a culture. We didn't exist. We were freaks. The Italian immigrants were suspicious of us. Spiritually, they didn't accept us. White privilege is the privilege not to experience racism; no matter how much of an ally you are, you can talk about racism without getting smacked in the face or spit on your body, or blood drawn.

Arab American artist Andrea Assaf describes a similar experience some years later, beginning life in Williamsport, in semirural Pennsylvania:

> I was profoundly "other" there. Not because anyone necessarily felt bad about Lebanese people, but they simply didn't know what I was. I didn't fit in their concept of community or identity; there was no Arab American community there at all. And, of course, being queer. I didn't come out until I moved to New York.

BIPOC, gender-expansive folks, poor or disabled people, are often simply not seen because their cultures exist on the margins. They are left out of the mainstream in the United States, have been erased, or neighborhoods are so segregated that we seldom encounter people of other cultures. Existence on the margins holds many contradictions and consequences of this invisibility, such as violence and poverty, as well as beautiful, influential subcultures and a more communal reality.

Ignorance about other cultures can lead to what Kathie deNobriga calls "toxic charity," citing minister/community activist Robert D. Lupton's 2011 book of that name. She gives Lupton's example of missionaries who go to Central America:

[They go] to paint schools or whatever, good work, but they really go down for themselves rather than for what people there actually need, people who house and feed them for two weeks to paint a school that doesn't need painting. They really need someone to dig ditches because of terrible drainage, but the people who go down may not want to build ditches.

Lupton talks about doing the right thing for the wrong reason or maybe the wrong thing for the wrong reason.

DeNobriga compares toxic charity to a dynamic in socially engaged art, sometimes known as "white saviorism," whereby privileged people work with others from cultures or in circumstances that they do not know in order to feel better about themselves and, in the worst scenarios, to impose their own worldview, values, and aesthetics. She emphasizes the importance of people working with groups outside their own interrogating their intentions to make sure they benefit those to whom they are reaching out. When projects involve building good relationships, there can be positive outcomes for all involved. It is more valuable to learn to engage with others across differences with sensitivity than not to do it at all. DeNobriga's warning is a reminder of the importance of reciprocity—for each party to hear how a collaboration benefits the other and act accordingly.

In a variation on seeing and being seen, performer Peggy Shaw, a white lesbian, describes being a young teenager in the late 1950s and early 1960s and "seeing herself"—that is, figuring out her identity—by watching and listening to Black male musicians:

To become who I was, I counted on early music, since I didn't have a family who was very progressive in their thinking. James Brown and Marvin Gaye, that's the first music I heard except for hymns, beginning at the end of the 1950s and into the 1960s, this incredible Black male music. I wasn't in touch with a lot of women musicians. I didn't even know there were any. So that's where I went to try to find my identity.

Shaw and Weaver come from a generation when most media was still created and programmed by cisgender white men (cisgender means that you identify with the gender that you were assigned at birth). They lacked models for themselves, so they had to use their imaginations to pull from different kinds of folks to cobble together an approximation of their identities. This is what people who don't often see themselves reflected in media sometimes have to do: cobble together and collage various influences to feel something like themselves, even if parts of it are not literally representative of their respective identities.

On the other hand, trying on the cultural expression of other people can sometimes reinforce stereotypes; witness the big nose and thick glasses one can buy at Halloween to go "as a Jew" to a costume party. People without firsthand experience of another group risk objectifying, misrepresenting, and/or co-opting those they don't understand. But that is not what Shaw was doing. Quite the contrary: She was looking for something that felt more like her.

Separatism and Integration: Who is "We?"

A number of theater companies have been formed as cultural wings of social movements. They tend to reflect the people the social movement most directly serves. An example is the Free Southern Theater (FST), founded in 1963 by three African American artists active in the civil rights movement—Doris Derby, Gilbert Moses, and John O'Neal. It was an integrated company for the first several years. But by the end of the 1960s, important questions had emerged as to who should lead a people's freedom movement, and if the company would send a stronger message if it were all Black. They experimented with both.

The FST was also part of interracial theater networks. O'Neal was among the original participants at the first meeting in 1976 of what became Alternate ROOTS—Regional Organization of Theaters South. It was initiated by the Highlander Research and Education Center with this goal, as described in the "History" section of ROOTS' website:

> To be a catalyst for grassroots organizing and movement building in Appalachia and the U.S. South . . . where leaders, networks, and movement strands come together to interact, build friendships, craft joint

strategy and develop the tools and mechanisms needed to advance a multi-racial, intergenerational movement for social and economic justice in our region.

While ROOTS was interracial from its beginnings, a core group of its white majority, though committed to equity in theory, habitually steered its course. It took years to develop processes to fully share leadership and undo the racism that comes from simply living and being conditioned in the United States. It was not enough to manifest good intentions by welcoming artists of various races into the same network. It took raising money to cover the costs of bringing a substantial number of artists of color to ROOTS and a commitment to foreground their aesthetics, such as ROOTS' hip-hop initiative beginning in 2003. It took not just choosing Black leaders; it also involved longtime, mostly white members concertedly sharing power with them. It took commitment from all when they faltered.

When building a large movement, much can be said for working across identities in coalition, so long as something central is shared, as white arts consultant MK Wegmann explains:

> The mission statement of Junebug [Productions] back in 1980, the value I took from [founder] John [O'Neal] even earlier, was that he wasn't a separatist. And that was a time in the Black community with a lot of split. People for whom gaining justice did not include working side by side White people. John was always a coalition builder. The idea of finding allies whether they work in a corporation, are a rich person, lawyer, laborer—the point was what you were trying to accomplish, not what your identity was, narrowly defined.

Through the 1970s and 1980s, the model of interracial alliances was building. Sharing some core social purpose was often enough to bring artists together. In the early 1970s, when Muriel Miguel wanted to create a theater company that foregrounded Native American women's experience, the other Native women she found to work with, in her eyes, lacked performance training. She then founded Spiderwoman with her two sisters, grounded both in songs, dance, and stories from Kuna/Rappahannock culture and trained in diverse performance techniques. She included several women performers with strong feminist ideals from other cultural backgrounds as well, including Lois Weaver and Peggy Shaw. Miguel and her sisters also offered theater workshops on reservations.

Dudley Cocke, white founder of Roadside Theater in 1975 in Appalachia, advocates for artists both exploring their own cultural roots and joining with artists from other backgrounds. He spoke about what poet and essayist Wendell Berry calls "local life aware of itself" (Berry 1972):

> We began in the 1970s looking at Appalachian identity, the intellectual, material, spiritual, and emotional traditions and features of our place. Paying attention to where we were. The critique at that time from the status quo was that it would lead to two thousand identities and no national sense of who we are as the American people. We always believed that drilling down into local life and understanding your local history and traditions makes it easier to then collaborate with other people who've done the same thing. Balkanization is the opposite of going deep into local life, which leads to the possibility of unification as we try to create a new American story based on putting these different local lives in conversation.
>
> That's what we've done with our intercultural work. We created *Betsy* with Pregones, a company grounded in Puerto Rican identity. It's about a Puerto Rican woman who discovers that she also has Appalachian roots. Many people with Puerto Rican roots who saw it felt their tradition deeply affirmed, and were also excited by seeing the commonality and connection with another culture. Same when we performed *Betsy* in Appalachia. A "both /and."

Linda Parris-Bailey, African American former director of the Carpetbag Theatre, experiences that company's relationship to both an African American and Appalachian identity:

> My communities are the disenfranchised. The Carpetbag Theatre is an African American organization, but we live in Knoxville, in Appalachia, in a place where we are at best 14 percent of the population. We know that other people suffer, and that's the community we're aligned

> with; shared values and shared experience of disempowerment, that's the community we serve. In Appalachia, in the Deep South. Because if you look at our work creating and shaping stories, a lot of that was in white Appalachia. We know our community is broader than African Americans. We are rooted in the stories of African American and other disenfranchised communities.

Leslie Ishii details her first experience of seeing herself reflected in art and the impact that had on her activism, subsequent professional career, and sense of solidarity with other disenfranchised groups:

> Back when I was a teenager, I was in the first reading about the [internment] camp experience at Northwest Asian American Theatre, written by Nikki Nojima Lewis. She was a very young child when she watched the FBI take her father away. Then incarceration happened, evacuation and incarceration during World War II. She had those formative years in the U.S. [internment] camp, Minidoka, in Hunt, Idaho. She collected stories from our community. It was the very first play that spoke to it and addressed the camp experience of our community. For many of them, how brutal camp was and having the Japanese language beaten out of them sent a message of forced assimilation when they got out. . . . They were being told, "Don't speak your language. Don't gather in groups. You'll be targeted again." That threat, when they were finally released, is partly why I think we became hypervigilant and assimilated hard.
>
> Unfortunately, the behavior we learned to not make waves probably contributes to the model minority myth. I feel like it also lends to why it's easy to hire us over other people of color who are darker than us. Colorism starts to come in. That's a powerful thing for us to know in the Japanese community. We've been looking at anti-Blackness in our own movements, and there's a way that we're understanding how we've been used as tools for white supremacy.
>
> Now the Japanese community, we don't roll without being in coalition. We support others because during World War II very few people stood up for us. That's always been true for me, from being raised that way and up to now. In my work and community organizing,

> we don't roll without coalition, without Native/Indigenous, without the Black community, without the Latine community, because we know separation of family; we know being policed. We know being mass incarcerated; my family knows being point-blank shot just for how you look.

K. Anthony Appiah has written about groups rescripting how they inhabit their identities rather than being boxed in by other people's perception of what those identities mean: "In order to construct a life with dignity, it seems natural to take the collective identity and construct positive life scripts instead" (Appiah 1996, 98). An example is the WOW (Women's One World) Café Theatre, a cooperatively run meeting place and performance venue for mostly lesbians, founded by Weaver, Shaw, and others in the early 1980s. There is multiplicity within the representation of lesbians across the varied performances associated with WOW, but they still chose to work toward more liberating, self-selected identities among lesbians, not within a broader group.

For forty years, Weaver was Shaw's partner in work (and much of that time also in life) through Split Britches, the company they started with Deb Margolin. Their first play, also called *Split Britches,* was based on three of Weaver's rural Virginia female relatives who never married. It was a reimagining of what their lives together may actually have been, a rich and at times raucous thing, in no way hampered by their being unwed.

Weaver elaborates on how in the early days of Split Britches, part of how they theatricalized their experience for audiences was by playing with images of celebrities and popular culture:

> Peggy and I have really embraced the idea of butch and femme, male and female, whatever that means. Not so much as our identity, but because it is amazing theatrical material for us to play with. How we think about the heteronormative—we wouldn't have said that word when we began, but we did sort of explode those stereotypes. We liked embodying them. We loved being James Dean and Katharine Hepburn or going into those fantasy places that we had probably unconsciously used to survive as queer women and transpose ourselves elsewhere. We loved being Neil Diamond and Barbra Streisand. It is

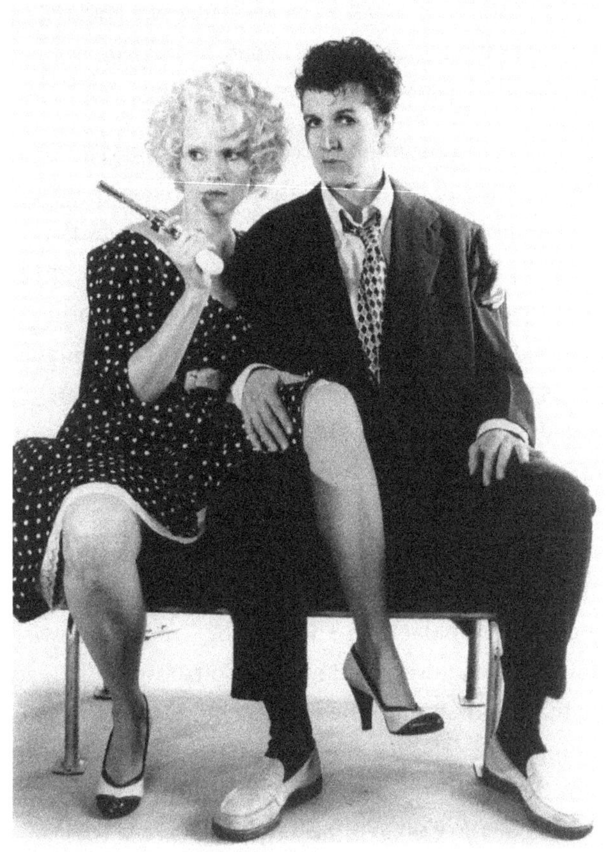

From the performance Lesbians Who Kill, *1993. Lois Weaver (left) and Peggy Shaw (right). Photo by Diane Ceresa. Courtesy of Split Britches.*

probably a love of popular culture that also led us into the love of the stereotype and the use of it.

Then, too, it's identifiable to a lot of people, it's accessible, if you want to play a lesbian couple and explode ideas of heteronormativity and how that impacts all of us. If you're Barbra Streisand and Neil Diamond, you don't have to explain that to anybody. But if you're playing a lesbian couple, you have to first explain that. Then you can get to the fun of it. It was an easy way in for a larger audience and it was fun for us because we grew up in the 1950s, fell in love with Hollywood, and had a fascination with celebrities. Without having to

> do what you have to do to get [celebrity status], we could put on the costumes and play it. It gave us an inroad, a structure, and a kind of storytelling that we didn't have to invent, that was already there for us.

Culturally specific ensembles provide a safety and an ease from not having to explain the soil from which they grew, but, rather, to celebrate it. Mirtha Quintanales wrote in *This Bridge Called My Back* that "those who have been racially oppressed must create separatist spaces to explore the meaning of their experiences—to heal themselves, to gather their energies, their strength, to develop their own voices . . ." (Moraga and Anzaldua 2005, 153). But Quintales went on to say that women must also gather across differences to form coalitions, to tackle issues in common by creating strong bonds with respect to shared goals.

An example of coalition building is the American Festival Project (AFP), founded in 1982, which initiated exchange among culturally specific ensembles: the African American Junebug Productions and Urban Bush Women, the Appalachian Theater, the Traveling Jewish Theatre, Latine-identified companies, including an offshoot of El Teatro Campesino and later Pregones, and the Liz Lerman Dance Exchange, as well as others committed to expanding who participates in art. According to their website, the Brooklyn-based Urban Bush Women, founded in 1984 by Jawole Willa Jo Zollar, is the only professional African-American women's dance company in existence (urbanbushwomen.org). Their dazzling combination of vernacular Black urban dance and African traditional influences celebrates and raises up the culture. Through AFP, these progressive white, brown, and Black artists performed for one another's audiences, facilitated workshops, and engaged in dialogue.

Not all artists who found homes in culturally specific companies sought collaboration across identities. The ethos moving into the late 1980s was to provide more opportunities for people of color who had been overlooked for many years because of the white dominance in every walk of U.S. life. White artist and consultant Arlene Goldbard describes her experience:

> I remember times in the 1980s when multiracial, multigender, multisexual coalitions were separating into their own categories. I was a

> consultant then to a lot of organizations of color who called me and said, "We love you, we want to work with you again, but could you recommend a consultant of color with your skills?"

Paul Bonin-Rodriguez, a Latine theater writer/researcher and former member of the Jump-Start Performance Company, is in favor of identity-specific opportunities, but not exclusively:

> Identity-based art making provides a place to start a conversation. It allows people to stand in their experience. The drawback is when we get confused and think that identity is the only thing we're defending. . . . I grew up in a home that aspired to assimilation, with two very culturally diverse and culturally rich parents who did not want us to talk about it, whitewashed it a bit, yet their parents spoke in their own languages and were just the opposite. So we didn't realize all we were until later, when I had to speak from the "I." I'm still learning to accept the "I." I feel both blessed and tired with identity work. I know it's going to put me through an emotional roller coaster, but I'm grateful because I need to hear it. How do we train each other to stay open to the conversation about identity, particular experiences, and the consequence of actions that have been going on for so long?

The word *multiculturalism* is a response to the challenges associated with diversity based on ethnic, national, and religious differences. It is about maintaining distinctive collective identities and practices, in contrast to "the melting pot," which advocates for the removal of what makes people particular in order for them to assimilate into the dominant culture.

A problem occurs when companies fuse together many cultural and ethnic traditions without the respect that comes from actually being from those cultures. The 1990s saw a mash-up of inspirations under the rubric of multiculturalism, with some artists using other people's identities as material for collaging new aesthetics and profiting from them. There were those who thought it was not only okay but a show of respect for those other cultures. Multiculturalism became a trend in the theater and performance world, with artists seeking exotic and obscure cultures to draw from. Given the power dynamics of racialized capitalism, resources and opportunities stay in the hands of the few. Cultural workers are trying to unravel this extractive system and mindset in favor of an approach that invites authenticity, self-determination, and integrity.

Applying What's Been Learned

Creating Organizational Frameworks

Since the late twentieth century, an articulated framework that was not always enacted emphasized JEDI(AB)—justice, equity, diversity, and inclusion, to which were later added accessibility and belonging—on the part of funders and cultural institutions themselves. It was intended to remove barriers that had long made access to substantial roles and resources in the U.S. performance ecosystem more difficult for women, people of color, disabled artists, gender-expansive folks, and people of nonheteronormative sexual identity.

The JEDI(AB) concept was often understood in a superficial way. The need for JEDI(AB), as Sicangu Lakota Nation playwright and director Larissa FastHorse suggests below, extends well beyond adding a BIPOC playwright to a theater's season or offering free tickets to community members with a particular connection to a current production.

> The Western theater world that I work in is so completely white-centered, and it doesn't realize it. Not just what you see onstage but the entire culture of it. When I'm working in a white theater, I do what I call Indian 101, where I make the entire staff, production, board members, front of house, ticketing, everybody, understand why their culture is so oppressive for a Native American person to walk into, that their lobbies, their policies, way before you ever buy a ticket, are oppressive and against our culture. . . . Look at the season, buy a ticket, show up, and watch a show, how we've had to completely suppress our culture a dozen times, just to show up. It's not a matter of "Why don't they show up?" It's that we have to deny who we are to participate in theater. Retraining the staff and everyone on how they need to change their space and change their culture to allow other

> cultures to participate fully within our own selves and not have to leave themselves behind when they show up in a theater.

What makes people comfortable even entering the very culturally specific space, rooted in colonial standards of respectability through decorum and civility, of a U.S. regional theater lobby? If the norm is, say, an unspoken dress code that other cultural groups don't know about, how will they not feel uncomfortable? Whereas in some cultures, audiences are expected to make comments out loud during performances, in U.S. regional theater culture, silence is the norm, other than laughing or clapping at culturally appropriate moments. Inviting one playwright of color into a theater's all-white season is a superficial and incomplete application of JEDIAB. It is the result of not only a lack of understanding about other cultures but a self-interest on the part of some theaters to align with funders' priorities as a way to keep money flowing in their direction without giving a lot of thought to the redistribution of power and resources.

Organizations may also have norms regarding a workshop facilitator's identity in relation to project participants. Jan worked at A Blade of Grass (ABOG), which supports socially engaged artists, from 2013 to 2018, engaging critically with the artists it funded. Conventional wisdom was that either the artist facilitating a project or a close cofacilitator needed to share some fundamental identity with the participants. This reflects an understandable fear that "outsiders" will objectify, misrepresent, and/or co-opt cultural groups they don't really understand. Jan relates that this concern extended to who was doing an evaluation:

> One of the ABOG projects I was meant to evaluate was about healing, and focused on women of color. I recommended that a female evaluator of color follow it instead of me. As a white person, I could heave been an obstacle to trust building and might have skewed a process that was about and for a group of which I am not fully a part. At other times, evaluating work by artists of other racial and cultural identity than mine has been embraced as a mark of respect, bespeaking relational solidarity with underlying social justice issues. Observing the work of Las

> Imaginistas, a largely Chicana collective on the Texas-Mexico border in Brownsville, was one such experience. I shared their grounding in activist performance, which generated much valuable exchange.

For Keryl McCord, director and founder of Equity Quotient, a short-sighted pivot in focus to DEI is problematic:

> The core of our work is not about diversity, equity, and inclusion. Because the lack of diversity, the lack of equity, and the exclusivity in the field are the results and outcomes of policies, practices, and rules in the way the field was built. We don't want to talk about DEI; if we want DEI, we're going to have to dismantle racism and other systems of oppression.

McCord explains that people in the arts, like everyone else, need to be retrained and reoriented if attitudes are to change and if they are to commit to DEI as an organizational frame.

Whereas superficial and incomplete JEDIAB initiatives tend to keep agency in the hands of people who have long held power, culture change means that the people who are meant to benefit are in positions to make necessary changes to these same ends. How does that come about? One level of change happens through the process and form of art making itself.

Community-Rooted Frameworks

Community refers to a group of people to whom you feel responsible and accountable and with whom you share some component of your identity—geographic home, race, gender/sexuality, circumstance, class, or other marker. By contrast, one might be in a shared ecosystem with a group of people, whose parameters may be much the same as a community's (shared geography, race, etc.), without a sense of committed responsibility. Issues of identity are deeply tied to artistic and social goals. Rhiana Yazzie, who directs New Native Theater in Minneapolis, says:

> It's impossible as a Native company to model white theater. You'd just get a bunch of people who aren't connected to their community. For some Native people, being in a play is a tool to continue to revitalize

> their language or be more connected to themselves, or overcome some of what comes with the history of colonization. . . . Biologically, as human beings, we learn because we have a mirroring system in our bodies. We learn to be human by watching others and by stories. That's why I'm totally for not wasting our time creating plays for white people to learn about us.

Toya Lillard, Black executive director of viBe Theater Experience in New York City, warns that the term *community* is overused, suggesting an accompanying responsibility for it to be meaningful:

> We use it too casually, as if sitting in a circle makes community. Do I trust you? Do you trust me? Do you believe me? Do you share anything in common with me? Is my presence an additive, the spice to your pot of stew? Is this a real relationship? Community is based on having some skin in the game, beyond allyship; you're an accomplice, beyond the finite show. For our young women in viBe, community means they hang out together before and after rehearsals, on the weekend. That's the kind of trust they need to write the vulnerable things they need to write. Community for them is survival. They can't survive in this world without pockets of safety and freedom.

There are artists who avoid all categorizations. Richard Elovich, a performance artist in the 1970s and 1980s, who then incorporated his art in AIDS activism, describes himself as "an outlier" at the first ACT UP meeting he attended and in the gay community more broadly partly because, he explained, "I also lived in the art world and there, you didn't want labels."

Some artists build theatrical communities in response to other forces that bring them together. For example, Gulf Coast artists of diverse racial identities worked together in the aftermath of Hurricane Katrina (2005), having all been impacted by the storm and its aftermath. There was, however, a clear racial dimension, given that, by and large, low-lying areas that tended to be hit the hardest were largely inhabited by people of color. Participant Nick Slie, who cofounded the interracial, experimental ensemble Mondo Bizarro with Bruce France, recounted that the group barely ever talked about racial difference:

> We were doing *Uprooted: A Katrina Project,* and a number of people, including John [O'Neal, who had a long history of racial justice activism], noted that while there were seven Black people and three white people in this production, we'd somehow gone through Katrina without ever having a substantive conversation about race. He was amazed at how pervasive that mystery is.

Mondo Bizarro and M.U.G.A.B.E.E. (Men Under Guidance Acting Before Early Extinction), a Mississippi-based multigenre musically driven performance group created by the African American brothers Carlton and Maurice Turner, decided to focus together on cross-racial dynamics. They chose not to make a piece of art, but simply to explore the subject together, as Slie explains:

> It became an artistic 3-D workshop about race on your feet. We guided participants through somatic practices and sociometric work about ancestry and race. The most valuable part was us getting together more to talk about race and dig into some of the darker history of our own communities.

The project also included a new generation of the largely African American Junebug, also New Orleans–based, under Stephanie McKee's leadership. They brought in the late John O'Neal, Black cofounder of Free Southern Theater and its reincarnation as Junebug, and Dudley Cocke, the white founder of Roadside Theater, as mentors to this three-way collaboration, which above all provided a space for conversation. They called the collaboration Race Peace, "a multi-generational performance project that deals with the debilitating fog of racism in an attempt to provide an opportunity for people to celebrate and explore common bonds, debate their differences, and lay the civic foundation to pursue solutions to the issues that impact their communities (www.mondobizarro.org/?page_id=157).

Identity issues are not strictly Black and white. M.U.G.A.B.E.E. also collaborates with Pangea World Theater, in Minneapolis, on the relationship between South Asian and African American performers. Individual artists and scholars have also furthered intersectoral efforts, an example being artist Andrea Assaf's work among Arab, African American, and Latine artists.

Disability activist Kevin Gotkin notes the importance of people with different marginalized identities joining together, recognizing that the bias against them is often on multiple fronts. Anti-Black racism is lodged at the heart of how ableism works and has developed in the United States: "Often the older generation, who are teaching us so much, feels that we are attacking something very core to what they've done [when we don't focus solely on disability justice]." Rather, Gotkin emphasizes "condensing all kinds of disability into a political force, and trying to model forms of solidarity, intersectionality, and justice."

Cultural critic Arlene Goldbard, now in her seventies, recognizes social media's role in spreading broad stereotypes about people with a total lack of nuance:

> Every day I read a ton of these giant racialized statements on Facebook: "White people do x. Black people are x." And it splits my mind open. It's true, some white people do this, some Black people are that. But it's a time when we should be learning that those categories are imposed by people who want to harm us, and we should be finding a different way, a modus vivendi, based on more particularities of identity rather than these big clumps of generalizations. That's what I would be doing and lending my support to if I were queen of the world.
>
> But instead, it's going the other way and splitting off. It's a total lack of trust that others have our best interest at heart and that there's kindness and compassion in the world. If we want to improve the social order to actually bring about compassion and justice, then there is a loss entailed by people who have unearned privilege, most of whom don't want to sustain a loss or give something up. So you can understand why people get into these reified positions of "This is who you are; you'll never change. Get out of my world." But I'm sad about it. I don't like the way it's going.

Numerous predominantly white ensembles are attempting to transform their working cultures to share resources and power and build community with BIPOC artists and organizations. For example, Mary Wright, an ensemble member of Touchstone Theatre, a community-informed company founded in 1981, recounted that while they seek to be responsive to a plurality of people in their home of Bethlehem, Pennsylvania, they are aware that as an all-white group in a culturally diverse town, they lack insider knowledge of what other groups want and need. They have long shared their resources by including other diverse local artists in the festivals that they produce, while continuing to make the art that they make (Wright in conversation with Cohen-Cruz, November 24, 2019). More recently, they have formed a working group with Latine community leaders to explore deeper, long-term collaborations.

Cross-identity collaboration has sometimes led to hurtful and demeaning slights. We knew a white European man who was able to cofacilitate a project with a group of Brazilian women because his partner, a Brazilian woman, was collaborating, and then took full credit for everything that happened. Some artists have gone to work with a distant community and lodged in a nearby hotel rather than staying in what they considered the substandard conditions that the community lives in. Some artists with not enough understanding of a community's plight in effect blame them for the challenges they face. Funders of socially engaged art need to ensure that grantees are capable and equipped to hold the physical, emotional, and spiritual safety of participants. This does not always mean that the artists are literally of the same race, gender, class, and circumstances, but that they have compassion for communities in which the work takes place and the skills to carry out sensitive, mutually beneficial relationships.

In the last ten years, collective awareness about self-representation and questions about using other people's circumstances as one's material has expanded. Peggy Shaw began to recognize her white privilege and that referencing Black artists—specifically Black male musicians—in her work could be seen as cultural appropriation. As a company, Split Britches decided to look at these nuances, and Shaw imposed the limitation on herself to no longer write about people of color.

However, raising questions about how artists draw on other people's identities in their work is one thing, and how they self-identity is another. In what might have felt like a kind of policing of some people by others in the same broad community, Shaw notes that she has been criticized as "a cop-out" by some trans artists for identifying as a butch lesbian rather than as a "nonbinary" person:

> I think the whole mood of the world, and especially the queer community, is dividing everyone up into sections and you can't cross the lines. It happened with the trans community and women's community. . . . You must remember what it was like to just have everything be up for grabs and ironic, and now there is no more irony.

Complexities of Identity

We draw on Kimberlé Crenshaw's idea of intersectionality (Crenshaw 2014), which focuses on overlapping identities such as race, class, and gender in order to understand the complexity of prejudices that people face. In what follows, we look at how social injustice and power intertwine in the face of inadequate understanding when sharing gender identity but not race.

In November 2019, for a book launch at Pioneers Works, Brooklyn, New York, white veteran feminist Gloria Steinem, eighty-five years old, and white journalist Ronan Farrow, thirty-two, discussed her *The Truth Will Set You Free, But First It Will Piss You Off!: Thoughts on Life, Love, and Rebellion* and his *Catch and Kill: Lies, Spies, and a Conspiracy to Protect Predators.* Event organizers commissioned the viBe Theater Experience, a group of Black girls, young women, and gender-expansive youth in their late teens and twenties, to create an original ten-minute performance as the opening act responding to Steinem's work.

American media dubbed Gloria Steinem perhaps the "foremost" leader of the women's movement of the 1970s, despite her acknowledgment of equally impactful women of color. It may have been that Steinem was easy for mainstream media to embrace; she's conventionally attractive, heterosexual, and articulate in a way that doesn't scare middle-class white Americans. Part of the white liberal flank of feminism, she nonetheless always challenged the second-class treatment of women and, importantly, avowed that even materially comfortable women were boxed

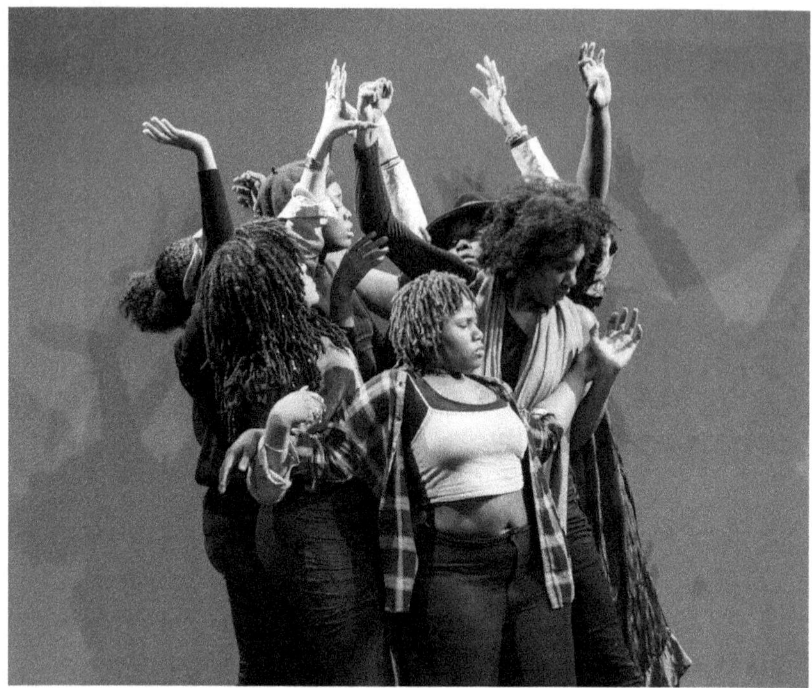

Monolith to Monarch*: Six young Black women grouped together, leaning in and on one another for support. Photographer: Richard Louissaint. Copyright March 2019 viBe Theater Experience.*

in by society's male dominance. Ronan Farrow's *Catch and Kill* is about news organizations' purchase of stories compromising influential people in order to bury those stories, such as those on Harvey Weinstein's sexual abuse of women in the film industry.

The viBe Theater Experience is based in New York City and offers free arts, leadership, and academic opportunities through writing and performing original productions about the issues they face daily. While there are women of color across generations who identify with feminism, the viBe members Jan met were not among them, perceiving Steinem and the 1970s women's movement as white-oriented and making no space for Black voices and bodies.

Attending the Pioneer Works event, Jan was struck that among several hundred spectators, she saw only one or two women of color. Given that Steinem valued Black participants in the women's movement, why had so few shown up? The animosity the viBe performers expressed toward seventies feminism suggested a response, as will become clear.

The viBe company performed on a bare stage with a large screen along the back, on which were projected quotes that Steinem had emailed them from her new book and to which the performers responded. To Steinem's "How many women are living out the unlived lives of our mothers?" one of the performers declared, "What a privilege it must be, to live a life that your mother couldn't." She recounted how hard her mom had worked while she struggled with her homework, both believing education was a way forward, but that her life was not so different from her mother's. Her so-called good education, in a white-dominated school, entailed denigrating her race:

> If it had been granted to me to fill a diversity and inclusion quota.
> If my teachers positioned me against the black kids
> it freedom if im still standin on an auction block. this one taller. Middle of the cafeteria. with my principal standing over my shoulder. And im reading off the morning announcements with that good n***uh voice but no one gives a shit half the black kids in our grade struggling to read.

The degrading experience of being Black in a white-dominated school is reminiscent of bell hooks' description of moving from a deeply supportive all-Black school to an integrated institution where her white teachers often shared the same prejudices against people of color as the society at large (hooks 1994, 3).

The next slide from Steinem's book read "We are all engaged in the task of peeling off the false selves, programmed selves, the selves created by our families, our cultures, our religion."

The company's response suggested that feminism has not encouraged that option for them as women of color:

> The other day feminism called me lazy and dumb
> And it was the first time I felt she was speaking her truth.
>
> She told me I was responsible for my own demise, that I can't sit with her and stop trying to make equality happen when all I ever did was wanted to be like her.

One of the performers then declared:

> I've swallowed my voice and choked on it a long time ago
> But aren't you happy that I'm cleaning this closet without being asked?

This raises the question, Who feels empowered by feminism to speak their truth? Agency is not equally available across race when hierarchical role expectations continue to be the norm.

This performer aspired to be not like a white feminist but like her own mother, so as to be, first and foremost, comfortable in her own skin:

> I just wish I can be all high-esteemed and confident like you are
> mommy. Teach me to be like that mommy.
> To live in the confidence of skin. comfort of flesh and skeletons

What important material, worthy of a discussion with people who *do* find something liberating in feminism growing out of the 1970s. But the event did not integrate the viBe performers at all. It felt tokenistic to have some young Black women on the stage without providing any exchange with the featured white authors.

Interviewing the young women a few weeks after the event, Jan heard that they found Steinem's book white-centered and disrespectful about Black issues. For example, the quote "If you don't vote, you don't count" blamed people who didn't vote, and in some cases couldn't, without recognizing the barriers to Black people (and poor people of any race) voting: gerrymandering, and workplaces that don't tell employees that they have a legal right to take time out to vote.

At the event itself, viBe executive director Toya Lillard was mistaken for someone who worked there. And while organizers had assured Lillard that the company would get a moment to meet Steinem, that never happened. As one of the viBe performers put it, "If Steinem is so passionate about this work, why didn't she come see us when we said her feminism wasn't reaching us Black girls?" Another performer noted that being in front of a white audience felt polarizing; Lillard compared it to a café where they are playing hip-hop but there're no Black folks, noting, "It had to be intentional to keep us at a distance and talk *about* us."

One of the young women summed up their general consensus:

> I don't expect much from white people. I don't think about feminism, but I believe in rights for all women. I had a gender studies class where they taught "The personal is the political." The issues that White women have seem petty—Black people just want to stop dying. . . . The atmosphere at that event was that everyone had to act as if everything was all right even if it was not. ViBe is the first space where I'm allowed to say what's not okay. Black women are supposed to say everything is okay.

The viBe Theater members' perception of feminism as a white movement and the lack of a public forum to discuss this perspective at the book launch is not atypical. Two social struggles that could well, and often do, support each other—antisexism and antiracism—are as often pulled asunder.

It's taken too long for many white feminists to recognize that what was a key cultural opening for some women was not so for all women. White and middle-class, Jan was in her early twenties in the 1970s, when the second wave of "the women's movement" took flight. It opened up possibilities she had not thought possible for her as a woman, such as eventually becoming a professor. It's not that it was illegal; rather, Jan had unconsciously bought into a sense of men as smarter than women, and had few women professors to prove otherwise.

The issue of pettiness in white middle- and upper-class women's issues in the 1970s women's movement is complicated. We each come to consciousness about inequity from our own experience, and though some people are, without a doubt, in more extreme circumstances, a person oughtn't be shamed because of the class they come from, but, rather, work to be aware of and act on behalf of people in more dire circumstances. Jan recounts:

> When I was in my twenties in the 1970s, a friend brought me into a women's consciousness-raising group. Like women all across the United States, groups of six to eight, in our case all white, though of different class backgrounds, gathered every week or two to talk about

> under-the-radar slights in our lives related to being women. Sitting around one another's kitchen tables, I found that unequal gender dynamics that I thought were particular to my relationships were, in fact, social, like why women usually did more of the housework than their boyfriends and why men tended to dominate political discussions. The women in that group gave me courage to ask my questions out loud. I tremblingly shared that I had been subtly taught to bolster men but nothing about supporting other women. We sought ways of dealing with men who whistled and made sexual comments about us in the street, making us feel that we didn't have the same right to public space.

While the above concerns are not as extreme as issues many people deal with, the personal is often a bridge to a larger consciousness and an expanded context. It's complicated that middle-class white women were having this shift in consciousness at the same time as many Black women were fighting for survival. But a movement is not about competing fragilities or oppressions, but, rather, about going forward, even if it is at different speeds and levels.

However, if one never expands beyond one's own circumstances, the contradictions are painful. How can a group be focused on liberating themselves without seeing their bad treatment of others? Tracing the history of white women who fought for their own liberation but not for Blacks, scholar Kimberly A. Hamlin writes, "By the 1910s, many white suffragists had come to believe that focusing on white women voting was the only way they could get the 19th Amendment through Congress" (www.washingtonpost.com/outlook/2019/06/04how-racism-almost-killed-womens-right-vote/).

Theater maker Cora Hook recounts attending the second National Organization of Women conference in 1977, when she was an Antioch student (Cora Hook in conversation with Cohen-Cruz, July 15, 2020). She arrived in the lobby, where various healthy food stands were set up, and the first exchange she observed was a white woman admonishing the Latina server at a yogurt stand that she hadn't been given enough. While the perfect is the enemy of the good, surely feminism was intended for all, not just for those who paid to attend the conference.

• • •

Numerous interviewees evoked another contradictory identity issue: the behavior of certain men committed to social justice but privately taking advantage of women. The very notion of gender equity is opaque to some, partly because many women may not appear to be at a disadvantage, given their education, economic stability, or professional accomplishment. Nonetheless, women have been historically positioned as auxiliary to men.

How do we deal with such behavior, recognizing that it is both a personal and, as the #MeToo movement has illuminated, a systemic problem that has been revealed to fester in nearly every profession? What of the good work that people who are sexually coercive in private may be doing in public? Does the commitment to self-critique and a belief in the capacity of people to change extend to individuals within a movement who have supported social justice in many good ways but in one terrible way have not? Activist Charlene Carruthers recounts how a Black man who was part of BYP100 (Black Youth Project 100), an organization that she cofounded, did sexual harm to a woman within that network. With first the woman's and then the man's consent, BYP100 initiated a community accountability process toward transformative justice that first protected the woman, then educated the man, and, third, generated a curriculum about sexual violence for incoming members (https://transformharm.tumblr.com). The organizational response is promising.

Interviewees also told stories of how theater culture becomes a cover for sexual abuse by those in power, be they directors or teachers. During her many years teaching in drama departments of universities, Jan has had countless young female, and over time, male students as well, confide to her of theater teachers overstepping a line with them, where the natural camaraderie of making performance together became coercively sexualized. (See also Ginzburg 2020.) They always begged her to not report it, fearing even worse reprisals.

Other than discussing how they could deflect unwanted attention, and raising the general problem with department administrators, she felt there was little that she could do individually. The culture of the workplace and indeed the profession needs to transform at the foundation. While protecting the individual being victimized is the first priority, the idea that people can learn from even terrible acts in their past is also important; the field of socially engaged arts is underpinned with the potential of individual and societal change. Recognizing how pervasive power dynamics are in U.S. society, how do we focus on necessary systemic changes?

If "We" Are…

If we are people who recognize the complexity of identity, we are likely to appreciate Andrea Assaf's experience:

> If I'm in a queer community, I have to navigate being Arab American, and vice versa. If I'm with people of color, I have to explain how Arab Americans are people of color even though legally white and how we got to this historical moment. It's challenging, but it can be very useful if you have an ethical framework as an outsider for what Urban Bush Women call "entering and exiting community." It's almost like Boal's joker role [in Theatre of the Oppressed]—you can facilitate without anyone claiming you, which allows a certain amount of freedom.

Assaf reminds us that being an outsider is sometimes a good thing. She gives the example of cofacilitating workshops with veterans with Linda Parris-Bailey, who invited her to direct *Speed Killed My Cousin*:

> I didn't understand military lingo or know what particular jokes meant, so that encouraged people to talk about things that would otherwise have remained unspoken. A workshop with younger veterans was one of the scariest things I had ever done, because they had served in the Middle East. I could see [distrust] in their eyes when they looked at me as someone visibly of Middle Eastern ancestry.
>
> That workshop was deeply important for me to do; who said, "An enemy is just someone whose story you haven't heard yet"? How do

we get through the idea that we are enemies? It was that experience, that mutual getting to know each other, through story circles, poetry, theater games. And it gave me a way to learn about addiction and mental health. which is important, given my family history. Doing that work with real people was healing for me personally, which is perhaps what kept me in it.

The political dimension was that people asked me why as an Arab American I was working with military veterans. I realized that it was a way to have an impact on people who don't already think the way I do. Especially leading up to and in the Trump era, a lot of people won't even walk in the door to a piece by someone with my name and face. But they will come to a piece written and performed by veterans. If people who trust me show up for me, and people who trust the veterans show up for them, we can have a dialogue with people who we think don't agree with us.

If we are people who lead with our values, we might take to heart and practice transformative justice (TJ), which Mia Mingus describes as "a political framework and approach for responding to violence, harm, and abuse. At its most basic, it seeks to respond to violence without creating more violence and/or engaging in harm reduction to lessen the violence." TJ can be thought of as a way of "making things right," getting in "right relation," or creating justice together. Transformative justice responses and interventions (1) do not rely on the state; (2) do not reinforce or perpetuate violence, such as oppressive norms or vigilantism; and, most important, (3) actively cultivate the things we know prevent violence, such as healing, accountability, resilience, and safety for all involved. It is important that in instances of harm we seek to understand private problems in relation to larger public issues and have built strong- enough relationships to go through this process together (https://transformharm.org/transformative-justice-a-brief- description/).

If we are people who can balance multiple allegiances, we might appreciate how Lanxing Fu, codirector of Superhero Clubhouse, explains what her collective does:

[It] unites ecology and theater, providing bridges, mostly in New York City, between those who are most directly impacted and vulnerable to present and future climate and environmental events with those who are more removed; and across disciplines—for example, people in artistic/creative fields and people in science and academic fields—and other divides in our society, like geographic ones and how they're connected to race and class. . . . I appreciate and understand why identity is important at this moment, to put dominant power structures on their head and revitalize. But it can also be harmful and reduce people and the complexity of movements. Ideally, we all hold different affinities, and people of multiple affinities work toward collective goals.

Black performer/writer/director Daniel Alexander Jones roots his ideas about identity, affinity, and art making in coming together around shared needs:

This is a thorny topic. I'm a bit of a transgressor here. I keep urging myself and everyone else to get off the auction block. All these definitions of who we are have to do with commerce, capitalism, and violent oppression. External definitions. I get it. I am Black and queer and have struggled my whole life in predominantly white institutions, with white people trying to tell me who I am and what we can do, and navigating their tears and their drama and white fragility.

And now—pedal to the metal, this coronavirus is a signal of something much bigger. I just heard a health leader saying, "This is bad, but we dodged the bullet. Wait until it comes in combination with a climate crisis like a hurricane." I'm not going to be checking identity cards when we're trying to get water. Some of us have to be willing to go beyond what I think is a fundamentally reactive space. Because I've lived through it, I can look back and say it's a poor mimeograph copy of the politics of the 1970s.

There is no part of my experience that is the same as [that of] someone who is dealing with questions of ableism or trans experience. My imperative is not to claim that I can know that. But how can we work with one another to do what we need to do? What is the means of creating space together that can welcome people, meet their

> needs, then be about our business? Auction-block thinking becomes a fear-based resistance to the violence we've all experienced. I will stand behind the bulwark of my identity so as not to retraumatize this wound. We all know about epigenetics, blood memory; it is a real thing we carry. But we have to work toward community. To that end, I keep going back to someone like Audre Lorde, who says we have differences and do things differently and must honor that fact. I can name the specificity of my identity and—let's go to work.

Facilitating across difference has an important role to play, as we are surrounded by world leaders, brazenly led from 2016 to 2020 by our former president, who rail against whole groups: people of color, immigrants and refugees, believers of other faiths, people of nonconforming gender and sexual identities. This has intensified with the digital divide, apartheid by algorithms, which siloes people all over the world into echo chambers of like-minded commentary and information that bolster their own opinions and may perpetuate violence and exclusion. Everyone has been given permission to do the same: shamelessly air and act on generalizations about those who may be of a different class, race, religion, sexuality, age, nationality, and political view, but to what end?

Arts consultant Holly Sidford gives another explanation for the growing gap between people of different identities and circumstances. She cites sociologist Robert Putnam's 2020 book, *The Upswing*, which looks at vast quantities of data since the late 1890s and charts the upswing in measures of social comity, positive race relations, more cultural equity, and less economic disparity, from the Gilded Age until about 1965. While it was not true for everyone and there were setbacks, it was, for many years, basically an improving picture for most people. Then around 1965, it started a very precipitous downward slope to today, when we are more riven by political, social, and economic divides than we have been since the 1890s. Putnam writes that we improved life for most Americans once and can do it again. But the anti–Vietnam War effort, the civil rights movement, the women's movement, all blazing in the 1960s and the 1970s, had the unintended consequence of creating divides that allowed the forces of inequity to take hold.

A perspective on the deep divisions of our times that has influenced director and professor Bob Leonard is philosopher Charles Taylor's theory of social imaginaries. It posits that humans carry around ideas about whole groups of people that are not based on reality or experience but that nonetheless produce concrete impacts—for example, difficulty in getting jobs or housing despite one's qualifications or greater police surveillance and violence. In a time characterized by sweeping generalizations about the "other," it's worth reconsidering the emphasis on art making solely with "one's own."

Native American playwright Larissa FastHorse and Michael Garcés, director of the Cornerstone Theater Company, collaborated on *Native Nation,* one play in a trilogy about Indigenous experience in North America that began with *Urban Rez,* which brought them into a geographic community not their own. When working across difference, Garcés emphasizes transparency:

> We enter saying, "I don't know how best to direct this play in this community. I have skills as a director, but I don't have credibility in this community." Community partners bring credibility to the table. We're never the experts. We wouldn't presume to do this show, we wouldn't have a show without them. You think you've done all these projects, you've earned credibility, and you haven't. History doesn't permit it and shouldn't. You have to learn it every time from scratch. It's really hard; it precipitates burnout in the field. It's also one of the joys, entering new every time. Sometimes you have to cop to a prejudice about a community or a person, which is hard. But it is this complexity and challenge that make me, as an artist, excited.

FastHorse reflects:

> Michael and I are simply there to take the skills and resources we have, whatever they are in each project, lay them out clearly, and ask, "Are any of these of interest to you? In what way?" Then, fulfill the community's desire, whatever that may be. That's the difference—we have no artistic desires or goals. It takes people a long time to believe

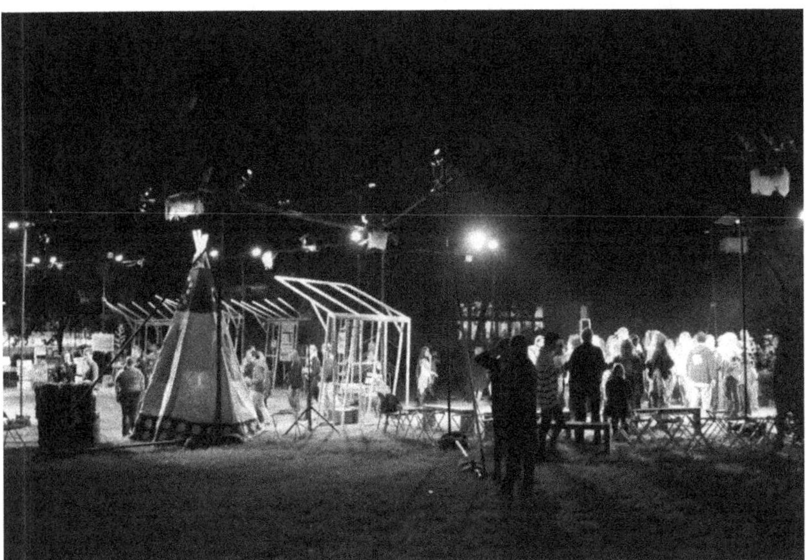

Audience and performers share space and interact in Cornerstone Theater Company's Urban Rez *in performance at Kuruvungna Sacred Springs in what is now known as West Los Angeles. Scenic design by Shannon Scrofano. Lighting design by Geoff Korff. Photograph by James Cheeks III. Copyright Cornerstone Theater Company, Inc.*

> that. If they said, "We just want you to spend this money serving us all Oreos and Kool-Aid for two years," we would say, "Great. That's what we'll do." The good news is when we're doing it in an Indigenous community, we get to go entirely by the Indigenous rules, protocols, and culture, as opposed to predominantly white institutions and white protocols and trying to inject Indigenous protocols into that.

Sometimes the issue of difference is more about other people's perceptions than about how the participants themselves feel, as Carlton Turner addresses in the context of his work with Sipp Culture:

> Some people in our small Mississippi town have been reluctant to share stories for fear of judgement. It comes with working in a strong faith-based community. We have nine churches and no grocery stores in town. People retreat to the comfort of spaces they see as their specific community, usually their church. There's a particular pastor

> who said he can't come to events we host if there's liquor, because of worry of what his congregants would think of him. So it's difficult to work with, say, the queer community, because people will think it's somehow unrighteous, not aligned with their Southern Baptist traditions. It challenges the ability to even see the spectrum in our own community. Our work is not faith-based; it's about identifying all the parts of who we are as being valuable and valued; you don't have to like or agree with the story, as John O'Neal said, but just respect it.

Turner noted that Sipp does indeed work with queer people in the community and has also hosted queer artists in residence. He asks:

> Who is interested in learning and expanding their community and who is trying to advance only their own causes? The latter doesn't require any type of transformation. The former requires you to be open to learning. I have come to understand the pastor as being the latter, interested in the idea of saving people and converting sinners into believers. Don't get me wrong: You can aspire to do those things and still be in a mode of expanding your knowledge and understanding. But if you aren't interested in learning with others, only teaching, then the work we do at Sipp Culture may seem counterintuitive.

Sometimes dialogue is not desired. While it was illuminating for Jan to sit down with the viBe company that performed at the Steinem-Farrow event, they had no interest in her or her perspective but only wanted to talk about their own. Jan could understand that:

> I've had plenty of opportunities to share my perspectives and they've had relatively few; plus, they've felt ignored or badly treated by white people. I nonetheless see a value in more cross-generational engagement within the field; to neither throw out everything nor be limited by what got us to this point. I'd love to hear younger practitioners and scholars consider and critique the work of my generation, and make their own proposals, so that rather than simply ignoring the learning from former years, we look at how it needs to grow and transform and what still must be unearthed to feed current and future generations.

Rad adds:

> For such exchange to be possible, the older generation has to discard a paternalistic attitude to younger artists, and both need to embrace egoless knowledge sharing, rather than hoarding, toward coalition and community building. We'd need to invest in learning new, complex ways of being together that can hold chaos through the process of trust building, that center healing and wellness, that consider a person's entire context, and set agreed-upon terms of transforming through conflict and disagreements.

We need to attend to contradictions within our field, like ongoing power imbalances around gender and race. We also need to recognize that for all the identity divisions, there are longings to come together across differences. We suspect that most of us have experienced the mystery of being deeply drawn to a culture or group of which one is not obviously a part. So as youth poet laureate Amanda Gorman said at Joseph Biden's January 2021 inauguration, we aren't "broken, but simply unfinished." Performance engaged around issues like these are signs of a robust practice with still much to do and much to contribute to our collective lives.

5 Community-Centric Civic Collaborations

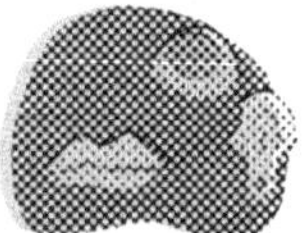

I was not surprised that I had to explain to professionals in fields like community development and public health what art could contribute to their sectors. But I had not expected that so many artists *would need such roles of art explained.*

—Jamie Bennett, then director of ArtPlaceAmerica, in conversation with Cohen-Cruz, 2020

My concern is what's deeper than the practical outcome: are people empowered, and do they see their own voice in this thing? Is there a poetic relationship that adds value for people there, not just an outcome for the mayor's office?

—Artist Rick Lowe, in an interview with Cohen-Cruz, "The Poetic Residue: On the Difference Between a Civic Action and an Art Project"

Here we focus on artists who ally with government, philanthropic, and business sectors in civic collaborations. Examples include retooling former manufacturing mills for public use; creating public events to bring people back to town centers by celebrating something particular to that place or marking a national holiday in a creative way; creating spaces and programs to hear local musicians and poets and simply to gather; and otherwise adding artistic skills to a mix of disciplines generating economic and social activity. How the artists work with the people impacted by these activities as well as the structural outcomes characterize their value.

Since the early 2000s, renewed attention and more funding for artists contributing to participatory problem solving have led to collaborations with the very groups to which many socially engaged artists would have been in opposition in the 1960s–mid-1970s—for example, government and business. Oppositional performance had been part of the zeitgeist of the 1960s– mid-1970s. It kept attention centered on the problems at that time: the war in Vietnam, racial and cultural inequity, worldwide nuclear armament, environmental degradation, and an overly materialistic status quo. Oppositional performance was epitomized by protest and dramatic images to embolden others to stand up to social wrongs. The expressive act was still core, but it was as likely to take place on a city street as in a theater.

A growing emphasis in the 1980s and 1990s on the local brought more attention to performance's role in building community and relationships. The language of dialogue was on the rise—rather than "preaching to the choir," addressing only those people who already agree (while also important), dialogue entailed engaging with people of differing opinions. An example is the four-year Arts-Based Civic Dialogue initiative, begun in 1999, that the Animating Democracy Initiative facilitated "to study current activity and best practices among artists and cultural organizations whose work engages the public in dialogue on key civic issues." The project drew inspiration from W. E. B. Du Bois, who said, "Begin with art, because art tries to take us outside ourselves. It is a matter of trying to create an atmosphere and context so conversation can flow back and forth and we can be influenced by each other" (www.animatingdemocracy.org/publications/papers-essays-articles/arts-based-civic-dialogue).

Some civically engaged artists find more in common with people from other sectors who want to improve people's everyday lives than with artists who work in institutional theaters and are not involved with the quotidian concerns of people outside the arts. They are seeking a different idea of success, with some eschewing aesthetic recognition entirely as they interact with diverse people and focus on cogenerating concrete enhancements to their lives. Such artists are aligned with both the people of a community—related by race, class, sexuality, geographic location, religion, and/or politics—*and* the institutions tasked with their well-being.

The notion of being of service has a spiritual dimension, and has been a crucial element of nearly every religious tradition. Basic tenets about being of service to one's community as an expression of faith, and an altruistic putting of others before oneself, have been associated with Muhammad, Jesus, the Peacemaker, Allah, Adonai, and Hindu gods. The spiritual framing often encourages acting from a generous place of interconnectivity as an expression of allegiance to a higher power.

A public servant is theoretically entrusted with attending to the good of all, typically through a governmental position. But anyone committed to serving the public good, including an artist, could be in that role. In the arts, the word *service* has tended to have a pejorative tinge, as if public-mindedness cancels artistic excellence. Commenting on an artist's "service" to a community has been a thinly veiled criticism. But commitment to the public good and to one's professional development are not mutually exclusive. Ideally, the exchange is based on relationship building and mutual benefit.

In what follows, we hear from artists and policy makers about the rise in artists embedded in civic initiatives since 2010. We see how the creative placemaking landscape has responded to criticism, and hear from artists who have participated in such collaborations.

Creative Placemaking, Creative Placekeeping

While it is not new for artists to collaborate with people in local government and other civic institutions, such efforts became more codified and better funded between 2010 and 2020 when framed as *creative placemaking*. Numerous initiatives paved the way, such as Leveraging Investments in Creativity, begun in 2003, which included how artists' skills could be used beyond strictly aesthetic spaces.

The term *creative placemaking* entered the cultural ecosystem through a 2010 white paper by that name for the Mayors' Institute on City Design. Coauthors Ann Markusen and Anne Gadwa defined it as "strategically shaping the physical and social character of a neighborhood, town, city, or region around arts and cultural activities." Private foundations such as Kresge rallied around the concept. The National Endowment for the Arts initiated Our Town grants to "support projects that integrate arts, culture, and design activities into efforts that strengthen communities by advancing local economic, physical, and/or social outcomes" (www.arts.gov/grants/our-town/program-description). In 2011, a collaboration of foundations, federal agencies, and financial institutions launched ArtPlace America, a ten-year initiative whose mission was "to position arts and culture as a core sector of community planning and development" (www.artplaceamerica.org).

While rightly praised as a catalyst for new sources of funding and for enhancing collaborations with people from disciplines other than the arts, creative placemaking was criticized by arts administrator Roberto Bedoya and others for often ignoring that places are already made, already have the character of their former and current residents. Historically, "community development" has too often been detrimental to longtime residents, code for gentrification that results in displacement, disinvestment, removal, and containment. In such scenarios, developers and people wealthy enough to buy property, rather than longtime residents, are the beneficiaries. Creative placemaking has sometimes been accused of "art washing," which cultural writer Stephen Pritchard describes as the use of art "to smooth and gloss over social cleansing and gentrification by corporations, developers, local authorities, arts organizations and communities themselves" (https://colouringinculture.org/uncategorized/artwashingsocialcapitalantigentrification/).

Erik Takeshita, who works in equitable community development, provides historical context for the *Creative Placemaking* report:

> It was the Great Recession. Barack Obama was coming into office. Rocco Landesman, chair of the National Endowment for the Arts, saw creative placemaking as an opportunity to think differently and more creatively about cross-sector partnerships, opening the way for more interagency funding for the arts. Given that cowriter Ann

Markusen is an economist herself, the context of the recession, and the federal mandate, the report necessarily had an economic focus.

Takeshita appreciates that the first director of ArtPlace, Carol Coletta, had a clear focus on getting those in local government, such as mayors and county executives, to buy into the work, think about economic returns, and support the development of "vibrancy indicators" that focused on economic contributions of the arts and culture. But Takeshita also sees flaws in creative placemaking's original formulation:

> We absolutely wanted investment in disinvested communities, but we had to do it in a way that wouldn't lead to unintended displacement, physically or spiritually. It's a both/and. Yes, we want more money to flow, these vacant buildings to be occupied, and more businesses to thrive, and we have to do it in a way that doesn't displace those already here. It's a much more complicated and nuanced conversation.

Takeshita credits critiques of creative placemaking for bringing attention to equity and justice. Most influential has been Bedoya's notion of place*keeping*, particularly concerning communities of color that had been and continue to be marginalized. Bedoya emphasized that places were in some cases being gentrified, with artists' contributions benefiting developers rather than longtime residents.

Bedoya warns that community development incurs dis-belonging when equity and justice are not foregrounded (www.giarts.org/article/placemaking-and-politics-belonging-and-dis-belonging). He avows that to be an ethical undertaking serving a truly public good, creative placemaking must integrate a commitment to those places' histories and an understanding of critical race theory and politics into its approach to planning and economic development.

Bedoya's comments and the ensuing field-wide dialogue exemplify critical community practice—that is, action based on a vision of society grounded in the ideals of social justice, social inclusion, self-determination, solidarity, and collective wellness. This approach to practice posits that social transformation is possible when people have a voice, power, and access to resources. It is grounded in an understanding that the roots of most community problems lie in patterns of systemic poverty, disadvantage, social exclusion, and oppression that are manifestations of structural inequalities and social divisions within society as a whole (www.scra27.org/ what-we-do/what-community-psychology/).

Creative placemaking was also criticized for promoting the "parachuting in" of artists from elsewhere—short-term involvement, with artists quickly entering a community and leaving again—rather than prioritizing the involvement of local artists committed to that place over time, even if outside artists provide additional ideas, expertise, and inspiration. The notion of "*making* a place" did not reckon with the value of local artists for project sustainability or knowledge of long-present layers of history. Ideologically, creative placemaking seemed to emphasize artists directing their individual visions as vetted by large institutions in a civic context, rather than as part of a holistic cultural commons, a paradigm that recognizes residents' needing a stake in the development of the places where they live and that they have shaped culturally and historically, whether or not they have economic ownership. Communities are upheld by the people who care about them.

Criticism by Bedoya and others has been taken seriously by leaders in the creative placemaking ecosystem. In January 2020, here's how Jan experienced the state of that field:

> I'm sitting at the Federal Reserve Bank of New York, in an audience of four hundred people, for a three-hour presentation on "Transforming Community Development Through Arts and Culture." Being here is uncanny for people like me, who've been on the ground with socially engaged art as practitioners, scholars, and teachers for many years. Those of us in our sixties and seventies began at a time when most community development professionals considered art and culture "the icing on the cake," if they considered it at all. Now it's got a name—creative placemaking. Witness its status here and now as a serious and useful approach nearly on a par with the contributions of other disciplines.

Leaders from the worlds of finance, municipal government, and public policy attest to creative placemaking's virtues. Serious funding streams—though still not enough—support it, with the rejoinder to get over the endless call to justify the use of money for art and culture; one simply has to look at what's been accomplished. Powerful people from civic sectors are becoming more conscious that not only the artists involved but also residents from the communities meant to benefit must be at the table with civic professionals, helping shape initiatives from the onset. Roberto Bedoya's critique has served as a reminder that the people who have lived in a place made it; it is a matter of maintaining, not creating, the places, and supporting the people who have lived there.

Whereas the norm is for artists seeking public funds to identify outcomes up front, acceptance of art, even in the context of creative placemaking, as a process of discovery is gaining ground. Panelist Penelope Douglas emphasized *rigorous experimentation,* a far cry from the days when those seated at the adult table (e.g., funders and development professionals) needed to know all intended outcomes up front, whereas those at the children's table—arts, culture people, and local residents—were long committed to discovery as projects unfolded. Host David Erickson quoted poet Pablo Neruda on *burning patience,* evoking the challenge of passionate work that takes a long time. The work's cross-sector nature, also underlined, requires various kinds of expertise and exists out of the siloes that keep old mind-sets in place when new approaches are needed.

Between creative placemaking's launch in 2010 and the event at the New York Reserve Bank in 2020, the value of equity has become more central, which ArtPlace's third director, Jamie Bennett, acknowledges:

> Context matters—Black Lives Matter, Occupy Wall Street, and other things that have been going on societally. ArtPlace and creative placemaking as a field were becoming responsive to that. Yes, we are building a new thing here and want to incorporate these other points of view and concerns. It's iterative; it'll only get better over time if

> people add to it, get on board and figure it out together, which is in itself an artistic process. We're putting something out, getting critiqued, changing it, then putting it back out. (Bennett in conversation with Cohen-Cruz, 2020)

Acknowledging Bedoya and others' concerns, Bennett identifies three displacements associated with gentrification: "The first is physical displacement in the form of eminent domain. The second is financial displacement in which property values rise but income remains flat and residents are priced out. The third is cultural displacement." He gives an example of a subtle form of this third phenomenon: "Consider public parks. They're free, so at least in theory, residents face no financial barriers to access. Yet bottles of water cost $7. That's a disproportionately large financial burden for a poor family, and it tells them that the park is 'primarily intended for rich folks.'" Bennett does not believe that creative placemaking practitioners can stop development projects. But by facilitating "cultural cohesion" from a "seat at the table," they can mitigate cultural displacement (www.insidephilanthropy.com/home/2019/5/30/ displacement-dilemma-do-arts-funders-exacerbate-urban-gentrification).

Performer and scholar Paul Bonin-Rodriguez praises Bennett's leadership of ArtPlace:

> Jamie Bennett came in and reorganized ArtPlace. He made it an open inquiry. [Research director] Jamie Hand's field scans [tools funders use to look at opportunities, needs, and funding gaps in a given field] are amazing. [ArtPlace organized the scans around ten sectors: Agriculture & Food, Economic Development, Environment & Energy, Health, Housing, Immigration, Public Safety, Transportation, Workforce Development, and Youth Development.] The research is creative, expressive, local, and validating. ArtPlace now functions in a spirit of abundance and generosity; it's not exclusionary.

The possibilities for artists to contribute to the world around them have expanded through creative placemaking's success in spurring on funders to support it and community developers to also benefit the people who live there, rather than focusing only on the economic profit that investors derive from building up a place.

Equitably Advancing Creative Placemaking/Placekeeping

What follows are some of the tasks of creative placemaking/placekeeping now, reflecting what we heard from artists involved in civic partnerships.

Recognizing Other Arts-Infused, Community-Connected Initiatives

The phenomenon of artists collaborating across sectors well before 2010 does not seem sufficiently well known to creative placemaking practitioners and advocates. Too many of the people we've met who are enthralled with the field seem to think they invented a role for the arts outside of strictly aesthetic spaces. Knowing about other socially engaged art instills humility, expands approaches, and aligns initiatives that integrate the arts to serve the public in different but also meaningful ways. Recognizing the various forms that socially engaged performance has taken is one of the purposes of this book.

Art contributing to one's community is part of a long tradition, arguably the first kind of art, when artists were also healers and priests, shamans, responding to multiple human needs. Jan defined community-based art as "artists, collaborating with people whose lives directly inform the subject matter, express[ing] collective meaning" (Cohen-Cruz 2005, 1). But the role of artists integrated in their communities has ebbed and flowed throughout history. The attitude in more recent times has often been patronizing, evoking a pat on the head but not taken seriously as social intervention *or* art. Then, too, the role of the socially engaged artist is not all-encompassing; even artists who eschew community involvement and see their role as socially distanced critics, or makers strictly within aesthetic contexts, have at times been welcome bulwarks against rampant commercialism.

Though part of a long tradition of art embedded in social rather than strictly aesthetic contexts, creative placemaking is grounded in community development. Whereas community-based art emphasizes long-term relationships in which artists collaborate with people impacted by the issues addressed, creative placemaking foregrounds artists' work with *institutions* that are tasked with the "public good" of a neighborhood, a distinct local population (e.g., children and families; immigrants), or a particular public sector (police, transportation, etc.). As committed as the staff members with whom the artists work often are, they are expected to represent their institution or agency in these relationships, not themselves, except for those at the very top of the chain, also in contrast to partners in community-based art. The civic base raises some longtime community artists' eyebrows—how can it support grassroots agency when the civic base is beholden to political structures and personnel for its very existence? Notwithstanding, both community-based art and creative placemaking are local endeavors that recognize the importance of building relationships with community members. An advantage of the civic base's institutional context is the possibility of bringing an initiative to a larger scale that serves more people through government's participation.

Preparations for Participating in Creative Placemaking

To gauge how artists and their cross-sector collaborators prepare for such work, one needs an understanding of how art in the context of creative placemaking is different from art in an aesthetic space where the partners are other artists. First, let us state that civic collaborations are not for all artists. Some artists thrive on spontaneity and taking a project wherever it goes. Overdetermining how art is to be of use and possibly overaccommodating civic agencies are at odds with some artists' practice. Jody Wood, for example, created a mobile hair salon that arrived at various homeless shelters and did residents' hair for free, providing residents with a marvelous experience of being cared for and seeing themselves differently. But she was uncomfortable making the experience something that happened every Thursday at 3:00 p.m., say, because part of its impact was its break from the routine. While interested in working in the civic sector, Wood needs to negotiate such matters.

In 2012, theater director Michael Rohd coined the term *civic practice,* which he describes as "projects that bring artists, designers, culture makers, and heritage holders into collaboration and co-design with community partners and local residents around a community defined aspiration, challenge, or vision" (thecpcp.org). He contrasts civic practice with both *studio* practice (e.g., artist-generated work with other artists) and *social* practice (work that artists lead with the participation of nonartists seminal to the project). This clarification was for nonartists as well as for artists who are used to working in strictly aesthetic contexts and did not always understand how they could apply their craft to community development.

Rohd distinguishes civic practice from social practice, which might look similar. The difference is intent and process: Is the project initiated by the artist or is a community seeking to realize its own vision? Perhaps social practice and civic practice exist in a continuum, such as when artists initiate projects that the community would not have thought of but totally embrace, like Wood's mobile hair salon. And what about projects initiated or controlled by a funder or civic agency? We look at the alignment of an artist's purpose and a community's needs, no matter who generates it.

Rohd avows that "with the right approach, the same tools and capacities that artists use to make art can be utilized to transform systems and improve the impacts of government and community-driven efforts and programs" (thecpcp.org). He engages with artists who want to work in civic practice by having them do the following:

1. Think about, analyze, and articulate their assets and what those skills are in themselves, apart from a performance context/the output they usually think of, but usable collaboratively in other spaces. Think of them as process tools that might be deployed so they are understandable by people, with the output nothing to do with performance.
2. Translate how they talk about their own practice into a language and framework they can share with people in other disciplines, that invite others to think more expansively about how the collaboration might work.
3. Pay attention to the ethics of self-determination and community development, and to positionality (e.g., who am I coming into this community?). Make power visible. Deal with issues that may come

> up concerning that positionality and race. Complications arise for artists working through institutions that are predominantly or historically white and have histories of settler colonial violence. Using a civic practice approach can be a kind of whitewashing of harm that an institution caused. That institution has to be doing its own antiracist work at the same time as the artist is doing civic practice. Otherwise, the institutional space will display, publicize, and make resources available while still benefiting from a white supremacist framework.

People from other disciplines, conversely, need to be prepared to work with artists. Rohd describes how he and his company members do workshops to that end:

> We spend time listening and asking questions: What do you do? What's your mission? What's your daily work? What do you hope to be next week, next year, in five years? We ask them [about] some of their aspirations, visions, challenges, obstacles, and current resistance. Company members then model what an artistic contribution might be to that, and the others will watch. We explain: "What we just went through was us using curiosity and imagination to add a creative dimension to something you are already working on. Which is probably different from how you've historically thought of artists contributing socially—making a space more beautiful, helping with communications." We demonstrate a more obscure way in, to open up the possibilities. What turns the conversation is listening and making an offer, and they say, "Oh, that's interesting. I never thought of that." That lifts you over a huge boulder.

Whatever process everyone goes through, the bottom line is the artist and other collaborators' values. A conscientious artist putting the community partner front and center does not in itself ensure an equitable outcome. There may be dominant members of a community with values that are at odds with equity for all. Taking time at the beginning to agree on underlying values and guidelines is time well spent.

Knowing Enough About One Another's Work to Collaborate

How much do artists and their civic collaborators need to understand what the other does and their field to work effectively together? Jan's exchange with Erik Takeshita provides some insights.

> **ET:** Artists working in municipalities need some baseline knowledge. But part of the secret sauce, the magic, is that I don't know too much about the other and their perspective. If you have too much similarity, you lose the power of the very thing we're seeking, which is a cross-sector diversity.
>
> More than knowledge or technical skills, people need curiosity, willingness to work with one another, humility; one of the hazards of expertise is we become set in our ways and think we know. The definition of insanity is doing the same thing and expecting a different result. If you want to have a different result, you have to do things differently. Whether you are a municipal government worker, a housing developer, or an artist, you have to be willing to step beyond your comfort zone, let go of the idea that how you usually work is the only way it can happen. Partnership suggests a mutual give-and-take. It's not about abandoning the need for technical expertise as much as being open to and intentionally engaging with a partner, giving up some of what you usually do and learning from the other. The whole must be greater than the sum of the parts of what either could do alone without combining skills. You need enough commonality of language and openness to affect and be affected.
>
> **JCC:** What do artists need to know about civic collaborations if they've had mostly studio practice?
>
> **ET:** That it is different from working in isolation in a studio. It's about being responsive to the needs of the community. To avoid emotional/psychological displacement, they must make sure the people there now are driving the development, leading the way. There are examples all over the United States where artists or developers say, "Oh, this neighborhood is abandoned and I'm here to save it." Well no. It may

> not be obvious to you what's there, but there are people there who know. When the developer or artist parachutes in from Mars, it's not so healthy. Work really driven by the community is the best work, and guards against this psychological and emotional displacement.
>
> Artists and their partners also need to know what each needs to be successful; what are the other's desired impacts? This will be a steep learning curve, understanding different ways of working, and will lead to some frustration. It takes more time and energy and a different energy. Know that you don't know what you are getting into; be prepared that mind shifts will occur.

Theater maker Mark Valdez, who frequently works across sectors, such as in his 2020 project about housing, goes further in his estimation of how acquainted the artists and their civic partners need to be about each other's work:

> [They need to know] enough so that if the project is not succeeding, they can see that maybe the art also isn't succeeding. You won't know that if you don't know what the art is supposed to be. Erik's point is that the partners aren't artists; they can't know about it, any more than the artists can know their [nonart] part, like the intricacies of financing. But I say they *must* know about each other, not the intricacies, but enough to keep the train on its track.

Equitable community development specialist Maria Rosario Jackson helped assess impact in a recent cross-sector collaboration, Valdez continues, which included teasing out "what indicators to look for. We're asking our partners what they need to see to believe this is working." He was also influenced by artist Marty Pottenger, who asks the mayors she works with in her projects embedded in municipal government what *they* need to see, which is often different from "what the theater people need or the funders want." The civic partner frequently seeks social outcomes—indeed, is required to do so as part of its accountability to whoever pays for it, be it a board of directors or taxpayers—while the artist is involved in a creative process or project, albeit often toward a social purpose. The artist must be willing to prioritize the community's goal without sacrificing artistic qualities. Core to the idea of both creative placemaking and civic practice is that art and culture bring something valuable to community development initiatives. Though the indicators they seek may be different, the collaborators need the same understanding of the kind of community development toward which they strive. Valdez adds:

> Ultimately, we're trying to keep artist collaborations with local governments going, replicate them, expand them. Make the case that this works so that cities will pay more attention to their arts organizations. How do we get the artists primed and ready so they can take advantage of these opportunities?

Though Takeshita and Valdez offer slightly different views about cross-sector collaborations, both describe necessary interactions between artists and municipal staff, especially up front, that require a real investment of both time and money.

Challenging Power Imbalances

A frequent frustration for artists collaborating with civic entities is uneven power dynamics. At its worst, art can end up being no more than window dressing, a congenial image of community without substance or sustainability. For example, artists may facilitate deep conversations with local residents using creative means and nothing may come of it. Like the tradition of carnival, civic practice can be used as a safety valve to let people with little power blow off steam but that ultimately keeps them "in their place."

The power differential is often heightened by the hierarchical structure within many large civic institutions and agencies. Whom, exactly, is one working with and where is the locus of decision making? If the agency has provided or is the recipient of the funding, it's more likely that final decisions will pass through its vetting process and it may bring in other people able to block aspects of the project even if they are not direct collaborators.

Contending with Governmental Accountability and Censorship

Even the most benevolent government agencies are subject to layers of accountability. While fully understandable, and better to be overaccountable than to have no outside checks and balances, having to answer to too many people puts government agencies under pressure to control everything that happens under their ageis. It too often leads to a level of censorship that may not be acceptable to a collaborating artist. Ricardo Gamboa describes navigating the complexity of the institutional context within which they were working with Black and brown youth from the South Side of Chicago under the aegis of the National Museum of Mexican Art:

> A program officer of After School Matters [partly funded with city of Chicago's money] came and then messaged the National Museum of Mexican Art that the youth should make sure their play did not critique the city or the mayor, or that they [would have] to fire me. I said, "It is not my place to censor their work." So we talked with the youth and we did an analysis of who's at risk and what would happen if we go through with this play. They came up with the idea to do a twenty-minute improv performance for grant compliance and then asked me if I could find a way for them to put on their show secretly. And we did.

Governments are risk-averse; artists are creatures of risk. Therein lies the rub.

Civic Collaborations

To allow a project that seeks to play a civic role to take wing before contending with governmental protocol, some artists begin directly with community members and approach government agencies for support later, after core decisions have been made. At other times, the access, resources, and other particulars of a municipal agency make it worth the challenge to collaborate from the onset. Examples of both approaches follow.

Artist-Driven Projects with Civic Agencies Among the Collaborators

Artist Rick Lowe was invited to participate in the 2017 iteration of the international art exhibit Documenta 14, which included a component in Athens, Greece, in response to the deluge of refugees forced from their homes in Syria and elsewhere in the summer of 2014. Arriving in Athens in 2015 to lay the groundwork, Lowe was shocked to see formerly well-functioning areas like Victoria Square inundated by refugees living there openly, having been forced from their homes in the south but with borders closed to the north.

Lowe had founded Project Row Houses (PRH) in Houston, Texas, in 1993. Through artists' restoration and conversion of several blocks of shotgun houses into studios and other resources for local residents, PRH has engaged neighbors, artists, and enterprises in collective creative action to help materialize sustainable opportunities in marginalized communities (https://projectrowhouses.org). An example is the Young Mothers Residential Program, which supports young mothers and their children living in some of the restored houses and participating in a Black parenting curriculum. So the conception of the artist as committed at once to the social and aesthetic was certainly not new to Lowe, who describes himself as socially *and* community engaged.

Lowe explains that he doesn't work anywhere that he'd "have to bring creative placemaking":

> . . . I like to think of places making themselves and the people there having the creativity within themselves to continue to make the places they are already making. It's not bringing anything there but rather elevating people's capacity to continue to do what they're already doing, making their place. Creative placemaking sometimes elevates the role of the outsider coming in to make it happen. It's a subtle difference to place myself to honor the placemaking that's already happening and the creative capacity already there. I work lightly within those communities to add a little focus on capacity. (Cohen-Cruz 2018, 18).

In the case of Victoria Square, Lowe admired efforts already under way among new refugees, but he saw a tension with longtime residents. Lowe describes his work as "a process of engaging a community of people: That's where the work is and the real value." He explores how to generate energy that inspires people to want to get involved creatively and, in this case, how to weave in the existing creative energies of Athens and more specifically Victoria Square, whereas in most cases, creativity is defined as individual. He began conversations with local artists, local businesspeople, students, and other residents, including a large immigrant and refugee population, and their support groups—who live, work, study, and/or have property in the neighborhood. They imagined together a way to support the neighborhood in the face of the challenges. Lowe shared enthusiasm for the community's vision of multicultural refugees contributing to a more vibrant neighborhood that, in turn, could seek more municipal support.

He created a container for what he came to call the Victoria Square Project (VSP), a physical building off Victoria Square where community-generated public workshops, exhibits, performances, and cultural celebrations are initiated by local residents and recent refugees. Neighbors have developed a broader sense of community and experienced positive contributions of the new arrivals, not just the challenges of people who need to share local social services. Lowe did not seek out a government partnership until the project was well under way. This positioned the municipality as the public servant, meant to respond to community residents, with the artist as facilitator. Lowe was both responsive to community members and proactive in proposing a particular cultural project to address it.

The VSP captured the attention of government officials partly because of Lowe's status as an artist—among other honors, he is a MacArthur Fellowship recipient—and partly due to his capacity to build relationships with people in many positions. But they stayed interested because of experiencing the high-quality multicultural events there. The person running for another term as mayor and other officials understood the message: "You can have a culturally diverse city, but you have to show respect and encourage that diversity to be a part of the city." Lowe and others at VSP then developed a proposal for government support.

Resident contributions were seminal to convincing the government to invest in the neighborhood. Lowe describes VSP as a *social sculpture*, the term that conceptual and political artist Joseph Beuys used for seeing society as a whole as a work of art to which everyone can contribute creatively. Working with community initiatives, local businesses, institutions, the municipality, artists, and other individuals and groups, VSP seeks to elevate the cultural and historical assets of this neighborhood. Lowe notes, "Each participant helps us better understand the cultural, historical, and political dynamics in this area." While Lowe made a space for the project and conceptualized it, his local partners determined what it actually is and does, in response to proposals from residents.

Artists Embedded in Municipal Agencies

At least since 1976, when artist Mierle Laderman Ukeles began her forty-plus-year partnership with New York City's Department of Sanitation, artists have been embedding their skills and sensibilities within U.S. local governments. In 2017–2018, Pam Korza and Jan researched U.S. municipal/artist partnerships. Jan notes:

> I was enamored by the possibilities. If the individuals in positions of power were open to what artists brought as conduits to community members' insights and bridges to their policy input, government's many resources could be brought to bear. Art's role in U.S. society could be expanded beyond recognition.

In the guide, Jan and Pam emphasize that artists and municipal agencies have much to offer each other but that such collaborations are not for all artists. Rather, they are for those "committed to applying their creative energies to improve social issues and community health." Municipal agencies offer artists "the opportunity to be immersed in community planning and action" through their "access to technical expertise and other resources, and connections to community leaders and constituents" (municipal-artist.org). The agencies can magnify the artists' impact, teach them how systems work from the inside, and expand their work possibilities. Municipal staff members benefit from artists' creative ways to increase and enhance civic participation; improve agency outreach and communications; think outside the box; deepen understanding of the community and identify ways forward; and improve workplace culture. Compelling examples of such collaborations can be found at that site referenced above.

For example, artist and activist Marty Pottenger was embedded in City Hall in Portland, Maine, from 2007 to 2015, launching Art At Work 2.0, a national initiative to put the power of creativity to work on behalf of local governments and the communities they serve. Over those years, research and conversations with city staff, unions, elected officials, as well as community members, helped identify problems that strategically designed arts projects might be able to address. Pottenger elaborates:

> My work focuses on two anchors with the potential to increase equity, understanding, and engagement. The first is relationships. The second is the potent impact that humans experience when they are creating something. They are two key elements that I've been experimenting with for almost fifty years. A crisis early on in my time in Portland revealed that city leaders did not have relationships—personal or professional—with grassroots leaders. Knowing the consequences of that disconnect, I designed Portland Works, six arts-based civic dialogue workshops that brought fifteen individuals from each "side" together over three months. Participants included city councilors, management, unions, the NAACP, and the South Sudanese, Congolese, Somali, arts, faith, and business communities, as well as our local "Occupy" movement.
>
> Essential to the project's design—dinner, key question, dialogue, and art making (poetry, collage, story circles, singing)—was the vulnerability each participant faced when making and sharing art together. It's tremendously powerful: the risks, the showing of yourself, the facing down of humiliation, the courage. It shreds the sense of official/unofficial because you are all having to share the poem you just wrote or collage you just made. This proved effective in a yearlong project to bring diversity to four neighborhood associations, as well as a project

> with the Public Works Department to address an increase in racial discrimination within the workforce. One point that I would make in pitching these projects to municipal leaders was that arts-based engagement had the potential to address the kind of problems--disenfranchisement, racism, silo culture—that employee barbecues will never fix.

For more on Pottenger's municipal/community work in Portland, see www.artatwork.us.

Jan was the evaluator for seven municipal-artist partnerships through the New York City Department of Cultural Affairs' Public Artists in Residence (PAIR) program, each embedding an artist in a city agency or office. The first was artist Tania Bruguera with the New York City Mayor's Office of Immigrant Affairs (MOIA). The project took place during the Trump years, a tense period, given the national government's unforgiving policy regarding immigration and New York City's more compassionate and progressive approach. Working in the collaboration's favor, MOIA is small and thus more nimble than large agencies. However, most local immigrants distrusted any governmental entity.

Bruguera focused on building trust between immigrants and MOIA through a project called CycleNews. It was grounded in the Mujeres en Movimiento, immigrant women who were part of the Immigration Movement International, an organization Bruguera had founded in Queens. Already accustomed to working with Bruguera, these women were educated by MOIA staff about city resources for immigrants, including free legal services, the New York City municipal ID, a government-issued means of identification that anyone living in NYC can obtain, and counseling on housing rights. Bruguera brought two artists from Las Migrantes, based in Germany, to work with the women on simplifying ideas for their bilingual (Spanish- English) handouts by communicating them with pictograms.

As participants in CycleNews, four women at a time wearing green vests and green backpacks bicycled to public places like markets and parks in immigrant-dense neighborhoods. They instigated conversations about immigrant services in a nonthreatening way to people they identified as immigrants. As important as the actual interaction was, the Mujeres' own educational process and the conversations they brought back to MOIA based on what the immigrants they spoke with needed most were also core. The project's success was assessed partly by the number of information sheets they handed out to people with whom they conversed. Contributing factors included that the actor/educators were aligned with other immigrants, they carried CycleNews out in public places, and MOIA's values aligned with those of the artists. However, the project never reached scale—that is, it was never replicated in other neighborhoods.

In 2017, Rad, as part of the Lost Collective (with Keelay Gipson, Josh Adam Ramos, and Britton Smith), four energetic and inquisitive queer Black and brown theater artists, was a NYC PAIR artist with the Administration for Children's Services (ACS). The ACS asked the Lost Collective to engage with thirty LGBTQIA2+ youth living in five foster homes to open up creative spaces in their lives. The Lost Collective had recently produced a hip-hop play about the experiences of a young queer person in the foster-care system, and proposed utilizing elements of the play to initiate a dreaming and healing process with the youth. The primary engagement was between the artists and the youth, with some participation of group home staff.

The four artists visited each of the five group homes and got to know participants through conversation, creative workshops, and field trips to LGBTQIA2+ cultural events, such as the Queer Liberation March. In response to the young people's interests, the Lost Collective artists taught them about do-it-yourself filmmaking on their cell phones. Together, they created short films that included the poetry and music the youth generated in their creative workshops that focused on their dreams and revelations about their past, present, and future. The Lost Collective also facilitated guest workshops, including a martial artist, a photographer, dance hall artists, and a teaching chef at each home, according to participants' interests.

The project culminated at the East Village's Nuyorican Poets Café, a long-respected venue particularly for poets of Latine ancestry coming up in New York. The youth presented their photographs and paintings, screened their videos, and performed live before an audience of almost one hundred ACS and Department of Cultural Affairs staff members.

This celebration represented a unique moment in which city officials focused their attention on these particularly marginalized voices (https://municipal-artist.org/profiles/profiles/public-artists-in-residence/).

Rad describes their experience as a participating artist:

> We came into the ACS at a contentious moment. The previous commissioner was stepping down and being replaced due to some allegations and continued issues in the child welfare system. They told us up front that our residency would be a great way to smooth over their bad press. Beyond a two-hour orientation with ACS, we had very little guidance in regard to understanding that system. We had a lot of support from our liaisons at Cultural Affairs, the staff at the homes, and the therapists at the private agency contracted to manage the group homes. I could sense frustration at many of our meetings; according to the staff at the homes, policies were being rained down from above at ACS by people who had never set foot in the group homes and didn't understand about the well-being of the youth in the same way the staff that worked with them day to day did. So not only were we dealing with navigating a complex system; we were also wading through the tension between the powers that be and the staff on the ground.
>
> While we made some incredible connections with the youth, connections that we still have today, at times it felt like we were glorified babysitters. The staff worked hard with us to try to create a consistent presence in their lives, but the way the system had been set up didn't allow for much ease, flow, or flexibility to work with the quickly changing needs and desires of the youth. I wish we had at least three years of funding, because it took one year to start to build trust with the youth and begin to understand the lay of the land. Then the residency was over just as more and more youth wanted to participate.

Jan adds her perspective as evaluator:

> For all its value to the young people in providing artistic experiences that stretched them and in which they could excel, the relationship between the Lost Collective and the ACS was not a partnership. Even though agency staff members were a concerned group of individuals under substantial pressure themselves, they had more power than

> the artists in shaping the residency. Partly because of the vulnerability of the population due to their age and circumstances, the staff was required to be hypervigilant that the Lost Collective not overstep. I remember agency concern about a report I wrote quoting the artists referring to themselves as "the gay uncles and aunties the young people never had." The staff feared that the artists might be perceived as too close to the youth, not at a professional distance, when they were brought on precisely because the youth lacked people close to them to open the world and support them. The project was worthwhile in its impact on a dozen or so of the youth with little guidance in finding their way in the world. But it would have taken more time and ongoing artist funding to make a systemic impact.

Municipal/artist collaborations in over two dozen U.S. cities and regions evidence that good work has taken place that neither collaborator could have done without the other. However, revisiting the Municipal-Artist Partnership Guide in 2021, having lived through the horrific police shootings of so many Black people in 2020, and well before then, and learned about the bad record of police nationwide since their very establishment, we now see the need to look at each agency and its purpose as the basis for assessing what an artist can do and if there can even be a real collaboration, given the fact that (1) an artist is a person and an agency is an institution controlled by people of differing intentions, and (2) some agencies may either not want or not be capable of systemic intervention from outside. These concerns are most contentious when artists work with police departments.

Artists Collaborating with Police?

> *The killing of George Floyd, in Minneapolis, cannot be wished away as an outlier.* —Jill Lepore, "The Invention of the Police," *The New Yorker*

Numerous artists have done thoughtful projects intended to improve relationships between police and community residents. We heard from some who were motivated by their own bad experiences at protests and in other contexts. However, the events of 2020 cast new light on the challenges involved. We begin by contextualizing such work with insights from Jill Lepore's *New Yorker* essay about the crisis in policing that these events made more visible. Lepore reports:

> In each of the past five years, police in the United States have killed roughly a thousand people. (During each of those same years, about a hundred police officers were killed in the line of duty.) . . . Urban police forces are nearly always whiter than the communities they patrol. The victims of police brutality are disproportionately Black teenage boys: children.

Lepore acknowledges that some individuals doubtlessly join police forces "to serve and protect" everyone. But, she avows, the problem is with the police as an enormous institution—"both the nature and the scale of the crisis and the legacy of centuries of racial injustice. The best people, with the best of intentions, doing their utmost, cannot fix this system from within."

Lepore argues that the police system is not broken—it is doing what it was created to do. She explains that police departments in the United States, though some linked to volunteer "watch" systems to protect neighborhoods, to which were added government constables, came into their own in the nineteenth century as a way to capture runaway enslaved people. States beginning with Virginia further established a set of rules known as slave codes, "for the good Regulating and Ordering of them."

By 1909, American policing was conceived as a kind of militia. "After all," explained police chief August Vollmer of Berkeley, California, "we're conducting a war . . . against the enemies of society." Lepore identifies those enemies as "mobsters, bootleggers, socialist agitators, strikers, union organizers, immigrants, and Black people." (This criminalization of Black people is analyzed in depth in the historian Khalil Gibran Muhammad's 2010 book, *The Condemnation of Blackness: Race, Crime, and the Making of Modern Urban America.*) Efforts to reverse this police department model have been uphill battles. For example, Lepore recounts:

> In 2014, after police in Ferguson, Missouri, shot Michael Brown, the Obama Administration established a task force on policing in the twenty-first century. Its report argued that police had become warriors when what they really should be are guardians. Most of its recommendations were never implemented.

Certainly not all Americans want police to be warriors instead of guardians, but how does a decentralized system made up of eighteen thousand separate law-enforcement agencies change? And is there a way for artists to contribute to this system in a positive way? While the subject is complex and merits an in-depth study, we include one example of an effort that seemed worthwhile for a period of time and why it was discontinued.

Performing Statistics (PS) is an art project in Richmond, Virginia, initiated by artist Mark Strandquist alongside Trey Hartt and Gina Lyles. It offers art workshops to young people impacted by the criminal justice system "to model, imagine, and advocate for a world without youth incarceration." Strandquist elaborates:

> The work included creating poems, videos, virtual reality experiences, and immersive installations with the explicit purpose and understanding that the exhibition would be used as a classroom to deeply engage with law enforcement (as well as social workers, teachers, politicians, and tens of thousands of viewers). Some of the pieces the youth created speak directly to police (though also to all of us), while others were more open-ended. We always framed the creative conversations around key audiences that the youth wanted to reach, asking, "What do you want to say to the police, to the mayor, to your principal that you think they need to hear?" (Mark Strandquist in an email to Cohen-Cruz, February 24, 2021)

One of PS's art projects pre-2020 involved the youth creating imaginary police manuals (reflecting the idea, closest to the problem, closest to the solution). The PS team contended that "the experts society needs to listen to in order to make progressive change are the people whose daily

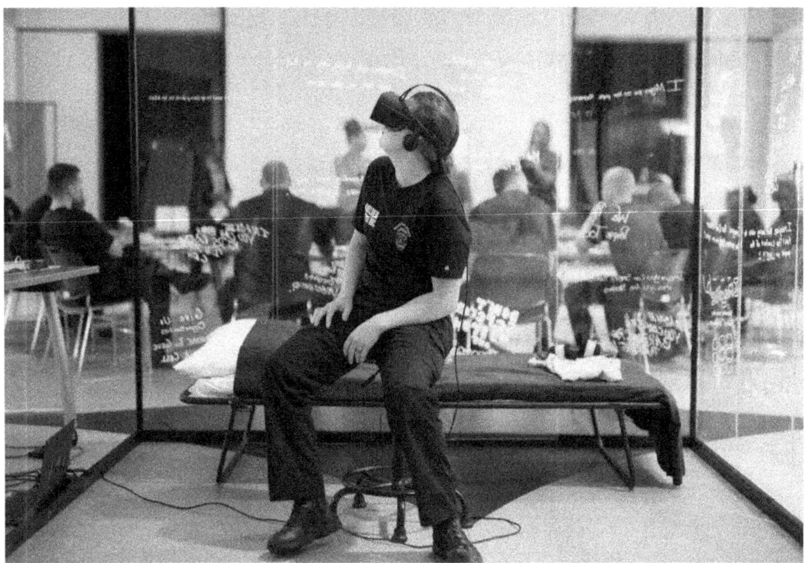

An officer in training watches PS's virtual reality film, ***Detained,*** *written and recorded by teens from the Richmond Juvenile Detention Center in PS's 2017 intensive summer advocacy program inside a closed youth prison. It speaks to their experience of being in a cell. Made in collaboration with Gary Hustwit and Maya Tippett from Scenic VR. Photo by Mark Strandquist, courtesy of ART 180.*

lived experiences are most impacted and would most benefit from that change . . . art is a vehicle that best expresses that vision and radical imagination" (*Performing Statistics: Reflecting on Three Years at the Intersection of Art and Activism,* 4).

Former Richmond police chief Alfred Durham was so impressed with what he learned from youth in Performing Statistics exhibitions and talkbacks that he instituted a half-day training program into which the youth's manuals were integrated. New recruits learned about "the effects of trauma and defusing tense situations that involve young people, and [were immersed] in the youth-voice materials created by Performing Statistics." Durham's goals were "to improve communication between police and youth, encourage officers to get to know people in neighborhoods on a first name basis, ensure that officers understand what drives today's youth, see officers mentoring young people, and see youth become advocates for police" (*Performing Statistics,* 51).

The youth were not directly involved in the training sessions, though the materials they developed were. Project director Trey Hartt explains:

> The idea is that young people are able to speak through their artwork when they physically can't be present. Not only because of the trauma associated with cops but also [because] some of the young people were still incarcerated when we conducted the training. (Trey Hartt in an email to Cohen-Cruz, February 24, 2021)

The next police chief was equally supportive of the half-day training. But there was resistance within the ranks. Hartt elaborates:

> We continued to have to repeat the purpose and impact of our training (in spite of . . . over 80 percent of the trainees highly recommending it to all of their fellow police officers). We never found our footing with the lower-level leadership who were gatekeepers to the logistics of the training. (Trey Hartt in an email to Cohen-Cruz, February 22, 2021)

The project's demise happened in the context of the 2020 public outcry regarding police violence. Hartt recounts that Richmond was spotlighted for "gross use of force violations on peaceful protesters." The Performing Statistics team kept its distance while the city cycled through several police chiefs. By the time stability returned six months later with entirely new leadership, the staff, Hartt recounts, had decided to end direct programming with law enforcement:

> We were tired of feeling like we had to convince the department that we were worthy, and wanted to invest our time and financial resources into building the world we want rather than trying to force change from the inside. This is when we became explicitly abolitionist. We also realized at this moment that while there were individual leaders in the Richmond Police Department (RPD) who were our champions, structurally their policies and practices never changed. For example, it required state legislation to force them to train their School Resource Officers in youth development, something we had been vocal about since the beginning of our training. In this past year, the RPD was

> more violent than it had ever been in recent memory. The change we wished to see was shallow.

Hartt believes it would take generations of new recruits before they could even hope to see changes. He says:

> [As artists,] we want to create a new world. We absolutely support organizations and initiatives that want to engage this work, but it's just not our lane. Our systems (like education, justice, public health, and law enforcement) are rotten because they are rooted in racism and white supremacy as extensions of slavery and settler colonialism. We are no longer interested in repairing a dying ecosystem. Rather, we want to build new ecosystems that can, over time, replenish the soil and hopefully repair the roots around them.

Because of what occurred in 2020, PS reframed its mission as youth prison abolition, which the team defines as "a world free from systems of criminalization, surveillance, and control. Abolition believes it is possible to build a world that centers human values" (www.performingstatistics.org/abolition).

• • •

Our reflection on artists collaborating with civic entities is complicated. When an agency represents a deeply flawed system, can one try to improve it from the inside, or is it more productive to try to create something else as an alternative and then see if a relationship is possible? The two meanings of collaboration—working with others to produce or create something; cooperation or willing assistance with an outside occupier—are a reminder of how risky and complex this territory can be.

Many artists shared with us various missteps that even the most multiculturally attuned among them have made. As the context of the work shifts, or we little by little understand more about deep divides in our society, we analyze our actions in a way we couldn't have before. What do we do with that knowledge? A good way to start is by being accountable for our missteps, exploring better ways of working, and bringing that new knowledge with us as we keep at it.

PART III
(Re)Generativity

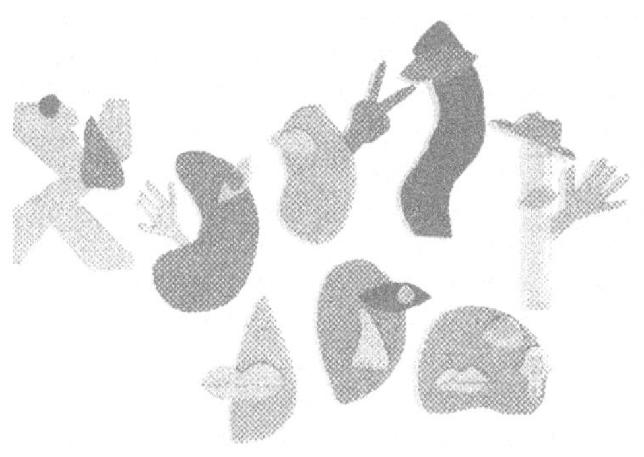

6 A Regenerative Life in Art

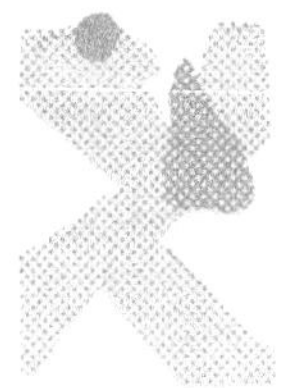

This is not hyperbole—girls join viBe Theater Experience to get physically, spiritually, and mentally free. Otherwise, there's no reason for us to come together, to speak the truths to power from the stage, to share vulnerable moments with an audience. It's for their own liberation and to engage other people around their liberation; the way they're not being free harms us all. Theater is a way to create more space in their hearts and minds and bodies and also in the world for themselves.

—Toya Lillard, executive director of viBe

Lillard's articulation of what participants get from viBe speaks to art making's large potential. Yet people perennially struggle to make art sustainable in their lives. In the wake of the NEA Four, the culture wars, and decreased arts funding nationally, a handful of foundation leaders were concerned about the system of support for artists, which had been impacted negatively by the ending of the NEA Fellowship program and subsequent cutbacks in state-level awards for artists. (See chapter 2 for a description of the NEA Four and the culture wars.) Among them were arts consultant Holly Sidford, then program director for arts, parks, and adult literacy at the Lila Wallace–Reader's Digest Fund, and Christine Vincent, then the Ford Foundation's deputy director for Media, Arts, and Culture.

With the Ford Foundation as a catalyst, Vincent and Sidford invited Maria Rosario Jackson to lead a research team exploring what artists needed for a sustainable life. Support eventually came from more than thirty-five other private and public sector donors, which, notes Sidford, "shows the extent of concern in the philanthropic community." That project, *Investing in Creativity,* was important in its breadth:

> It looked at artists as members of numerous communities—artistic and professional, cultural, economic, political and technological. It considered artists as freelance workers who need income, health insurance, appropriate space and equipment, professional networks, and validation. It looked at how artists live in specific places . . . and what could help more of them succeed and contribute to their communities. (Sidford, Cornerstones, www.lincnet.net/1491)

The ensuing research was the first step in launching a ten-year initiative, Leveraging Investments in the Arts.

Eighteen years later, we address here the ongoing problem of insufficient support for artists, focusing on those committed to social uses of their work. We build on Jackson et al., also framing artists' needs largely, looking at what they need to live, rather than only to fund a given project. But whereas Jackson et al. focused on a sustainable life, our interviewees reflected on a *regenerative* one, continually improving upon their conditions, rather than just keeping them going. In what follows, we try to unravel some of the tensions between surviving and making a life/ walking one's values that we heard from artists across the fifty-five years we are looking at. We include alternatives to a capitalist mode where possible, while appreciating that artists have to make a living. The chapter is organized around markers of regenerative lives in socially engaged performance and the challenges to attaining them that the interviewees emphasized.

Embracing One's Calling as a Socially Engaged Artist

It's especially important to understand one's calling within art as a basis for making decisions about one's life. Take theater director and professor Bob Leonard's experience:

> I was doing a play with the Washington Theatre Club while protests against the Vietnam War were happening in front of the embassy just down the road. Tear gas was seeping into the building, which was awful but also emblematic—we were doing this play which had nothing to do with what was going on in the street and we had the residual consequence of tear gas. And I didn't have time to march against the war. I had a family; I had to work. But I was struck by how particularly irrelevant I felt that particular night—it wasn't the play; it was a great play. It [was] that I wasn't where I was supposed to be. I eventually took another direction and found I could go where I needed to go, and make theater that was satisfying—not entirely; I wanted it to be better every time, but I was realizing my own intentionality.

Leonard found in community-engaged performance a congenial context in which to balance his multiple priorities, rather than buy into the idea that an artist should care for nothing but art. The excuse of having no time to be involved in social justice issues becomes irrelevant in a field that is hyphenated in whatever way the individual choses.

Here's how the sense of a calling arose for Marty Pottenger:

> I understood the power of performance from [the time I was] very young, making up, directing, and producing performances from when I was five years old to twenty-five. That's when I made a full-on commitment to women's liberation, lesbian liberation, and racial justice activism. Like so many of us here in the United States, I had been taught that the "arts" were not central in working people's lives. That the arts were for those with a level of economic resource that most of us would never have. Ten years later, I was learning about artists, singers, and playwrights, like Victor Jara, Mercedes Sosa, Miriam Makeba, and Bertolt Brecht, and realized that those who seize illegitimate power begin by seeking control over the military, with its destructive power, and the artists, with their constructive power. The clarity that art was that powerful and that it belonged to all of us was enough to compel me to start performing again, my activism feeding the roots of my art making, and the other way around.

Jan asked Pottenger about the most important features of the art she's gone on to make over the thirty-plus years since, to which she responded:

> After years of making solo performances about growing up female, about construction work and public works projects, I realized that performances could not only reflect, reveal, and inspire but that they could become a place where people, onstage as themselves, could tackle whatever needs tackling. I created performances like *home land security,* where Portlanders appear as themselves—a man whose home is a tent, a mayor, a tribal member, a priest, three refugees from South Sudan, Iran, and Somalia, a fire chief, a state senate president, a NAACP leader, and a multigenerational Franco elder. They not only reveal the inequity, confusion, isolation, and fear that [are] both shared and unique but also foster resilience, connection, clarity, and the courage to take the risks necessary to transform our collective circumstance. And yes, we also get to appreciate, explore, and celebrate ourselves, each other, the beauty and the victories that come to us, as well.
>
> We are different when we are making art. A part of us becomes engaged that is often left out in our day-to-day lives. It is what I strive to bring into play in all my Art At Work projects. The English language doesn't describe it well, so I often have to settle for calling it "creative engagement" or "art making." This is the most important understanding from the art I've made for almost fifty years: that performances focusing on critical community experiences—current, past, or approaching—can be powerful ways to reveal and heal, or to identify what needs changing and generate the determination to do what's necessary, or to find enough common ground to interrupt the divisions. (See also www.artatwork.us/projects/.)

Once one is making a life doing the kind of art to which one is committed, metrics can be found to help one assess it. Too often, however, the metrics used in art do not get to the heart of socially engaged practice. Typically, assessment focuses on a final product, like a play or dance concert or exhibition, and adopts the terms of formal aesthetic categories, when an artist may be more interested in, say, a workshop process or adhere to nonmainstream aesthetics.

With the participation of socially engaged artists and evaluators, the Animating Democracy Initiative (ADI) generated "Aesthetic Perspectives: Attributes of Excellence in Arts for Change" to explore ideas of excellence that run through art that is as much about *what* it accomplishes concretely (effect) as it is about the artful ways it does so (affect). ADI identified eleven attributes (www.animatingdemocracy.org/aesthetic-perspectives). Of particular relevance to much socially engaged performance are communal meaning, cultural integrity, disruption (e.g., "challenges what is by exposing what has been hidden, posing new ways of being, and modeling new forms of action"), openness ("subject to influence and able to hold contradiction"), risk taking ("subverting dominant norms, values, narratives, standards, or aesthetics"), and stickiness ("achieves sustained resonance, impact, or value"). Whether adopting Animating Democracy's criteria or that of others, it's important that partners, together, articulate indicators that signal the degree to which their desired results are emerging.

Exchange with others plays a crucial role during an art project's development. Liz Lerman designed the Critical Response Process to put artists in control of feedback during the development of a work. Lerman was partly motivated by first reflecting on the nature of so many bad experiences in giving and receiving feedback. She also spent time talking to people about what was the essential nature of their relationship with those whom they could really listen to and take any kind of criticism. So in her process, the first step is meaning: "Responders state what was meaningful, evocative, interesting, exciting, and/or striking in the work they have just witnessed" (https://lizlerman.com/critical-response-process/), reflecting Lerman's recognition that when we have just made something, we first need to hear what was meaningful to people before we can hear what did not work for them.

When educational programs integrate not only practice but also the study of socially engaged art, or recognize the value of other than mainstream traditions, they are validating a broad range of choices an artist might make. When newspapers and journals cover more than work presented in conventional spaces, by trained artists, for art-savvy audiences, they, too, are contributing to the validation of a larger conception of art.

When college and university tenure committees assess community workshops that artists/scholars have facilitated in addition to shows they've made in aesthetic contexts, they, as well, are providing necessary support for socially engaged artists. (For validation of socially engaged artists and scholars within universities, see https://imaginingamerica.org/ scholarship-in-public-knowledge-creation-and-tenure-policy-in-the-engaged-university-a-resource-on-promotion-and-tenure-in-the-arts-humanities-and-design/.)

Choosing Where to Live at Various Points in One's Development

MK Wegmann regrets that many artists feel the need to leave the South and move to big cities:

> I always felt it as a defeat when artists left New Orleans to go to New York. It was frustrating that they couldn't see a way to sustain their work here. It was always a goal for me to work toward an environment where artists could stay where they were, continue to be part of their home community, do their work, and not feel they had to go elsewhere for validation and for sustenance, for money.

For Otrabanda members Roger Babb and Rocky Bornstein, the move from New Orleans to New York was more about the community they needed than validation and money. Otrabanda was grounded in the work of European avant-garde directors Tone Brulin, Jerzy Grotowski, and Eugenio Barba. For ten summers, they also did a river raft tour down the Mississippi River, performing free shows in a popular style for largely Black audiences along the Mississippi Delta from St. Louis to New Orleans, where they eventually settled. The combination of the avant-garde and the popular was part of what made Otrabanda unique, and there's no doubt it was nourished by living in New Orleans.

But they had reasons to move to a larger city four years later.

> **Bornstein:** Living in New Orleans was great—our housing, the food, the music, our friends. But I felt we couldn't develop. We had really

limited interaction with other young artists. Even though we worked with musicians, it was not who we were. Everything we did was with Otrabanda; we didn't play around with or develop our skills with anyone else.

Babb: As soon as we got to New York, I did a show at the Public and Rocky got work with major dance companies. This was extremely fulfilling; there were all these people we had access to. Everything we wanted to happen, happened, in terms of our artistic development.

On the other hand, some artists who originally thought they *had* to go to New York to develop as artists made totally congenial homes elsewhere. In the early 2000s, Seed Lynn, for example, found a community of like-minded, supportive artists partly through Alternate ROOTS and the National Performance Network, in the South, where he was living. He gained access to those communities thanks to Roberta Uno and the Ford Foundation's funding of hip-hop artists, discovering colleagues, mentors, and a community of people who engaged around his work. He was relieved that he did not have to go to New York to be nourished as an artist.

John O'Neal graduated from a college in Illinois in the early 1960s and was about to move to New York to become a playwright when the Freedom Summer happened. He thought he'd spend one summer in Mississippi and then move to the Northeast. But he never left the South and made an enormous impact there, first as part of the cultural wing of the civil rights movement and later through other artistic efforts toward racial and economic equity. And he found lifelong colleagues who challenged and supported him there.

Other artists have tried New York and other large cities, and chosen to leave. Double Edge Theatre headed out of Boston to rural Massachusetts, where the collective has developed an entire philosophy of community-engaged theater. So while community and networks are important, it's not obvious where one will find it. It is certainly not always in New York.

Artists who are queer or otherwise marginalized growing up in small towns have not always felt safe. Some went to big cities, where they were not such a minority and could live more freely. Now that consciousness has grown, people can often stay safe outside of big cities. They may still be nurtured by the expansiveness of artistic expression in cities and either move there permanently or for a period of time. Some artists ultimately feel they have the most to contribute to the place they are from, where they may have deep relationships and certainly a deep understanding of the place.

Finding Community

Community in the sense of support from others who have been slighted because of racism and other social violence came up frequently in our interviews. Toya Lillard, executive director of viBe Theater Experience, captures that priority when she emphasizes the support the girls of color whom she works with give one another, which serves their shared purpose: "We always come back to liberation. The driving purpose is to get free."

Meaningful relationships with various kinds of communities figure largely in what regenerates socially engaged artists across time. It's not unusual for such theater makers to develop strong relationships with one another, form ensemble companies, and settle in places where they can put down roots. Ensembles sometimes go so far as living communally, as Jan experienced:

> In 1971, when I was in the NYC Street Theatre/Jonah Project, we were very focused on workshops in a maximum-security prison. We got so involved with some of the participants that several of us from the company rented a house and lived communally, with the idea that as people got out, they could live and work with us. We could also live cheaper and devote more of our time to our collective work.

Artists also seek like-minded colleagues through organizational memberships. The National Performance Network, founded in 1985 to address artistic isolation and economic restraints "that constricted the flow of creative ideas within and among communities, independent artists, and locally-engaged arts organizations in the United States," is also a source of regeneration for artists who attend annual meetings year after year. The same is true of the National Association of Latino Arts and Cultures, founded in 1989 as "a national advocacy organization for an under-served Latinix arts sector."

Associations work both within the field, connecting artists and cultural workers to one another, and across fields, connecting artists to people not primarily in the cultural sector but sharing some other important priority, such as ArtPlace. Some associations are regional, such as Alternate ROOTS, created in 1976 by and for southern theater makers who have tended to be more independent and politically progressive than those in the mainstream. MK Wegmann describes the importance of ROOTS being in the South in the 1970s: "The fact that ROOTS was a place where Black and white people were working together was so great. In the South in the 1970s, finding integrated environments was almost impossible."

Wegmann, past president and CEO of NPN and past chair of the ROOTS Executive Committee, explains that such intermediary institutions contribute to sustainability, "building a coalition of people and having the ability to get money at the national level and give it out at the local level." She emphasizes how important they are for small, locally based entities to access national funds. She compares her hometown of New Orleans to most places in the United States that lack robust funding communities and are in effect "funding deserts," particularly for progressive work. They depend on national and international funding. Without access through an intermediary to robust philanthropic and government support, which varies from state to state and city to city, Wegmann notes, nonprofit organizations of all stripes struggle:

> That's just as true for a theater company trying to do Shakespeare, Tennessee Williams, or recycled Off-Broadway plays; there is virtually no financial sustainability in the United States. That leads you to private philanthropy, but if you don't have that robustly locally, you can't survive. ROOTS has held on to national funding for more than forty years; NPN, approaching that. Which is pretty remarkable given the whims and vagaries of how the national philanthropic community behaves.

Jackson et al. elaborate on communities and networks:

> They facilitate access to sources of validation, material resources, training and professional development, and dissemination of artists' work. They provide emotional support for people pursuing a profession that, for many artists, often has little status. And they are essential in giving artists a political voice. Some are value-driven; others are pragmatic. . . . They include various configurations of artists themselves; closely knit associations of institutional directors, curators, and administrators; intellectual clubs and networks of a city's top government, business, and arts gatekeepers; "old boys" and "old girls" networks; ethnic networks; and social scenes. (Jackson et al. 75)

Many artists and organizations benefit from local institutions. Small community networks can impact artists' work, like the YWCA giving subsidized office space for girls-serving organizations, including viBe early on. Shared space also provides organizations with a community that may share other resources, such as a grant writer, bookkeeper, or conference room. Or the artists might be the engine of a collaborative venture. Community Forge, in Wilkinsburg, Pennsylvania, was founded in 2017 by eight young adults to revitalize the former Johnston Elementary School as an asset for the region. They developed it with the community to contribute to a more equitable economy, providing a place for kids, employment opportunities, a venue for sustainable businesses, and an accessible space for all who live there to use.

We found, like Jackson, that the opportunity for artists from small towns and rural communities to showcase their work in places that are more used to art has been meaningful to them, as well. Indeed, as first director of Alternate ROOTS in the 1980s, Ruby Lerner played an important role in connecting the community-centered work of many of the southern artists at ROOTS with her New York art community.

Jackson et al. note that external validation that is in sync with an artist's work is also important, rather than trying to be recognized by art outlets with a narrower view. They found examples of artists responding "to the shortcomings of mainstream validation mechanisms by creating alternative forms." This is strongly evident in socially engaged art communities, where alternative critical forums have emerged, most notably the online Community Arts Network in the 1980s; HowlRound, out of Emerson College; and Rescripted, a Chicago-based, artist-led, interactive commentary on the state of the arts, including reviews, dialogues, and essays. There are also informal validation mechanisms, such as random conversations, that keep aspirations alive, because, as artist Nick Slie put it, "you often can't stir things by yourself."

Learning to Communicate About One's Work Beyond One's Immediate Circle

Unlike the image of artists as outsiders, at odds with the people around them, those committed to social justice typically work collaboratively with a broad spectrum of others toward equitable goals. To that end, artists and diverse members of the public need contact with one another. Artist/public contact is especially necessary, Jackson et al. also found, when the work is less understood as part of the whole picture of art. Liz Lerman asserts that the Dance Exchange, the company she founded, was as likely to perform in senior centers or with workers at a shipyard as at the Kennedy Center, a Washington, D.C., performance venue: "It was a matter of getting people to understand there was value in art in unexpected places, responding to a need. So we had to learn how to talk about it."

Art embedded across sectors requires orientation for the public and for funders. Uniting ecology and theater, Superhero Clubhouse, for example, makes original performances for adults and families that participants perform in schools, theaters, parks, and museums; facilitates "eco-performance workshops" for people with a range of experience to creatively explore climate and environmental justice together; brings eco-theater education to schoolkids; and offers an annual paid fellowship for people of various disciplines to collaborate together on a performance for environmental justice.

Codirector Lanxing Fu describes the problem they have had being situated between more familiar categories:

> A challenge to funding and more is that we do not fit in with the more activist-minded in terms of environmental work because we

> aren't doing direct action and advocacy. We want to work with people in different disciplines, but we don't fit the most familiar science/art model, which is a lot about communicating science. We're not as interested in art as a vehicle for educating the public about science. We feel more aligned with socially engaged or community-based artists with the awareness that in New York we are straddling many different communities, not in service to one, and that presents its own challenges, raises its own question.

Local universities can be a source of reciprocal support. While some institutions of higher education are insensitive to smaller and nonmainstream cultural institutions, others are extremely responsive. Imagining America (IA), for example, is a network of colleges and universities that "brings together scholars, artists, designers, humanists, and organizers to imagine, study, and enact a more just and liberatory 'America' and world." It is a place to find "one's peeps" within a higher ed context that promotes extending out into local communities. Its members provide resources to local arts and cultural organizations and, in turn, become more integrated into their surrounding area.

Students benefit from the availability of local cultural experiences and artists benefit from higher education resources, as Linda Parris-Bailey testifies:

> For eight years, Carpetbag was the resident theater company at Knoxville College, the HBCU [historically black college or university] where we were founded. I'd spent many years trying to convince college presidents that this was a good idea; we do have a national reputation. Finally, one said, "Oh! This is a good idea!" The resources were extraordinary—they had them and we knew how to use them, so what a perfect marriage. We had college interns; we had a youth festival with nine hundred kids. A great eight years. But Knoxville College, like HBCUs all over the country, suffered decline. The college lost its accreditation, ran out of operating money, and was being shut down. We lost that resource, and we no longer had a facility to do programming. So boom boom boom. Unsustainability is so much a part of the story.

Having Representation in Relevant Policy Decisions

Some artists become interested in communicating with people who are in positions to make structural changes that impact them, or at least in being represented in such circles. As president and CEO of NPN, Wegmann became very interested in policy, seeing it as basically making sure "you had a seat at the table." She quotes Carol Bebelle, founder of Ashé Cultural Arts Center in New Orleans: "If you don't have a seat at the table, you might be on the menu." She pointed out that the culture wars of the 1980s, where liberal and conservative ideology battled it out, demonstrated that the arts in any arena—local, regional, state, whatever—rarely have a seat at the table, making sustainability so difficult.

Wegmann used her leadership role to make cultural policy a formal program at NPN:

> Having a voice at the policy table is part of the responsibility of an intermediary organization. I was active not just at Grantmakers in the Arts but also with the advocacy organization Performing Arts Alliance. Also crucial was participation in the NEA panel system and site-visit system; they were ways to be active in policy in a huge way, because as an individual on a panel or site visit, you could bring an issue about equity to a panel that could lead to changes in guidelines. [Municipal arts manager] Roberto Bedoya said that policy is a system of arrangements, and that it's important to help to make it a system by which people benefit. I strongly believe the people affected by a policy should have a voice in that policy.

Sustainability of arts and culture is related to the sustainability of a people itself. In Baltimore, the Arch Social Club, in response to a "brutally repressive racial environment," was founded in 1905 and incorporated in 1912:

> Black people at the dawn of the 20th century were savagely pushed to the political, social, cultural and economic margins by a combination of white folkways and state statutes. Out of necessity, African Americans sought collective survival in the construction of a parallel civil society.

> Schools, churches, benevolent associations, commercial enterprises, cultural venues and every conceivable social institution that addressed the exclusionary nature of the broader white society and day-to-day needs of Black folk were forged—often in the face of de jure, race-driven harassment and humiliation. (www.archsocialclub.com)

Indeed, the tradition of African American social aid and pleasure clubs in the South came into existence when insurance companies wouldn't cover people of color, who therefore organized associations—such as the Zulu Social Aid and Pleasure Club in New Orleans—to raise money for funerals, et cetera. (www.archsocialclub.com/history).

Solidarity economy artist Caroline Woolard expands the idea of community or network to any larger context in which one's work sits:

> If you are an artist who thinks about short-term projects like a performance, or a painting, or sculpture, I encourage you to look at the infrastructure that holds that up. Is it a gallery? Is it an event space? Is it some school? How could they be aligned with your values, with your deepest longings and desires? The things that hold up my sculptures and short-term events are collectives and long-term self-organized initiatives. I think of the sculpture or the performance as a shiny and short-lived apple on a tree. The tree trunks and branches are the collectives and the long-term work we do together to make those things visible, to make them circulate, to talk about them. It's important that the trunk has the same value as the artwork, because otherwise we're just holding up institutions that are not making the world we want to see. It limits the impact we can have, because the sculpture will probably only be looked at for a few seconds or a minute.
>
> I also think about how those collective initiatives are nurtured and sustained, about roots and mycelium and these daily practices that really are how we shape ourselves and shift the work that we want to do. [That leads to] thinking about deep listening and all of the skills that are required to be in spaces of cooperation that are not taught or reproduced in most institutions where people are not valued equally at all.

Woolard suggests that networks are not just the concrete connections we make with others but also the visible and invisible infrastructure that undergirds those organizations.

Making a Living

What would it mean to proactively focus on who could benefit from what an artist does, rather than try to fit oneself into existing ways to make money? Clear Creek Creative in rural Kentucky, for example, builds community and creates its own markets, largely on its rural property, describing its goals as follows: "[Codirectors] Carrie Brunk and Bob Martin work with people and organizations to envision and enact a better world. We lead with our art, cultural and community organizing, transformative facilitation and stewardship of the land." They host anything from "local farm-fresh performative feasts to rustic artistic residencies and learning exchanges to all sorts of other productions, festivals, celebrations and more." They also tour and perform elsewhere. So whereas the word *market* sounds like a structure based solely on financial remuneration, Clear Creek suggests a relationship based on sharing particular goals. An artist might seek markets sometimes and congenial contexts at others.

One way to find audiences and collaborators is to develop a model and then broadcast it. Liz Lerman muses that while a broad public embraced the company she founded, Dance Exchange, which evidenced the power of people of all ages and backgrounds dancing, their economic model, which expanded markets, was understudied:

> Our idea was, sell your knowledge, not your dances. We had a touring engagement model. I told presenters that everyone in the company could do two things a day in the community. Although later it was three weeks or six months, in the initial period it was one-shot deals, which could be life-changing but weren't enough. People were happy for me to do a concert piece as a culmination of the time there, but we also would have been in schools, prisons, rehab centers, whatever. Jawole [Willa Jo Zollar, artistic director of Urban Bush Women] shared

> the intention that everyone who came through our companies should be able to do a number of things: teach, collaborate, listen, be in a community setting, help [people] do something they want to do. We were unique and therefore people were interested. Now many, many people can do what I just described.

Scholar and performer Paul Bonin-Rodriguez, in a similar vein, speaks about the residency model that expanded his market and sustained him when he was touring solo performances in the 1980s and 1990s:

> Within a few years of beginning to write my own performance material, my work went into two spaces. The economic engine that kept me on the road and what became my artistic practice was the residency model that NPN [the National Performance Network] did a lot to pioneer: making it part of the visit to not only perform but also give talks, workshops, do community visits, make small pieces with people, that model. And secondly, with Jump-Start [the company he was part of] there was maintaining a space and doing projects. So there was my economic versus my social engine. I wanted to make a living as an artist. The social projects are the ones you're always seeking more resources for and the economic ones have resources coming in. I hadn't been prepared to think about that.

Markets associated with nonprofit work and those that exist for commercial work are not mutually exclusive. A number of playwrights whose work is produced at regional theaters, like Tanya Barfield, Aurin Squire, Monet Hurst-Mendoza, Bekah Brunstetter, and Theresa Rebeck, also write for television, especially given the explosion of "the Golden Age of TV," with streaming services and cable channels willing to take on more complex subjects over the past decade. Nonprofit venues often allow greater artistic freedom than commercial ones, allowing writers to stay true to their creative impulses; television offers expansion to larger publics and better pay. Indeed, while working on this book, Rad was earning money acting in the recurring cast of *Betty*, an HBO series about the transformative relationships of women skateboarders in a male-dominated scene.

Our research confirmed what Jackson and her coauthors found in 2003: Potential markets for socially engaged artists are not strictly arts-based. Lerman gives this example:

> We were asked to come into universities to help them with their own engagement work in their local communities. We began to help the arts centers on these campuses work across the whole school. So the work began to move inward as well meeting the external needs of these big institutions.
>
> At some point my own interests as an artist began to evolve into what and how communities might be a part of the work. Again universities proved useful grounds for research and experimentation. Meanwhile, other artists at the Dance Exchange were continuing to work in communities of aging and health, as well as staying very local in our Takoma Park, Maryland, home.

Mark Valdez, former director of the Network of Ensemble Theaters, speaks to the pitfalls of cross-sector partnerships:

> If you're doing cross-sector work, you try to access funds from the partnering sectors. I thought, This is great; I am doing a housing project and can try to access money from these sectors. The problem is the giant gap in understanding art-based projects. When I try to talk to housing funders—they fund housing projects, not art—they understand a very narrow, very specific thing, and art doesn't fit. The amount of time and work to explain it is tremendous—and that assumes that the funder is even open to the discussion. If you're just an individual, you don't have that much time or capacity.

Sometimes a person with formidable commitment and entrepreneurial skills provides a home for artists' work. A visionary in creating a community and a market for international and noncommercial theater, Ellen Stewart was, in 1961, a Black fashion designer and artist with friends in experimental theater. She created La MaMa Experimental Theatre Club for them in her basement, which has continued to be a force supporting such work, expanding into two buildings in Manhattan's East Village.

Generating Material Support

Material support consists of more than cash. Jackson et al. include financial *and* physical resources that artists need for their work: space—which might be donated by a local church, say; equipment—which may be shared with other organizations, and materials to make one's work; employment, health insurance and other benefits, awards and communication mechanisms. Weekly newspapers, podcasts, social media, public radio, and public television, important mechanisms of validation, may also be routes to material resources (e.g., audiences) as are ethnic-specific media, for artists whose subject matter is so aligned.

Longtime cultural critic and organizer Arlene Goldbard talks about the perennial problem of short-term and insufficient funding for art inflected by social justice, which she attributes to the lack of a U.S. cultural policy:

> What are the conditions that make something permanently insurgent? So it's always fucking emerging, and now we're too old to emerge, but the money is still going to the emerging. I look at that as there's never been a meaningful cultural policy in our country. The people who were in charge of arts funding either didn't feel inclined politically or were not led by their own curiosity to give more than a little money. Only enough to fail, not to flourish or build. If you get on one of those trains, you get a big grant for a little while; then it's over. If you define the field as non-elite art forms and participatory art, then you can see the recurring pattern—like Lila Wallace giving all this money to jazz for five years, then nothing more—it's always like that.
>
> A consistent truth has been that people in largely underresourced projects and organizations have to spend an inordinate amount of time to stay afloat, doing a huge amount of paperwork—which funders use as a culling mechanism, to reduce the number of applicants— applying for things they may or may not get, and it's hugely significant in relationship to the amount of time it leaves to make the art.

MK Wegmann is also a critic of nonpermanent mechanisms of art support, referencing ArtPlace America, which was founded as a ten-year initiative to infuse funds into art and cultural contributions to community organizing:

> I disagree with their premise—let's do this for ten years, then take it away. In foundation philanthropy, the people [whom] artists deal with have no power, authority, or control. They are only in staff positions for that moment and they are not the deciders. If they happen to have a board at the moment that will go along with their activism, the money goes there. If they don't, the money goes away. The cognizance that philanthropy and donor-designated funds are depriving the public sector of what otherwise would be tax money to benefit them is a fine point that most people just can't wrap their heads around. The point of foundations is to shield the owners of that money from paying taxes, so they have control over their money instead of participating in the civic arena.

Valdez sees as bleak a picture:

> Across the field, the economic models don't work. Same thing we've been complaining about, same conversations over the twenty-four years I've been at it. There aren't enough funders; they are funding very specific things; they don't understand this work. I'm curious, at this particular COVID moment—it's exposing the problems with our economy and capitalism for everyone. The solution is the government giving everyone money. We'll see what of that sticks. I'm fortunate that I have relationships with funders and they'll take my calls. I can pitch and they'll give me advice, but I'm of a small privileged few. That's not a solution; that's just luck.

Other than from a handful of funders committed to what is known as "diversity, equity, and inclusion," there has traditionally been even less funding for artists of color. While the events of 2020 shook up the field in this regard, director and writer Linda Parris-Bailey critiques the perennial second-class state of arts funding for people of color:

> The field is like the country. We often try to deny that because we feel as if we are this progressive wing, and in some ways, we are,

> but it doesn't seem to trickle down to an economic reality, and that's hard to crack, especially at this time, with the top 4 percent of cultural organizations getting the vast majority of the money. In recent years, I've seen some serious attention to this inequity by certain organizations. That effort is in the context of the larger economy and larger discussion of race. These things are historical realities. And cracking that is also part of our job.

Underlying many problems in the funding world is the power imbalance between artists and foundations. Some philanthropists who support racial justice ask would-be grantees to do work that they aren't always doing internally themselves. Former director of Alternate ROOTS Carlton Turner, who is well acquainted with art and social justice funders, relates:

> Some foundations establish diversity, equity, and inclusion programs, often funding white institutions to do such work with communities of color, so in effect asking communities of color to do the work without being funded directly. The foundations have to accept change themselves, not just facilitate other people's changes.

Here the funders' identity around money/class is at odds with their identification with social justice. Being groomed to make decisions for others because their money positions them to do so, they do not always go through a necessary process of self-scrutiny regarding their own values or consult with the people meant to benefit because of the habit of wielding power. What is in effect power hoarding and gatekeeping are among the basic tenets that allow patriarchy and white supremacy to thrive, because these keep the means of cultural production out of the hands of the cultural workers unless they cater to those in power.

In *Winners Take All: The Elite Charade of Changing the World*, journalist Anand Giridharadas critiques the philanthropic sector in depth. He describes it as a context in which "the rich and powerful fight for equality and justice any way they can—except ways that threaten the social order and their position atop it." He asks, "Why, for example, should our gravest problems be solved by the unelected upper crust instead of the public institutions it erodes by lobbying and dodging taxes?" He points toward an answer: "Rather than rely on scraps from the winners, we must take on the grueling democratic work of building more robust, egalitarian institutions and truly changing the world. A call to action for elites and everyday citizens alike" (www.goodreads.com/book/show/37506348-winners-take-all).

Darren Walker, president of the Ford Foundation, entitled his book, online resource, and forum *From Generosity to Justice*, echoing Giridharadas's probing distinction between the two. Walker posits that whereas "generosity is focused on helping someone in need, justice is about solving the problems that created the need. A healthy society needs both, but we believe it's time to dedicate more resources to the fight for justice . . . and consider philanthropy as a tool for achieving economic, social, and political justice." It demands that all members of society recognize their privilege and position, address the root causes of social ills, and seek out and listen to those who live amid and experience injustice (www.fordfoundation.org/ideas/ford-forum/the-future-of-philanthropy/from-generosity-to-justice/).

Activist artist Ricardo Gamboa, whose practice includes storefront theater in Chicago, is among those seeking to bypass foundations entirely:

> We had institutional funding, but we also had entrenched relationships with the community. It became about piecing together a model to fund a project that relied upon [the community]—not in-kind. It's not that language of the nonprofit world. It's community sustainability. It was all very intentional: "How do you take these nonprofit foundation dollars, [and funnel them as direct] dollars to households? . . . Why is that not the model? Why was it ever the model to let these nonprofits [be] gatekeepers? . . . That's within these very historically racist ideas that people of color are incapable of self-governance and you can't trust them with money. [What we do] is not going to look oriented toward the idea of fiscal austerity, which is a white one.

Certain regions of the United States are also typically at a funding disadvantage. Georgia-based arts consultant Lisa Mount explains:

> The South has been extracted from rather than invested in. Atlanta is a funding desert compared to, say, Cleveland, Ohio, on a per capita basis. Not as bad as New Orleans (the worst of all), but nowhere near what it oughta be for a major city. Old money here has tended to be very conservative. A Rockefeller-size foundation down here would be the Woodruff Foundation in Atlanta [, which] only gives to bricks and mortar. I was talking to a guy today who is trying to repurpose his Woodruff capital grant so there's a tenant for the building they've spent some of that money on renovating. Are we saving the buildings or the organizations?

Socially engaged performance has expanded what an artist can do in social contexts, but that does not necessarily help with material sustainability, especially in places without foundations. Carlton Turner of Sipp Culture in Mississippi explains, "Our funding comes mostly from beyond Mississippi, from national sources like ArtPlace, Surdna early on, Mellon, and hopefully will continue with Ford. We have to figure out how to generate more resources where we are."

Erik Takeshita, who worked at ArtPlace America, agreed with the then Roadside Theater director Dudley Cocke that "funding for community-based art began going downhill in 1981, in the context of general anti-community policies, like expansion of prisons." Takeshita saw anticommunity policy as part of a general trend of smaller government and privatization.

On a more hopeful note, we, like Jackson et al., found that recognition for what civically engaged artists contribute to other sectors has greatly increased in the twenty-first century, expanding how artists can make their livelihoods. Support entities, including ArtPlace America, significantly funded community-based artists in the context of community development during ArtPlace in America's ten-year life (2010–2020). During the last year, these entities shifted their focus to how initiatives they have supported could be ongoing.

There are also opportunities specific to artist and organizational expertise. Girls Write Now, for example, describes its mission as "serving a culturally and educationally diverse community of girls and gender non-conforming youth (mentees)—90% of color, 90% high need, 75% immigrant or first generation, and 25% LGBTQ+/gender non-conforming—Girls Write Now mentors underserved young women to find their voices through the power of writing and community." In the course of enacting that mission, 100 percent of the participants have gone on to college. Through their "Writing Works" program, they have been "growing a writing and technology pipeline into the schools and industries that need your talents most . . . mentor[ing] young women and gender expansive youth to be creative thinkers, clear communicators, and competitive candidates for the trails they choose to blaze—across all industries from publishing and advertising to entertainment, finance, and beyond (www.girlswritenow.org).

Artists looking for other ways to organize their economies are reemerging. In their forthcoming book, *Ways of Being,* Caroline Woolard and Susan Jahoda explain that what in the United States might be called an alternative economy is known elsewhere in the world as the solidarity economy. They trace the latter's roots to the global South (the *economía solidaria*) in the 1990s. It is also called the community, workers', social, new, circular, regenerative, local peace, and cooperative economy. It "unites grassroots practices like lending circles, credit unions, worker cooperatives, and community land trusts to form a base of political power," placing "people before profit, aiming to distribute power and resources equitably."

Woolard calls herself a solidarity economy artist and says:

> Rather than believing that the economy (if we define economy as the ways in which we meet our needs) is a monolithic entity that cannot be altered, I aim to cocreate equitable systems that privilege communal well-being over personal gain. I try to make art projects within systems that are aligned with my values.

Solidarity artists and economists are working together toward a just transition that subverts the current art economy into something that can hold artists in all their complexities and needs and is aligned with their values. Some collective initiatives toward that end include Creating New Futures, The People's Cultural Plan, Cultural New Deal, Artists Dismantling Capitalism, Build from Here: The Future of Ensemble Theater, Ways and Means of We Economy, Anticapitalism for Artists, and many more.

To further illustrate this direction, we quote at length from a 2021 report, *Solidarity Not Charity*, prepared for Grantmakers in the Arts (www.art.coop) by Natalia Linares and Caroline Woolard:

> Artists and culture-bearers need more equity ownership of their own assets (land, buildings, equipment) in order to ensure greater stability amid crisis, to enable long-term planning, and to provide time for experimental work. The arts and culture sector requires shared infrastructure so that the sector can develop peer-reliant ecosystems. Places like Double Edge Theatre, Sol Collective, and the Caribbean Cultural Center are navigating the pandemic with integrity, relationality, and community-respect precisely because they have equity ownership and shared infrastructure. The relationships these culture-bearers and artists are able to build with their neighbors builds democracy and creates room for mutual support in the face of devastation and loss. New types of peer-driven, ecosystem-oriented finance are emerging to make these types of equity, infrastructure, and relationship-building possible. At the heart of this work is solid peer governance and committed, deep relationships, built over years and across sectors and movements.
>
> • • •
>
> In this moment of crisis and uncertainty, grantmakers can make a "big bet" on the power of Solidarity Economy practices and institutions that artists and culture-bearers are building. The December 2020 Americans for the Arts' COVID-19's Impact on The Arts Research & Tracking Update states that the top three needs for artists are: (1) unemployment insurance, (2) food/housing assistance, (3) forgivable business loans. This is what all people need, and what artists need. According to the Brookings Institute, creative workers are experiencing historic precarity. What can be done? Forgivable loans, affordable housing, and dignified jobs—when structured as solidarity-based, cooperative insti-

tutions and networks—have been shown to withstand crises because they are built with self-determination and community-response from the outset. These entities emphasize self-help, dignified livelihoods, and community wellbeing instead of profit for external shareholders and are underexplored in the United States.

* * *

Shifts in grantmakers' mindset, practices, programs, investment/endowment, and policy advocacy to support interconnected, locally-rooted models of community ownership and democratic governance to flourish in the arts and culture sector and beyond. This repairs inequity in the sector and allows those who have been most harmed by our current systems to achieve cultural, economic, and political power.

Expanding Where, Why, How, and with Whom One Works

The integration of artistic and community commitments in socially engaged performance has expanded the broader field of nonprofit theater in terms of where, why, how, and with whom artists make work. This was evidenced in the responses to a research survey (howlround.com/participatory-research-results-and-further-questions) conducted over HowlRound, an open-source platform where people from different points on the theater spectrum, although largely socially progressive, connect. Reading these comments, posted during the incredibly reflective year of 2020, we wonder if some of the values expressed here will circulate more in the nonprofit theater world moving forward, and we turn to those findings now.

Asked about skills and orientations that the expanded field calls upon, most cited was listening. Comments included, "not bypassing someone else's brilliant idea because it doesn't fit the image I have of what a person from a specific place or background might say. . . . Building on what people are already doing instead of imposing one's own ideas." In response to guiding principles, we heard variations on caring for the community/participants with whom you are working. Respondents elaborated on this idea, stating these sentiments: Do no harm; cultivate respect; seek out mutually beneficial engagement; honor people in their place of belonging and the expertise and knowledge already present in the community;

recognize that a theater belongs to its community, whose residents need access, ownership, authorship, participation, and accountability; and arrive with a framework and/or philosophy, not an agenda.

Also prevalent in survey results was putting one's work in a larger, systemic context. Respondents emphasized examining their racial and financial privilege and making changes in what they did based on equitable access. They spoke of decolonizing, cultivating an equity lens, and working both bottom up and top down.

The skill of collaborating with more than other theater artists came up frequently and, with it, working with the unexpected and remaining flexible. Also expressed was the desire to develop a sense of when to step back and foreground community voice, to facilitate intergroup dialogue and storytelling, and to become more responsive to the moment and the needs of specific communities. Others wanted to cultivate adaptive leadership, humility, and the sharing of power equally with community partners; to make space not just to critique but also to envision the world we want; and to meet one's basic needs to support one's dreams, rather than getting so caught up in survival as to lose touch with one's dreams.

Many respondents cited concern about a particular social issue, even if they still aspire to work in regional theater or with an ensemble company. They wanted to bring art into other contexts, including neighborhood-based social services, organizing, interactions with young people, and environmental activism, and expressed a general desire to have more social justice impact and make theater where more people see themselves represented and can be part of it. They also sought greater synergy of *e*ffect (activism) and *a*ffect (art), especially regarding race, class, gender, and colonialism. Some wanted to explore art's therapeutic capacity more deeply; others felt the need to do something different because of COVID-19.

Respondents expressed the desire to have their theater making to do the following:

- Show viewers the beauty around them: What people love, they protect.

- Express interconnectedness: We are all players in one another's stories; theater at its root is socially, civically, and community-engaged. Identify shared needs: Coexistence means including humans as part of nature.
- Integrate equity values: coalition building across racial and class identities.
- Include the community's self-representation: A thriving community must be supported primarily from within—by its members, resources, and capacities, for the present and future; establish cultural specificity, with community members' stories intertwined with their art.
- Embrace both effect and affect: Have both an emotional affect and a material effect; "stories of the many" are both artful (affect) and produce knowledge (effect).

Other touchstones that came up: that process is as important as a end result; that it is necessary for the work to include risk, joy, justice, liberation, healing, curiosity, and discovery; and that collaboration allows our most radical, inventive, adventurous selves to shine through.

Aligning One's Values and One's Art

When artists' inner values are aligned with their outer practice, they can sustain *themselves,* even through lean times, whether or not they have community, material support, or anyone's validation. Socially engaged art allows space for people to align their internal desires with their external professional life. Some call this a spiritual alignment, while others call it being in flow, but it can be an almost euphoric feeling of usefulness that fills one's life with purpose and meaning.

Because personal values may be expressed in so many ways in theater making across fields, socially engaged artists may be said to live their lives in public. They are as likely to align their social and artistic passions when performing a community-informed play, facilitating a workshop at a local community center, or participating in a political demonstration. Interacting with people at these different venues opens up possibilities of dissipating prejudices, slowly yet crucially, about whole groups of people in the face of actually encountering them.

Gloria Miguel of the Kuna/Rappahannock Nations recounted a woman coming up to her after a show and saying that she had expected an all-dance-and-song performance; she had not expected stories, especially stories about women's experiences that she related to and that left her in tears. This kind of exchange happens more frequently when artists interact with a range of people and not just with those who self-identify as "into the arts."

Regeneration in Practice: Double Edge Theatre

Double Edge offers an example of how a company and the various communities with which it interacts validate one another, provide markets and networks, and offer ways to continue and advance lifelong learning. Founder Stacy Klein has this to say about Double Edge's sustainability:

> DE was founded as a laboratory theater and was never dedicated to the moneymaking ideas of theater institutions. At a certain point we decided to move to a farm and become self-sustaining; we did not want to be in the race of competition for a very small pie. We were self-funded for many years. Our ensemble has very low wages and many of us chose to have outside jobs. We now have a garden and a greenhouse for almost year-round vegetables. We are developing the farm and solar energy. We don't want to depend on corrupt corporations for our sustainability.
>
> Over the last maybe ten years, we have good earned income from our work, a solid barter system and community support, and foundation support, particularly to develop our community endeavors. Because we are working with almost exclusively local businesses that believe in us, we can negotiate and navigate rough times. Local family foundations also are lending a hand. We have decided that our ensemble and the staff, who have been here for years, will be the focus of our endeavor. We are not starry-eyed about our survival, but

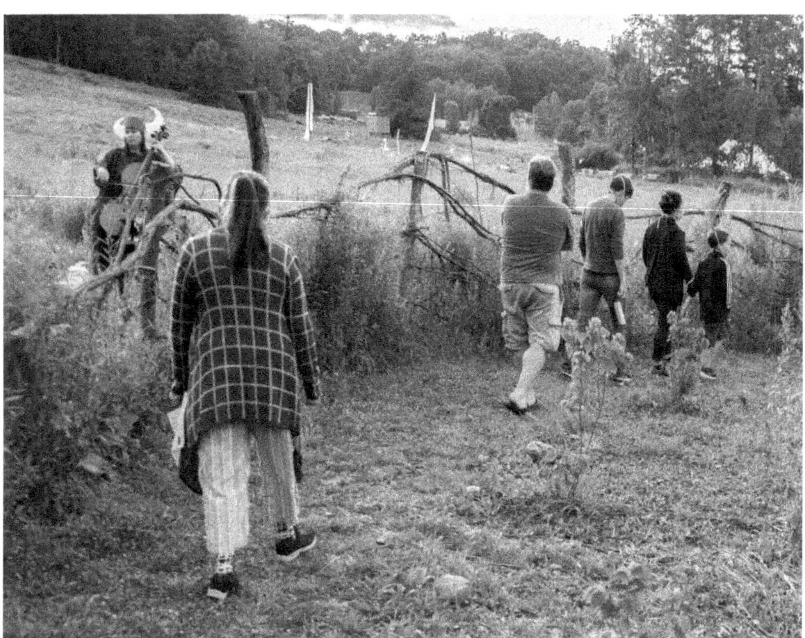

6 Feet Apart, All Together. *Dylan Young playing cello as masked audience members walk through the labyrinth located on Double Edge Theatre's Farm Center during their Summer Spectacle performance of* 6 Feet Apart, All Together. *in 2020. Photo by Kim Chin-Gibbons. Copyright 2017 Kim Chin-Gibbons. Courtesy of Double Edge Theatre.*

we are working hard to ensure that we and our community (to which we contribute a lot economically) are safe. Advice I would offer to anyone, whether they own property or not (as I don't think that is a panacea) is LOCAL LOCAL LOCAL and focus on your ART and your sustaining creativity particularly for these times.

Codirector Carlos Uriona elaborates:

The integration of many participants of the Double Edge experience as a village—or community, as it is not limited to a geographical site—enables the ensemble to diversify income streams and ration expense lines. We turn work relationships into virtuous cycles, instead of the vicious cycles that happen with monetization. The exchanges are multiple and complex, which allow us to obtain a good portion of our necessities through a bartering system. Some of this is visible in the

> way we use the housing, the performance spaces, the shops, and the office space as a multiple-function habitat, which also includes one hundred acres of beautiful land and pastures.
>
> Examples of the larger supportive community during the COVID-19 pandemic include Greenfield Savings Bank, which held back our mortgage payments for three months until we could get it together, and gave us our PPP loan the day the program [took effect.]. Bread Euphoria has donated all their leftover bread to us for the past eight years. Greenfield Markets, Natural Roots, River Valley Coop, Good Bunch, and Diemand Farms Chickens all made sure we had food and, in the case of the latter, gave out chickens at wholesale price for our entire summer endeavor.

In turn, Double Edge looks to share its assets with other local cultural groups. It has "gifted a space to the local indigenous community, Ohketeau—an autonomous Center for Indigenous Culture, in addition to a guest artist/ Ohketeau kitchen" (DE-Case-Statement-April-2021.pdf, 13). Ohketeau partnerships include:

- Living Presence of Our History: an educational in-person and livestream series on the present day and historical roots of Native People of Western MA and subjects such as mascots and symbolism affecting issues of identity and representation.
- Indigenous Artist in Residence: combined support of an artist selected annually.
- Commissioning of co-director Larry Spotted Crow Mann's original performance *Freedom in Season* at the DE Farm.
- Fiscal sponsorship and business assistance (DE-Case-Statement -April-2021.pdf, 14).

A close relationship between one's work and life enriches both. Lois Weaver of Split Britches captures that dynamic:

> What I made has become a methodology for living for us: We worked out our challenges by making work about those challenges. Our work parallels a lot of the ways our community has lived through certain

> challenges, like around lesbian and transgender identity. I'm proud that we have created a method of working where we trust what we have, don't reach for what we don't have, work with what we've got. And then we make something from it.

Writing this book has provided us with a learning opportunity, not just filling in gaps in our socially engaged performance knowledge but also contending with our separate perspectives, which are both individual and generational. It has required humility and patience on both of our parts. It required letting go of the entrenched system's prioritizing the self-authored monograph in favor of an opportunity to learn from many people's experience. And it has been, in a word, regenerative.

7 The Year was 2020

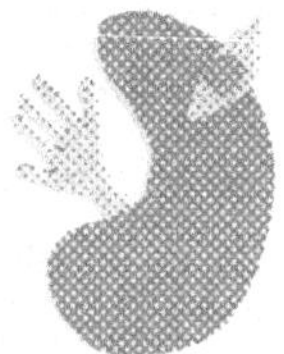

A riot is the language of the unheard. . . . [I]n a real sense our nation's summers of riots are caused by our nation's winters of delay. And as long as America postpones justice, we stand in the position of having these recurrences of violence and riots over and over again. Social justice and progress are the absolute guarantors of riot prevention.

—The Reverend Martin Luther King, Jr., "The Other America," speech given at Grosse Pointe High School, March 14, 1968

Uprisings need artists to access that felt sense of the world, like communicating with images, and opening up your own and other people's hearts because you have a vulnerability and a truth seeking that can be contagious. It's important to . . . resist and protest along with building and creating.

—Artist Caroline Woolard

In January 2020, the first murmurings of a potentially deadly virus hit our shores. At first, there was denial. Then panic and fear dropped in, with a sprinkling of doom. Quarantine began with the uncertainty of being sheltered in place indefinitely. Face-to-face human contact beyond one's immediate "pod" disappeared, from the simplest interactions to the shuttering of what were considered all but "essential services": schools, most businesses, live arts and sports events, unnecessary medical procedures, sit-down restaurants . . . the list goes on. Many who continued working outside the home risked serious health consequences and were left without child care; many who could not keep working faced eviction. Many created interdependent mutual-aid networks.

Tectonic reverberations were set off by the extraordinary reality of every person on Earth impacted by the same threat . . . but unequally: the extent of our nation's polarization was displayed, and great uprisings against state-sanctioned racialized violence unleashed, generating enough force to open a portal into the next world, as novelist Arundhati Roy writes:

> Historically, pandemics have forced humans to break with the past and imagine their world anew. This one is no different. . . . We can choose to walk through [the portal it opens], dragging the carcasses of our prejudice and hatred, our avarice, our data banks and dead ideas, our dead rivers and smoky skies behind us. Or we can walk through lightly, with little luggage, ready to imagine another world. And ready to fight for it. (www.ft.com/content/10d8f5e8-74eb-11ea-95fe-fcd274e920ca)

In the sudden space of suspended life as we knew it arose calls for institutions to transform themselves, and create systems of accountability. Mass protests followed police killings of George Floyd, Breonna Taylor, and others; we experienced the rancor of a divisive presidential election, witnessed public gestures of racial reconciliation, and lived through the spiral of loneliness caused by the inability to observe important markers in our lives and the need to spend a holiday season in isolation. As the New Year commenced, we careened from the insurrection at the Capitol to the glimmer of a functioning government returning and the readying of mass vaccinations.

We write to you from inside the whirlwind of this portal, this liminal space between worlds. It is a space of reckoning that is restoring collective memory from historical amnesia: of the structural inequities and social division caused by decades of extraction of wealth and labor from people of color, dispossession of lands and genocide of Native peoples, displacement of peoples from the global South, mechanisms of disfranchisement, the epic growth of prisons and detention centers, terrorizing governmental policies, privatized public schools, hospitals, and public resources that have produced scarcity, environmental health hazards, poverty, and underground economies regulated through violence. We are gasping for air in a country built on intersectional oppression.

With this epic-scale backdrop, we present a glimpse of how theater and performance makers have been navigating through this portal, questioning what came before, and imagining what could come after. Catalyzed by the events of 2020, numerous artists have been compelled to situate themselves in a context that is larger than their individual aesthetic visions or even their previous community and social engagement. We begin with a scan of immediate performative responses to the circumstances of the pandemic, artists' growing consciousness of the possibility of seeing their work on the world stage, the rise of resistance and loss, and we culminate in the sense of the future that we heard from many of our interviewees.

Performance During the Pandemic (Winter/Spring 2020)

At first, many artists just tried to continue being artists. Some chose to ignore the form of the computer screen and pretend they were in a theater with people in front of them, while others fused theater with digital storytelling. Those who had been working digitally already flourished in the new environment. Kevin Gotkin, disability justice advocate and artist, remarked, "When everyone started using Zoom, it allowed us to use our community's knowledge, because [people had] done a lot with technology and remote access, and taken it to the next level." They had had no choice but to organize virtually, as much cultural programming is not accessible to people with disabilities. So many cultural organizations moving into digital technology was a nonetheless bitter reminder that accessibility could have been chosen a long time ago.

Some theater makers adapted works in progress to the digital environment. Lois Weaver and Peggy Shaw's *Last Gasp,* intended for the stage, became a film set in an empty house in Haudenosaunee territory (upstate New York). Superhero Clubhouse, led by Lanxing Fu and Jeremy Pickard, partnered with the Bushwick Starr, an experimental theater venue in Bushwick, Brooklyn, to create a digital version of Big Green Theater program.

For over ten years, members of Superhero Clubhouse have been teaching eco-playwriting, "a holistic approach to theater-making that centers climate and environmental justice in content, process, and production," to public elementary school students in Lenapehoking (Bushwick) most impacted by environmental racism. Guests ranging from Native knowledge keepers to climate scientists and Bomba musicians have helped bring students' ideas to life. At the end of every school year, the plays are performed at the Bushwick Starr by professional actors for a public audience, the young playwrights, and their communities. But in 2020, they made a live-action Zoom film that utilized the Zoom square as a multidimensional stage by smartly playing with angles and entrances, guided by Sadah Espii Proctor. The amazing props, puppets, and sets by Yijun Yang and Lexy Ho-Tai were made from garbage in people's apartments (www.youtube.com/watch?v=5-ouxlq7Skw&t=3s). Written by kids, for kids, the digital performance was a loving reminder of the "before times" and a welcome escape for kids who so acutely bore the weight of being sheltered in place.

For You Productions has addressed the often tragic consequences of quarantine on elders in isolation by creating beautiful collaborative performance films. The Artists & Elders project connects elders and artists of many different mediums from around Turtle Island, creating and exchanging art in the spirit of gift giving (www.foryou.productions/march-october-2020).

Melecio Estrella and Panching Pedrin cocreated a film that weaved together Melecio's movements with Panching's memories, prayers, and poems set at some of their favorite places to commune with nature. Beatriz Escobar & Berta created a Zoom Carnaval in a living room in Rio de Janeiro by learning the traditionally performed dances and songs.

On the web platform Twitch, River Ramirez, comedian, performer, and visual artist, hosted *Art is Easy,* bringing a jolt of humor and pathos to a participatory digital art piece. The live-sound composer engaged par-

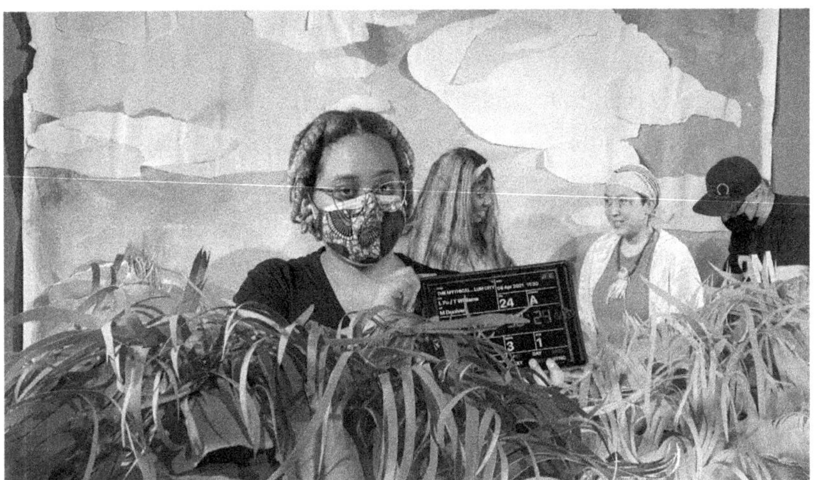

Production coordinator Rachel Denise April slating for the filmed adaptation of The Mystical Jungle and Luminescence City, *an eco-play written by students at P.S. 152 in Queens. This Big Green Theater Queens production, in spring 2021, was a collaboration between Superhero Clubhouse and the Astoria Performing Arts Center. Photo by Lanxing Fu, courtesy of the photographer.*

ticipants in story making via a chat room by offering questions, prompts, and improvised contextual connective tissue.

For years, nightlife has provided a go-to therapeutic, community-building, and safe way for many LGBTQIA2+ people to interact. With all such interactions curtailed by the pandemic, many parties moved online. Body Hack utilized the digital commons to transform their QTBIPOC and sex worker–centered performance and dance parties into an act of international solidarity with an artist and DJ lineup that brought folks together from around the world for collective catharsis and camaraderie aimed at mutual aid and structural material change.

Along with the weight and the losses that the pandemic brought, the conditions of quarantine brought some unexpected pleasures. People had access to live performance and art experiences from all around the world, albeit mediated now over the Internet. More broadly, for those with the privilege to work from home or to collect Pandemic Unemployment Assistance, the quarantine was also a welcome relief. Many interviewees recounted the space they had to reflect on their prequarantine lives, the positive impact that time had on their well-being, and the opportunity to imagine the lives they wanted to live. We hold the contradiction of something so painful for many bearing unexpected fruit for others.

Some made substantial life changes. A number of artists sought to participate in making pandemic-related policy decisions at the city, state, and national level and lent their efforts to various political organizing endeavors. Shouting into their virtual megaphones about an arts sector and governing body that failed them, some artists stepped into new roles as community organizers to fight for systemic changes in their industries and/or the larger world. Some were propelled to divest from unresponsive institutions they had been attempting to build relationships with and instead shifted their energies toward grassroots movements and coalitions. Carolina Dỗ, cofounder of the Sống Collective, shares her experience:

> When the lockdown happened, we heard crickets from the people whom we had invested so much of our souls and creative and intellectual power in. No one was, "Hey, are you guys okay? Can we take the bonds that we've been hoarding to help you pay rent?" None of that.
>
> In some ways, artists are realizing we've been complicit in machines [that don't serve us]. Like Hollywood: How many cop shows? How many prison shows? How many projects that you do as an artist so that you can get paid but that put [negative] images of our people out there, that inform how we are treated on a societal level?
>
> Artists were coming out with [statements like] "This is how I've been exploited. This is how I feel." For so long the consensus was, Keep your head down, do the work, because without these institutions you are nothing, instead of realizing, Wait a minute, we make these institutions. We're the reason they get those diversity grants.

Some artists left big cities, returning to smaller hometowns to lower their expenses and start again. An actress we know left NYC with a renewed purpose to be of service and became a social worker. A stage manager who had been frustrated with the inequitable theater industry found joy in his new meditative routine as a mail person. Youth theater maker, scholar, and single parent Dana Edell recounts:

It lasted two months in a 1.5-bedroom apartment with my one-year-old and three-year-old while trying to work full-time, terrified to get in the elevator with the stroller to go outside because my kids did not understand "Do not touch anything!" So, much to the likely horror of the teenage version of me who had left Wilmington, Delaware, for life in the "big city," I accepted my parents' generous offer to spend the summer in the house I grew up in, with plenty of indoor space and a wondrous backyard filled with fox, deer, and fireflies.

I slowly began seeking to find partners to make theater. The racially segregated city I left in the 1990s had not changed much, though looking at it through my 2020 vision, I saw opportunities to engage with privileged white teenagers—like I had been—and became more and more inspired by the connections and solidarity I felt with them, and the urgency to use my privilege, resources, and twenty years of experience creating activist theater to create a new project here, where I'm from. As a white woman who has spent most of my adult life collaborating with Black and brown teenage girls in New York City, connecting with white girls to rehearse in the same Jewish Community Center where I went to elementary school, I feel a sense of belonging and solidarity that is new to me, and deeply powerful. (Edell in an email to Cohen-Cruz, May 3, 2021)

Freedom Dreaming (Summer 2020)

Is it possible to share the feeling of being lonely or alone as a way to make new forms of collectivity? Loneliness is endemic to the affective life of settler colonialism. It is also an effective commons that demonstrates a world that isn't quite right. Loneliness in fact evinces a new world on the horizon.

—Billy-Ray Belcourt, *This Wound Is a World*

BREONNA TAYLOR. GEORGE FLOYD. BRAYLA STONE. MERCI MACK. SHAKI PETERS. DRAYA MCCARTY. TATIANA HALL. BREE BLACK. We say their names. *Axé.*

For many artists, it became impossible to keep their professional lives separate from the world in which such violence is commonplace. Throughout history, artists have pumped hope back into spirits by working in tandem with movements—civil rights, LGBTQIA2+, Occupy, #MeToo, Black Lives Matter, to name a few. Artists aligning with the prison abolition movement are now in that historical tradition.

The call for abolition has existed since the slave trade began, but the current fight for prison-industrial complex (PIC) abolition finally has its spotlight on a national stage. The fires of resistance that had been tended by a few on the ground turned into a wildfire spread by many, a burn that was necessary and a long time coming. We imagined the day would come when calls for abolition would enter the mainstream, in maybe five or ten years, but here it was being debated and discussed on the evening news.

Prison-industrial complex abolition is a vision of a restructured society in a world where people have everything they need: food, shelter, education, health, art, beauty, clean water, and more, things that are foundational to our personal and community safety (We Do This Til We Free Us). Through various creative and education initiatives, Chicago-based abolitionist, scholar, and educator Mariame Kaba invites people to question why these systems exist at all, and believes especially that the hip-hop theater gives "the message a common heartbeat, a rally cry, a conversation starter, to disrupt patterns and old ways of thinking."

Minneapolis was a focus of this national reckoning. Meena Natarajan and Dipankar Mukherjee, co–artistic directors of Pangea World Theater in Minneapolis, describe how the killing of George Floyd in their very neighborhood and the pandemic more generally affected them:

> **DM:** How is it different now? Our sense of immediacy. We don't have front and back burners, only one burner. Reenvisioning.
>
> **MN:** Everyone has to help develop policies. We need to have a percentage of BIPOC ownership, make sure these buildings, over this three-street area [much of which got burned down by white supremacists during the protests following Floyd's murder], where people of color can own land that was historically denied.

There have also been arts administrators, who manage cultural spaces, who mobilized their resources to support the needs arising in 2020. Performance Space 122 (PS 122) in New York City, for example, paused all public programming to redirect their budget to artists and organizers to do with as they saw fit. Both PS 122 and JACK, "a performance meets civic space" (www.jackny.org), in collaboration with We Keep Us Safe Abolitionist Network, turned their spaces into food-distribution centers and mutual-aid and information hubs. These actions birthed new narratives of possibility for cultural centers as bridges between people, community organizers, the city, and the world.

In response to community organizers who wanted artists in their work but perceived them as lacking understanding of justice movements or thorough systems analysis, Rad organized Media Tools for Liberation with Izzy Sazak, Lilleth Glimcher, and Francisco Perez. This was a workshop series on how artists could support economic justice and abolition movements with good propaganda. Through presentations, discussions, think tanks, and creative experiments with radical economists, abolitionists, healers, and water protectors, over 350 artists utilized their skills to offer creative solutions to build steps toward our shared goals. Playwrights initiated collaborations with graphic designers to make abolition comics for kids, illustrators partnered with poets to make other graphic formats for adults that reached millions, and harm-reduction workers collaborated with comedians to make videos that broke down hard-to-understand concepts into digestible formats. JACK and You Are Here provided support. These collaborations made it clear that there is an inextricable necessity for artistry in organizing and organizing in art.

Reg Flowers facilitated "12 Steps to Anti-Oppression," a virtual creative improvisational exercise modeled after the twelve steps of Alcoholics Anonymous. It invited folks to begin to heal from internalized white supremacy by admitting that they "suffered from symptoms of white supremacist beliefs and internalized racism and were in recovery through this process" (https://jointheprogram.org/).

Together with many other grassroots cultural organizations and groups, the Black Visions Collective not only articulated a "People's Budget," proposing cuts to the Minneapolis Police Department, but also generated graphics, videos, popular assemblies, social media campaigns, TikTok presentations, and participatory performance mourning rituals. It organized a beautiful mourning celebration for George Floyd that included a giant multiblock-long altar where people could add their offerings to honor those lost to police brutality.

Daniel Park gives an example of creative support to protests in Philadelphia:

> One of the best moments that I had last year was seeing the Bearded Ladies Cabaret. They're a queer cabaret performance company. During COVID, they got a truck and converted it into a traveling cabaret venue. They brought it to one of the big rallies and drove along with the protest, so that folks who were chanting had this quality sound system to amplify their voices. Music was playing, and it turned the protest into a parade in this really beautiful, energizing way. It was like, "Yes, this is a place where I want to be." It's not just a bummer and sad.

Responses to Loss (Fall/Winter 2020)

In the wake of the great uprisings, the level of unprocessed grief in this portal between worlds that was 2020 emerged thick and palpable. Some friends who live near hospitals could see the trucks piled high with bodies and smell the pungent odor of death. These ripples of grief seemed to grip many of our spirits, a reminder of the thousands of lives lost.

Larissa FastHorse describes the devastation that COVID has wrought on her people:

> We're losing languages in this country because so many elders have succumbed to COVID. They live in these incredibly remote areas and because of COVID, people didn't know that they needed help. Our reservations often lack electricity and Internet. It's just crazy. I hear people talking about the positives of this time: "So many good things have happened. It's been a reset." If you mean that it killed off thousands and thousands of our people, then I guess it's a reset. If you mean that our children are even further behind and have been abandoned by the school system . . . that in South Dakota, a friend's nephew on the Pine Ridge Reservation had to be flown to Denver because they had no ICU COVID beds left in the state . . . If you mean that, then I guess it's a reset—of some horrible thing.

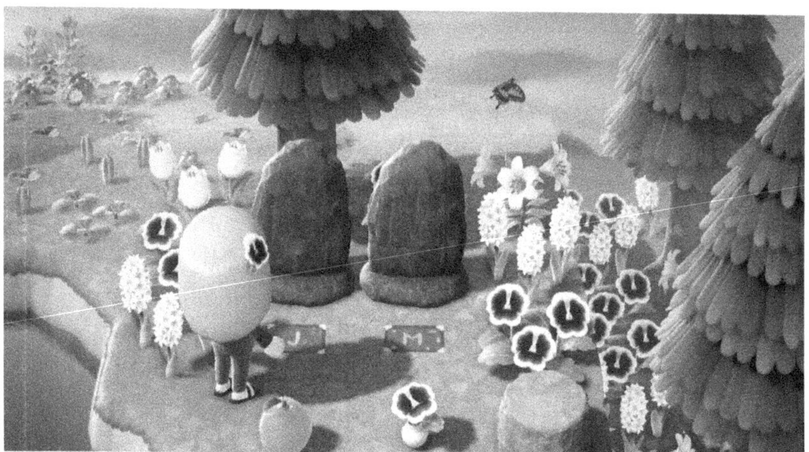

Characters from the Nintendo Switch video game Animal Crossing visit loved ones at a digital queer burial site for queer players. Players discussed and explored their ideal grieving space and what that looks like outside of the confines of our typical world. Players were encouraged to come dressed in their true gender presentations with their chosen names, which they might not otherwise be able to do in their real-life burial plots. This was especially cathartic for players in a time of grieving while sheltered in place during quarantine. Photo courtesy of Stefanie Grosekemper.

Our ceremonies for mourning were inaccessible in person and the leaders of our country offered no days of national mourning. Live-streamed funerals felt far away and alien. How can we honor a life in the absence of our rituals? Some artists created virtual spaces to process this grief: dance-based vigils to move grief through the body led by BUFU: By Us for Us; the virtual Dia de Muertos altars; digital games like Animal Crossing, where people create altars, shrines, and community cemeteries to honor someone they loved and lost. Death doulas Alua Arthur and Lashanna Williams recommended making playlists, videos, tangible touch-based memorials, meditations, and story circles (www.orderofthegooddeath.com/funerals-dying-in-absentia-inspiration-tips-during-covid-19).

By late 2020, live performance was returning at a growing scale (beyond the occasional performances in parking lots and in large open spaces with small groups of masked spectators that had continued throughout the pandemic). In NYC, council members, led by Laurie Cumbo, worked in conjunction with the Parks Department to create an inclusive process for artists to perform outdoors, even as the winter winds still blew. Permits had previously been difficult to access for individual artists who are not part of formal groups or institutions.

A few months later, NYC Mayor Bill de Blasio announced the City Artist Corps, a New Deal Works Progress Administration–style program providing $25 million in funding for about fifteen hundred artists creating outdoor performances and other forms of public artwork around the city. We'll see how it pans out. This isn't system change and it isn't a long-term solution, but we hope it can bring some solace and joy to people who have been in grief and isolation for over a year, and perhaps be extended and expanded.

States, too, are initiating programs to support artists in their full humanity rather than only on a project-by-project basis. In New York State, for example, the following initiative was announced in spring 2021:

> Creatives Rebuild New York is a three-year, $125 million initiative that will provide guaranteed income and employment opportunities for up to 2,700 artists throughout New York State. These two components will work to alleviate unemployment of artists, continue the creative work of artists in partnership with their communities and arts and cultural organizations, and enable artists to continue working and living in New York State under less financial strain. (creativesrebuildny.org)

Emboldened to Imagine (January–May 2021)

Fueled by the pent-up energy of ten months of quarantine, the manifestation of what people imagined and hoped for was as devastating in some cases as it was inspiring in others, depending on one's worldview. Indeed, 2021 began with the Capitol insurrection on January 6, manifesting compounded feelings laid bare by decades of perceived entitlement coupled with resentment for what hadn't delivered ebbing even further away, and bursting forth in a performance-level tantrum. It vividly demonstrated that even those with political power are not immune from the wrath of those who feel themselves wronged.

For some, the needle was moving from *if* abolition was possible to *when and how* to begin the transition to a culture of abolition. By May 25,

2021, one year after George Floyd's death at the hands of Derek Chauvin, more than thirty states and dozens of large cities had created new policies limiting police tactics or enforced those already on the books (e.g., banning neck restraints, like the kind that Chauvin used on Floyd, and requiring police officers to intervene when a fellow officer uses extreme force, which did not happen in the situation with Floyd (*The New York Times* Morning Newsletter, May 25, 2021). Some went further. The mayor of Cayuga land (Ithaca, NY), Svante Myrick, for example, developed a plan to abolish the city's police department and replace it with an agency made up of armed "public safety workers" and unarmed "community solution workers," which would dispatch certain calls to people trained in mental health.

Rad's mother had been working for years on initiatives toward abolition with the Black Lives Matter movement in Broward County, Florida. In the spring of 2021, BLM Broward finally saw some results when a Black woman, one of their leaders, was appointed as the new "emergency call liaison." Her role is to build out a system and task force that diverts 911 calls to their appropriate social services providers, which will result in a significant decrease in the policing of Black and brown people. These are some tiny steps toward dismantling the system of incarceration and punishment on Turtle Island.

The calls to abolish police and prisons and to shift those resources to housing, universal health care, living-wage jobs, universal basic income, green energy, and a system of restorative/ transformative justice were once a pipe dream but are materializing into reality. They are now a generative driving force in a massive network made up of many movements that have been hard at work for decades. It makes beautiful sense that in a land made up of so many nations, this growing network of movements, which address a broad range of struggles, would take root through decentralized, *emergent strategies,* adrienne maree brown's term for "building complex patterns and systems of change through relatively small interactions" and as "an adaptive, relational way of being" (brown 2017, 2). There's a place for everyone when the small is seen as a building block for the large.

Here's what some of our interviewees imagined coming out of the pandemic:

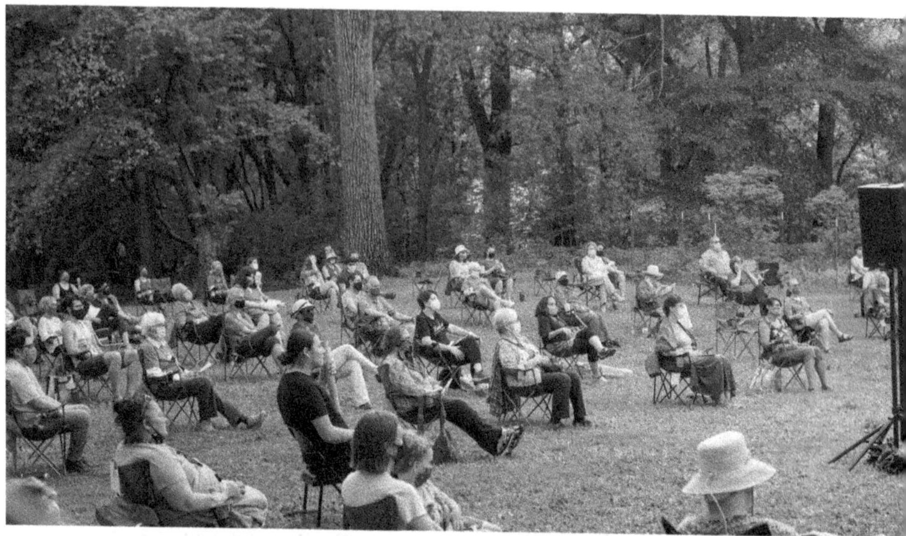

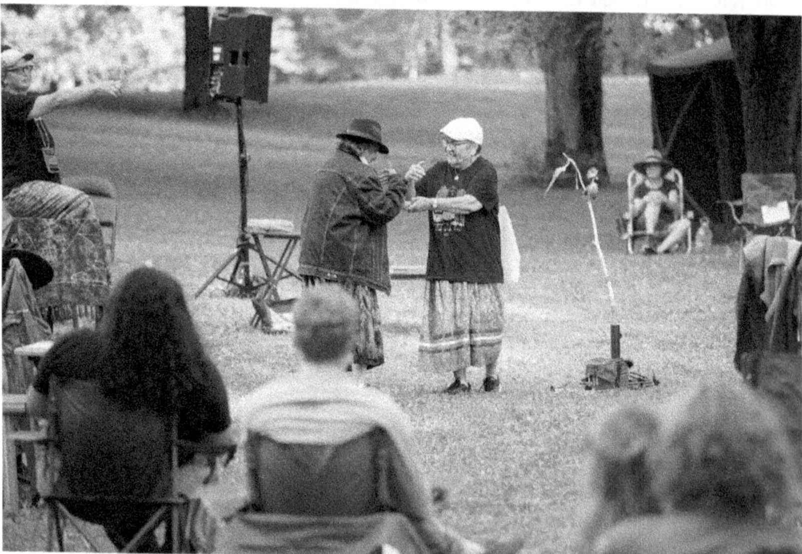

Two views of The Missouri River Water Walk*, a performance chronicling Sharon Day's and five other women's water walk the length of the Missouri River, from Three Forks, Montana, to St. Louis, Missouri, fifty-three days later. Written by Day with Dr. Roxanne Ornelas and directed by Dipankar Mukherjee. With songs in Ojibwe, Dakota, Lakota, and English and stories of healing historic wounds and the women restoring their relationships with the land and one another. Performed at Hidden Falls Regional Park, May 21–23, 2021, for 100–150 people per day socially distanced from one another. The youth in the first photo are from the Ikidowin Youth Ensemble. The performers in the second photo were water walkers. Photographs by Bruce Silcox. Copyright Pangea World Theater.*

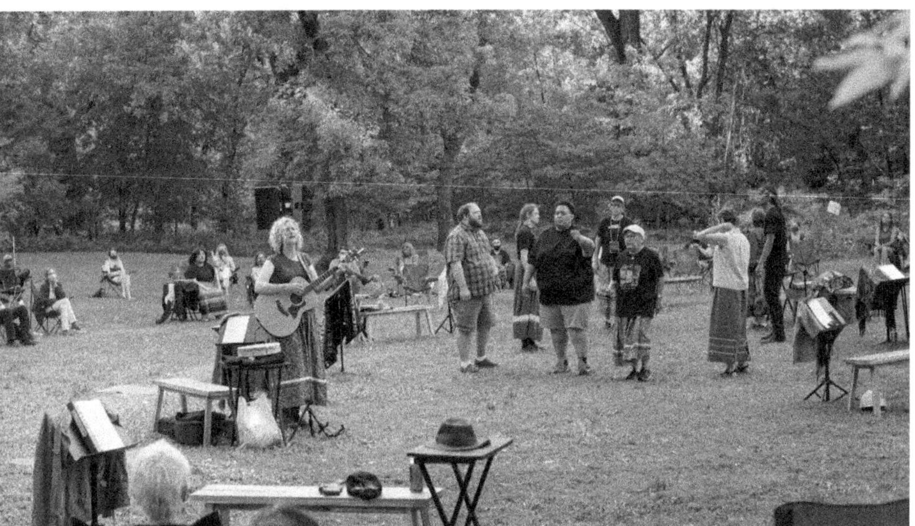

Sharee Clark: "My vision is for community centers to have gymnasts, karate teachers, photographers, and others, all teaching our youth something that may enhance their talent, the gifts that they already have, or show them something different. Show them that they are valued. There are resources in the community that can do that. During the protests, we linked with the directors of a white children's theater that our kids have been priced out of. They said they want to make what they do accessible to our community."

Arlene Goldbard: "Most of my livelihood has come from speaking engagements and consulting projects, virtually all of which were canceled during the pandemic. The upside was that I got to focus on a series of paintings and essays that will be part of a new book. Now I'm noticing colleagues here and abroad questioning whether they want to go back to expending carbon, time, and resources flying somewhere to gather for a conference, and organizations questioning whether they'll have the resources to engage a consultant. So postpandemic, my big question is whether to embrace the change, cut back, and focus on my solo work–is this the right time in my own life as well as our collective life to do that? I trust the answer will emerge."

Larissa FastHorse: "I would [like to see] every theater answerable to the people on whose lands they're standing."

Leslie Ishii: "I imagine our healing circles continuing, supporting each other to be fully healed from internalized oppression. But what if we didn't have white supremacist culture constantly pressing? Can you imagine? We must strive for what we can imagine—for our liberation."

Ricardo Gamboa: "We don't live in Earth. We don't live in the present. We live in infinity, and that means all possibilities are possible. It is really important to move without certainty. Often movements break down, artistic or activist ones, because of the insistence on certainty. . . . We think of the radical as a static position, when I think it's a relation and a response to the context that you're given."

Carlton Turner: "Twenty twenty is the year never to be forgotten. Many organizations and businesses closed their doors, some of them for the last time. The impact of the pandemic on Black and brown communities exacerbated the inequity that we already knew existed. As most organizations struggled to find their footing in this new and temporary reality, I feel like Sipp Culture doubled down on our mission to provide food, support, and strategic thinking to Black southern folks. 2020 brought the entire country to a pace that is native to Mississippi. At this pace we thrive."

Some artists look forward to picking up work they had been absorbed with before the pandemic, which already had a socially engaged component. Others want to reenvision what theater and performance can do in the world that they want to live in. Others are in an in-between space, as expressed in this exchange:

Mike Lew: I've noticed that throughout COVID there's been this funny sense that we miss theatre, but we don't miss a lot of the lifestyle around theatre. Why is that?

Rehana Lew Mirza: It's like a relationship that was not equal in a lot of ways. And when you're forced to break up, you start to have the distance to analyze what wasn't working and why. So then you're like, *Do I even want to take theatre back?* (Lew and Mirza 2021)

We heard three approaches to arts and culture system change that while not new had intensified over 2020:

1. Holding (predominantly white) cultural institutions that have not only done harm in the past but also are funded by "dirty money" (war, weapons, prisons, etc.) accountable by disrupting and dismantling them as they are, with calls for equity and justice through material redistribution of money and power. An example is the Strike MoMA movement, a coalition seeking to end the Museum of Modern Art's dependence on private donors such as Leon Black, whose financial ties to war profiteering and convicted sex offender Jeffrey Epstein led to his resigning as board chair (though he remains a trustee) and demanding a more equitable institution.

2. Institutions themselves looking to diversify proactively. Some of these efforts began well before 2020. For example, the National New Play Network (NNPN) contacted arts consultants Lisa Mount and Keryl McCord in 2017, wanting to become a more equitable organization. Together, they worked on a strategic plan through an antiracism lens, and as a result, NNPN completely changed their board structure. "Core Members"—many of whom were NNPN founders and nearly all white—had received the majority of the benefits of organizational membership and had guaranteed seats on the board. Core Members are no longer guaranteed seats on the board, half of which is now composed of people of the global majority. NNPN continues to work on power sharing, more equitable grant-making structures, and other efforts to realize the vision articulated in its strategic plan.

    Of the other organizations that McCord and Mount work with, some are still in the learning phase, some are changing policies and practices, and a few are rebelling against this work (usually quietly) and maintaining the status quo. How will we choose to engage with those who refuse to transform? In sum, notes Mount, "Most organizations are finding some way to 'hike the horizontal'—borrowing Liz Lerman's phrase—and engage with both staff and community in ways that are much more egalitarian."

    Proactive organizations are generating new models, infrastructure, and processes that center communities in their wholeness; see

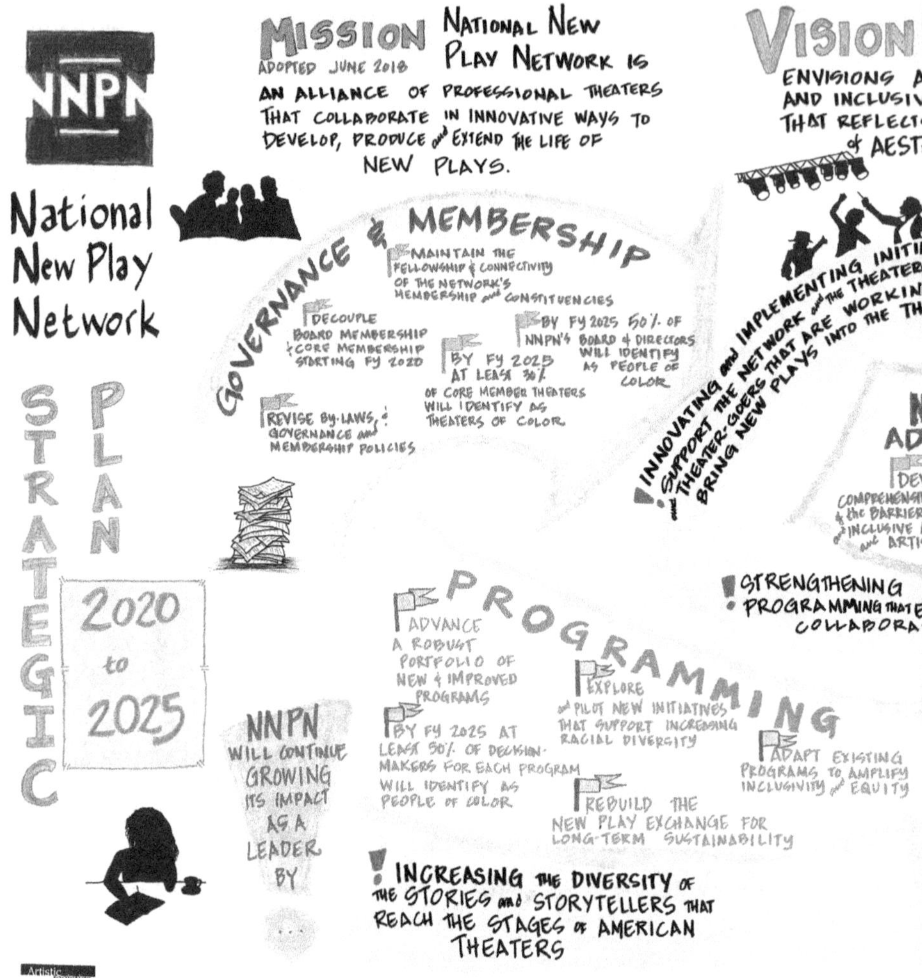

Strategic illustration by Lisa Mount for the National New Play Network. Courtesy of Lisa Mount.

the description in chapter 4 of Charlene Caruthers and BYP100's community accountability process toward transformative justice as an example.

3. Developing equitable and expansive cultural funding nationally. Groups focusing on this effort include Creating New Futures, The People's Cultural Plan, Cultural New Deal, Decolonize This Place, Art.Coop, Workers Arts Project, Hollywood Labor, and Ways and Means of We Economy.

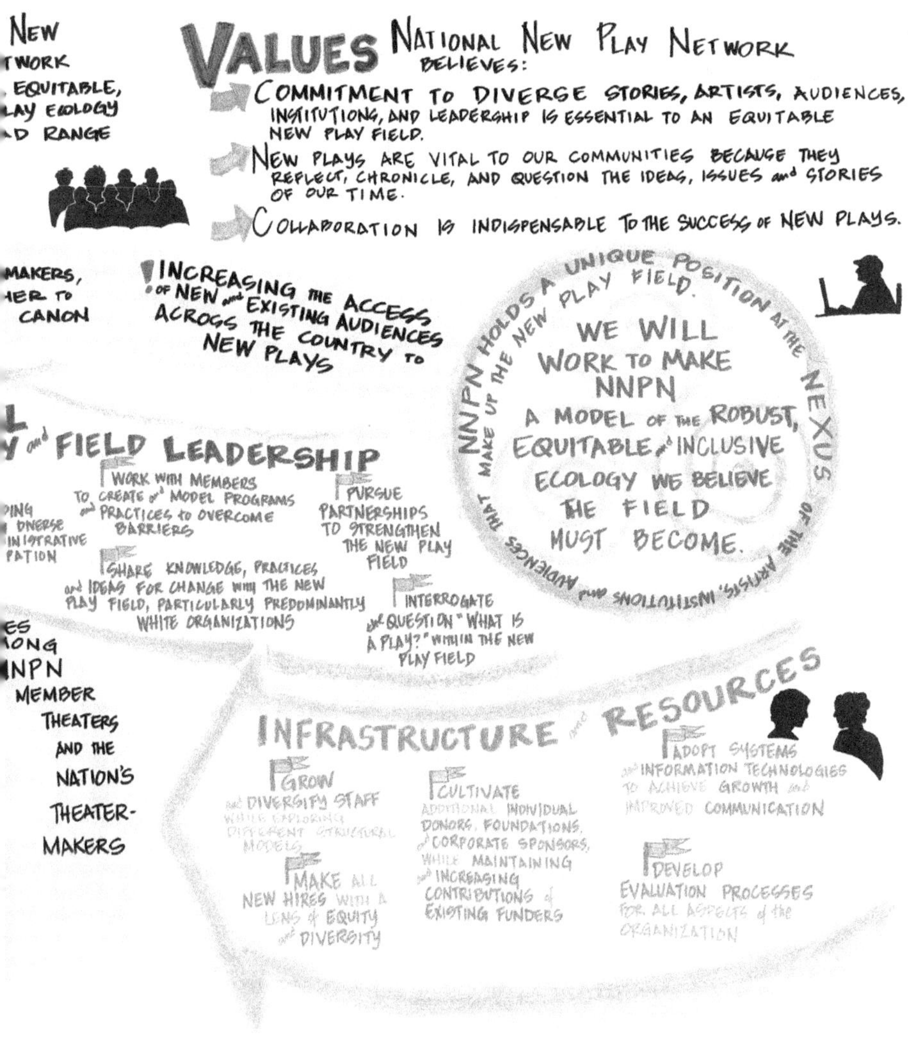

The efforts described above require artists to know about more than their art. In his course Anticapitalism for Artists, self-taught educator and theater maker Chris Meyers warns:

> Without a careful analysis of what's going on, arts workers risk internalizing the same destructive ideologies that ultimately undergird the problems we cry out against. . . . It's high time we acknowledge that the politics of all artworks, including theatre, are not just the content of the art—the characters and the story, in our case—but the values of

> the institutions that present them, the behavioral norms of those on stage and especially in the audience, the finances of access and influence, and who's in the physical building and how they were invited in, not to mention the building itself and the land on which it stands. These are all matters of class. (https://howlround.com/art-work, April 20, 2021)
>
> May 14, 2021. The Center for Disease Control announced that people who have been fully vaccinated no longer need to wear masks inside or out. While this may or may not be good advice, it is another sign that we in the United States are moving out of the pandemic. COVID diagnoses here have gone down and immunization has gone up, but herd immunity no longer appears to be a viable solution, as so many resist the vaccine for a myriad of reasons. So some continue to wear masks, keeping one another's well-being in mind.
>
> As 2020 and its immediate aftermath in the first half of 2021 come to an end, so, too, does the writing of this book. It was quite a leap to undertake this collaboration, given the different places that the two of us are in our lives. Jan was writing more reflectively, looking back in light of what she has done in the field and where it is now; Rad was writing more aspirationally, on their path but with more attention to where they want to go from here. Rad now looks forward to an ever-blossoming life in loving justice-rooted systems change, cultural work, and socially engaged performance, and Jan to a different direction in her writing and more time for involvement with her grown kids, one with a young child and the other with a food truck.

Despite all we do not know about what comes next, we believe that artists will continue to show up for their communities in unique ways: bridging divides, through strategies of shock or awe, offering story medicine, singing beauty into the crevices, dancing across dimensions, and enacting what they want to be impossible and possible. They will continue to imagine alternative futures and offer humorous escapes, to connect the dots and make spaces and structures in which more and more of us will feel seen, heard, and validated as part of a great mosaic that holds us in all our complexities and humanity.

Acknowledgments

We are grateful to the following people and organizations for supporting this book in many ways.

Lanxing Fu and Liz Lerman, for reading an early draft of this manuscript and discussing it with us.

ArtPlace America, for supporting this undertaking intellectually and financially, providing funds that freed up our time and underwrote publication costs.

The following people whom we cited based on conversations and emails: Jamie Bennett, Bryan Brayboy, Charlotte Canning, Randy Cohen, Houston Cypress, Dana Edell, Dioganhdih Hall, Trey Hartt, Cora Hook, Stacy Klein, Mark Strandquist, Delanna Studi, and Mary Wright.

The organizations that generously provided photographs, all at no fee, and the contact people who helped us find the images: Anne Basting and Carol Varney, TimeSlips; Christina Maria Xochitlzihuatl Patiño Houle and Ruben Garza, Las Imaginistas; Mark Strandquist and Trey Hartt, Performing Statistics; Meena Natarajan, Pangea World Theater; Jose Torres Tama; Stephanie McKee and Damia Khanboubi, Junebug Productions, with thanks to the Amistad Research Center; Normando Ismay of Café Bizzoso, Alternate ROOTS; Toya Lillard of viBe Theater Experience; Laura Donnelly, Cornerstone Theater; Carlton Turner, Sipp

Culture; Laura Petree and Lois Weaver, Split Britches; Muriel Miguel and Deborah, Spiderwoman Theater; Leslie Ishii; Laxing Fu, Superhero Clubhouse; Carlos Uriona and the marketing people at Double Edge Theatre; Lisa Mount, with thanks to Nan Barnett of National New Play Network; and Stefanie Grosekemper.

Jan additionally gratefully acknowledges Dana Edell for ongoing writerly support and the Brooklyn Central Library writers group for camaraderie as this book took shape.

Bibliography

Appiah, K. Anthony. "Race, Culture, Identity: Misunderstood Connections." *The Tanner Lectures on Human Values* 17 (1996): 51–136.

Atlas, Caron, and Pam Korza, eds. *Critical Perspectives.* Washington, D.C.: Americans for the Arts, 2005.

Berry, Wendell. "The Regional Motive." In *A Continuous Harmony.* New York: Harcourt Brace Jovanovich, 1972.

Belcourt, Billy-Ray. *This Wound Is a World.* Minneapolis: University of Minnesota Press, 2019.

Boyd, Andrew, and Oswald Mitchell. *Beautiful Trouble.* New York and London: Or Books, 2013.

Blackburn, Simon. *Ethics: A Very Short Introduction.* Oxford: Oxford University Press, 2001.

Brayboy, Bryan. Desert Skies Symposium talk. Arizona State University, February 18–20, 2021.

brown, adrienne marie. *Emergent Strategies: Shaping Change, Changing Worlds.* Chico, CA: AK Press, 2017.

Caro, Robert. *The Power Broker.* New York: Vintage, 1975.

Chang, Jeff et al. *UP from the UNDERGROUND: Documentation of the Ford Foundation's Future Aesthetics Program, 2002–2014.* https://artsinachangingamerica.org/future-aesthetics-report/.

Cohen-Cruz, Jan. *Local Acts: Community-Based Performance in the United States.* New Brunswick, NJ: Rutgers University Press, 2005.

———. "The Poetic Residue: On the Difference Between a Civic Action and an Art Project." *A Blade of Grass Magazine,* Issue 1: "Where?" 2018. https://abladeofgrass.org/articles/poetic-residue-interview-rick-lowe/.

Crenshaw, Kimberlé. *On Intersectionality.* New York: The New Press, 2014.

Davis, Lizzy Cooper. "The Free Southern Theater's Story Circle Process." In *Creating Space for Democracy*, edited by Nicholas V. Longo and Timothy J. Shaffer. Sterling, VA: Stylus Press, 2019.

Dougherty, Sarita. *A Textbook for the Ecocene.* Los Angeles: Co-Conspirator Press, 2020.

Flanagan, Hallie. *Arena.* New York: Benjamin Blom, 1940.

The Free Southern Theater, Thomas Dent, Gilbert Moses, and Richard Schechner, eds. *The Free Southern Theater by the Free Southern Theater.* Indianapolis: Bobbs-Merrill, 1969.

Freire, Paulo. *Pedagogy of the Oppressed.* New York: Continuum, 1968.

Gard, Robert. *Grassroots Theater.* Madison: University of Wisconsin Press, 1999.

Gardner, Howard. *Frames of Mind: The Theory of Multiple Intelligences.* New York: Basic Books, 1983.

Ginzburg, Randy. "Setting the Stage for Sexual Abuse: How Theater Pedagogy Makes Students Vulnerable to Sexual Harassment." February 25, 2020. https://medium.com/@randy.ginsburg/setting-the-stage-for-sexual-abuse-c8daf7ce0f56.

Hamlin, Kimberly A. "How Racism Almost Killed Women's Right to Vote." *Washington Post,* June 4, 2019.

hooks, bell. "Essentialism and Experience." *American Literary History* 3, no. 1 (1991): 172–83. www.jstor.org/stable/489740

———. *Teaching to Transgress.* New York and London: Routledge, 1994.

Jackson, Maria Rosario et al. *Investing in Creativity. Urban Institute, 2002.* https://www.urban.org/research/publication/investing-creativity.

Jackson, Shannon. *Social Works: Performing Art, Supporting Publics.* London: Routledge, 2011.

Lepore, Jill. "The Invention of the Police." *The New Yorker,* July 13, 2020.

Lerman, Liz. *Hiking the Horizontal.* Middletown, CT: Wesleyan University Press, 2011.

Lew, Mike, and Rehana Lew Mirza. "What Theatre Do We Want to Return To?" May 27, 2021. https://howlround.com/what-theatre-do-we-want-return.

Lewis, David Levering. *The Portable Harlem Renaissance Reader.* New York: Penguin, 1994.

Linares, Natalie and Caroline Woodard. *Solidarity Not Charity,* Report prepared for Grantmakers in the Arts (www.art.coop), 2021.

London, Todd, ed. *An Ideal Theater.* New York: Theatre Communications Group, 2013.

MacAloon, John. *Rite, Drama, Festival, Spectacle.* Philadelphia: Institute for the Study of Human Issues, 1984.

Markusen, Ann, and Anne Gadwa. *Creative Placemaking.* Washington, D.C.: National Endowment for the Arts, 2010.

Mehler, Michael Peter. "Percy MacKaye: Spatial Formations of a National Character." Ph.D. diss., University of Pittsburgh, 2010.

Neal, Larry. "The Black Arts Movement." *The Drama Review* 12, no. 4 (Summer 1968): 28–39.

Performing Statistics report. Art 180, 2019. www.performingstatistics.org/educator-resource-links?rq=report.

Quintanales, Mirtha. "I Paid Very Hard for My Immigrant Ignorance." In *This Bridge Called My Back,* edited by Cherrie Moraga and Gloria Anzaldua. Albany: State University of New York Press, 2005.

Skoots, Rebecca. *The Immortal Life of Henrietta Lacks.* New York: Crown, 2010.

Thompson, James. *Digging Up Stories.* Manchester, England: Manchester University Press, 2005.

———. *Performance Affects.* London: Palgrave Macmillan, 2009.

Truscott, Cristal Chanelle, and Greta Gabriel. "Good Theatre Got Soul: Exploring Dr. Cristal Chanelle Truscott's SoulWork Method."

CONTINUUM: The Journal of African Diaspora Drama, Theatre and Performance 4, no. 2 (December 2017).

Tworkov, Helen. "Agent of Change: An Interview with bell hooks" *Tricycle Magazine* (Fall 1992).

Van der Kolk, B. *The Body Keeps the Score: Brain, Mind, and Body in the Healing of Trauma.* New York: Penguin Random House, 2015.

viBe Theater Experience. Company collective creation commissioned for Gloria Steinem Book Launch. Pioneer Works, Red Hook, Brooklyn. November 5, 2019.

wa Thiong'o, Ngugi. *Decolonising the Mind: The Politics of Language in African Literature.* Portsmouth, NH: Heinemann Educational, 1986.

Willett, John, ed. *Brecht on Theatre.* New York: Hill and Wang, 1957.

Zarrilli, Phillip B. et al. *Theatre Histories.* New York and London: Routledge, 2006.

Index

Page numbers in *italics* indicate Figures and Photos.

About the Contributors

The interviews that we conducted greatly informed this book, both through direct quotes and by helping us think through the breadth and depth of our subject matter. We thank everyone who participated in an interview with Jan or Rad for their time, dedication, and thoughtfulness.

Andrea Assaf (she/her) is a playwright, poet, performer, theater director, and cultural organizer. She's the founding artistic director of Art2Action, Inc. Her awards include a 2011 NPN Creation Fund Commission, the 2010 Princess Grace Award for Directing, a 2007 Hedgebrook residency for "women authoring change," and a 2004 Cultural Contact grant (U.S.-Mexico Foundation for Culture).

Caron Atlas (she/her) offers over three decades of experience integrating arts, culture, civic engagement, and social justice across the United States, with cultural organizations, artists, foundations, higher education, policy centers, and networks. She has broad and deep citywide and national networks. She currently directs Arts & Democracy and Naturally Occurring Cultural Districts NY (NOCD-NY).

Roger Babb (he/him) was for many years a playwright/director with the Otrabanda Company, performing popular theater along the Mississippi River and avant-garde work in experimental venues. He has worked as an actor for Joseph Chaikin, Jim Neu, Julie Taymor, Meredith Monk, and many others. He has taught at Princeton, NYU, Swarthmore, and most recently at Mount Holyoke College.

Ron Bechet (he/him), former chair of the Department of Art at Xavier University and first director of its Community Arts Partnership Program, has exhibited widely. He has served on the Joan Mitchell Foundation and Imagining America boards. He's contributed to many arts and youth programs in New Orleans and received the New Orleans Mayor's Arts award in 2006.

Seth Bockley (he/him) is an award-winning writer of plays, screenplays, and fiction, and a theater artist specializing in literary adaptation and new work development. He teaches at the University of Chicago.

Paul Bonin-Rodriguez (he/him) is a writer-performer and dancer from San Antonio who has toured extensively throughout the United States. His writings include *Performing Policy: How Politics and Cultural Programs Redefined U.S. Artists for the Twenty-First Century.* Paul is an associate professor of Performance as Public Practice and LGBTQ Studies at UT Austin.

Rocky Bornstein (she/her) was for many years a performer and choreographer with the Otrabanda Company, performing popular theater on the Mississippi River and experimental theater in venues nationwide. Her choreographic work was supported by the National Endowment for the Arts and the New York Foundation for the Arts. She danced and collaborated with many downtown New York dance companies. She is now a physical therapist working in New York City.

Sharee Clark (she/her) is cofounder of Freedom Fighters in Wilkes-Barre, Pennsylvania.

Bill Cleveland (he/him) founded the Center for the Study of Art & Community, which develops creative partnerships that help build caring, capable, and equitable communities. The Center's podcast, *Change the Story/ Change the World,* chronicles art and community transformation across the globe. Bill's books include *Art in Other Places, Making Exact Change, Art and Upheaval,* and *Between Grace and Fear.*

Dudley Cocke (he/him) is the former artistic director of Roadside Theater, a part of rural Appalachia's Appalshop. His essays appear in *An Ideal Theatre, The Routledge Companion to Art and Politics, The Roles of Art and Culture in Community Change,* and elsewhere. He received the 2002 Heinz Award for Arts and Humanities.

Kathie deNobriga (she/her) is a founding member of Alternate ROOTS, an organization for community-based artists in the South, serving as its executive director for ten years. She led community theaters in North Carolina for a dozen years and acted with a Tennessee-based ensemble. She served as council member and mayor for Pine Lake, Georgia, and currently works as an independent arts consultant.

Carolina Đỗ (she/her) is an actor, playwright, producer, and community organizer. She is cofounding artistic leader of The Sống Collective, whose mission is to nurture a community of artists whose work explores questions of identity, race, intersectionality, immigration, and the refugee experience.

Jill Dolan (she/her) is the Annan Professor of English, Professor of Theater, and the Dean of the College at Princeton University. Among other books, she is the author of *The Feminist Spectator as Critic, Utopia in Performance,* and *The Feminist Spectator in Action.* Her blog, *The Feminist Spectator,* won the George Jean Nathan Award for Dramatic Criticism. She has received numerous teaching awards and the Distinguished Scholar Award from the American Society for Theatre Research. She was inducted into the American Academy of Arts and Sciences in 2016.

Stephen Duncombe (he/him) is a professor of Media and Culture at New York University and the author and editor of six books on the intersection of culture and politics. Duncombe, a lifelong political activist, is cofounder and research director of the Center for Artistic Activism, a research and training organization that helps activists create more like artists, and artists strategize more like activists.

Richard Elovitch (he/him) is a performance artist who joined ACT UP and turned his skills to AIDS activism. He is a specialist in program design and development on HIV/AIDS and substance use in the United

States and internationally, with expertise in harm reduction and innovative drug-treatment services.

Larissa FastHorse (she/her) is of the Sicangu Lakota Nation. She is a 2020 MacArthur Fellow, writer, choreographer, and cofounder of Indigenous Direction, the nation's leading consulting company for Indigenous arts and audiences. Larissa has created a trilogy of community engaged plays with the Cornerstone Theater Company: *Urban Rez, Native Nation,* and *The L/D/Nakota Project,* set in Larissa's homelands.

Ben Fink (he/him) has led cultural organizing and grassroots economic development projects in several states, building long-term collaboration between communities that have been divided along racial, political, and rural-urban lines. In 2020, Ben was recognized by *Time* magazine as one of "27 People Bridging Divides Across America."

Lanxing Fu (she/her) studied theater and environmental science. She codirects Superhero Clubhouse, a multidisciplinary community that creates theater to enact climate and environmental justice, cultivate hope, and inspire a thriving future. Her work as an artist and teacher centers around meaningful integration of ecological justice and art into community practice.

Ricardo Gamboa (they/them) is an award-winning artist, activist, and academic working in Chicago and NYC, creating radically politicized work. In Chicago, Ricardo is a member of the Free Street Theater, the Goodman Theatre Playwrights Unit, a resident playwright at Chicago Dramatists, and founding adult creative partner of the controversial, politically charged ensemble the Young Fugitives. In NYC, they are a fellow of the EmergeNYC program at the Hemispheric Institute of Performance and Politics and a member of the New York Neo-Futurists.

Michael John Garcés (he/him), a Cuban-American playwright and director, is a recipient of the 2020 Doris Duke Artist Award. He has been artistic director of the Cornerstone Theater Company, an ensemble based in Los Angeles, since 2006. Among the many works he wrote and directed with the company is *Los Illegals,* created in concert with day laborers and domestic workers.

Ryan Gilliam (she/her), executive director of FABnyc and Downtown Art, is an artist and organizer with forty-plus years' experience working on New York's Lower East Side, where she created 120 original performance projects with local youth. Ryan cofounded FABnyc to fight the displacement of local cultural groups, and now leads efforts to strengthen cultural participation through public art projects and community partnerships.

Arlene Goldbard (she/her)—provocative writer, speaker, social activist, consultant, and blogger—works for justice and compassion in spheres from the interpersonal to the transnational. Her books include *Crossroads: Reflections on the Politics of Culture; New Creative Community: The Art of Cultural Development; Community, Culture and Globalization; The Culture of Possibility: Art, Artists & The Future; Clarity; The Wave.* She is Chief Policy Wonk Emeritus of the U.S. Department of Arts and Culture.

Meggan Gomez (she/her) is a theater maker, facilitator, and activist. She has served as executive director at Theatre of the Oppressed NYC, as theater conservatory director at Working Classroom in Albuquerque, New Mexico, and is currently assistant vice president of faculty and creative practice at the New Jersey Performing Arts Center.

Kevin Gotkin (he/they), researcher, artist, and activist, studies endurance and the ritualization of ableism in American culture. He is currently focused on histories of the telethon, danceathon, walkathon, and hackathon in the United States. His essays appear in the *IEEE Annals of the History of Computing, Disability Studies Quarterly, the Journal of Video Ethnography, and Porn Studies.*

Groundwater Arts (Ronee Penoi [she/her], Annalisa Dias [she/her], Anna Lathrop [she/her], Tara Moses [she/her]) shapes, stewards, and seeds a just and decolonized future through creative practice, consultation, and community building. The team began the Divest to Invest campaign and the Green New Theatre initiative.

Leslie Ishii (Yonsei, she/her) serves as the artistic director of Perseverance Theatre on Tlingit Aani, colonially known as Juneau/Douglas, Alaska. She has performed in TV, film, and theater productions with legacy POC theaters and on Broadway. Her other positions include cochair of the

ConFest Steering Committee, board president (2020–present) of the Consortium of Asian American Theaters and Artists' National ConFest, founder of the National Cultural Navigation Theatre Project, and NNPN board member. She received the Los Angeles Women's Theatre Integrity Award, SDC Standout awards, and has been a DDCF and NEFA grant recipient. She is on the Core faculty at artEquity.

Maria Rosario Jackson (she/her) focuses on comprehensive community revitalization, systems change, arts and culture in communities, and dynamics of race and ethnicity. She's worked with philanthropy and government organizations on strategy, program design, research, learning, and evaluation. She's an institute professor at Arizona State University and is affiliated with the Herberger Institute for Design and the Arts and the Watts College of Public Service and Community Solutions. In 2021, President Biden nominated her to be chair of the National Endowment for the Arts.

Lynn Jeffries (she/her) designs puppets, sets, and costumes. She is a founding member of the Cornerstone Theater Company, which produces original plays with, for, and about communities in Los Angeles and beyond. Since 2003, she has collaborated on numerous spectacles with satirical puppeteer/performance artist Paul Zaloom.

Denise Griffin Johnson (she/her), president and director of community engagement of the Arch Social Community Network, has extensive experience as a community organizer. She is a cofounder of CultureWorks Baltimore, a member of the national network Alternate ROOTS, and a cultural agent with the U.S. Department of Arts and Culture (a nongovernment entity).

Daniel Alexander Jones (he/him) makes theater, music, and live performance with a wide range of collaborators and audiences. He is the creator of Jomama Jones, a mythical music diva. He has received a Doris Duke Artist Award, a United States Artist Fellowship, a Mellon Foundation Creative Research Fellowship, Creative Capital support, and the 2021 Pen Lifetime Achievement Award.

Suzanne Lacy (she/her) has long promoted dialogue and collaborations with communities. Since the 1970s, she's used organizing strategies and media interventions to galvanize discussions about feminism, violence against women, racism, labor rights, et cetera. Her large-scale performances bring together diverse participants. She is a professor at the University of Southern California.

Aaron Landsman (he/him) is a theater artist, writer, teacher, Abrons Arts Center Social Practice Artist in Residence, recent Guggenheim Fellow, and Princeton Arts Fellow. His performance works have been presented in the United States, the UK, Serbia, Norway, and the Netherlands. With Mallory Catlett, he has coauthored a book, *No One Is Qualified,* about democracy, participation, and performance; it will be published in 2022 by the University of Iowa Press.

Robert Landy (he/him), Ph.D., is a pioneer in the profession of drama therapy, has been a professor of Educational Theatre and Applied Psychology at New York University, where he founded the Drama Therapy Program . Robert has more than forty years of clinical experience within institutional, community, and private settings, and is an accomplished theater and visual artist.

Bob Leonard (he/him) directs the MFA program in Directing and Public Dialogue at Virginia Tech. His work includes ensemble-developed performances as an expression of public voice and interactive theater techniques in partnership with local initiatives on race to animate public dialogue and civic imagination. He is the founding director of The Road Company (1975–1998) and cofounder of Community Arts Network.

Shaun Leonardo (he/him) is involved with multidisciplinary work that negotiates societal expectations of manhood—namely, definitions surrounding Black and brown masculinities—along with its notions of achievement, collective identity, and experience of failure. His performance practice, anchored by his work in Assembly—a diversion program for court-involved youth at the Brooklyn-based, non-profit Recess, where he is now co-director—is participatory and invested in a process of embodiment.

Liz Lerman (she/her) is a choreographer, performer, writer, speaker, and a 2002 MacArthur Fellow. Over four decades she has generated personal, intellectually vivid, and up-to-the-minute artistic research for participatory performance in concert, with community, and on-screen. Liz developed the Critical Response Process in use across disciplines and is currently building the Atlas of Creative Tools, a digital commons. Liz teaches at Arizona State University.

Debra Levine (she/her) was an early member of ACT UP and has written extensively about AIDS activism and queer demonstrations of care during the early years of the HIV/AIDS crisis. She taught in the Drama Department at New York University, at Barnard College, and is currently director of undergraduate studies and lecturer on theater, dance, and media at Harvard.

Toya Lillard (she/her) has directed plays, developed curricula, led advocacy efforts, and implemented innovative teaching artist training programs both in and out of New York City's schools. Toya served as director of School Programs for the New York Philharmonic's Education Department, as executive director of viBe Theater, and is now Arts Education Program Officer of the Pierre and Tana Matisse Foundation.

Timara Lotah Link (she/her) revives arts rooted in her Chumash community and teaches them to Native Peoples throughout California. Primarily a weaver, she also makes baskets, fish traps, bows, seed beaters, headdresses, cradles, boats, traditional houses, dolls, hats, jewelry, musical instruments, et cetera. Each new skill is a small piece of culture she returns to her community.

Todd London (he/him) is an educator, artistic instigator, theater historian, and author, most recently of *If You See Him, Let Me Know* (a novel) and *This Is Not My Memoir* (with André Gregory). From 2014 to 2018, he was executive director of the University of Washington's School of Drama, and prior to that, he spent eighteen seasons as artistic director of New Dramatists. Todd was the first recipient of the Theatre Communications Group's Visionary Leadership Award.

Seed Lynn (he/him) is the founder and lead listener of Storyographers, a narrative health and justice practice located in Chicago. He earned a BA in creative writing at University of Tennessee and honed his listening skills as a cultural worker/organizer at the Highlander Research and

Education Center. He was introduced to ROOTS through the Hip Hop Artist/ Activist Fellowship and credits the Carpetbag Theatre ensemble for developing his earliest sense of both of art and activism.

Keryl McCord (she/her) is the founder of Equity Quotient, which provides dismantling- racism training, and organizational planning and development through the lens of racial, cultural, and ethnic diversity. She previously worked with such organizations as Alternate ROOTS, the New Jersey Symphony Orchestra, the African Grove Institute for the Arts, and the National Endowment for the Arts.

Gloria Miguel (she/her) is from the Kuna/Rappahannock Nations. She is a founding member of Spiderwoman Theater, the long-running NYC-based Native feminist theater company, and has been a writer, actor, and activist for over seventy-five years. Gloria has toured extensively and has facilitated workshops and lectures throughout the world. She received an honorary DFA from Miami University and, in 2020, the Clara Lemlich Award honoring incredible women activists.

Lisa Mount (she/her), director of Artistic Logistics, works as a consultant with nonprofit arts organizations and facilitates dynamic meetings for groups large and small. As an independent artist, she produces, directs, and performs. Earlier in her career, she toured with the DeLuxe Vaudeville Orchestra as rhythm banjo player, and was managing director of 7 Stages Theatre in Atlanta.

Dipankar Mukherjee (he/him), a director from Kolkata, has over thirty years' experience directing. He cofounded and is co–artistic director of Pangea World Theater, a progressive space for arts and dialogue in Minneapolis. His aesthetics have evolved through his commitment to social justice, equity, deep spirituality, and relevant politics. Dipankar strives to disrupt inherited colonial, racist, and patriarchal modalities and collaboratively searches for alternate ways of working.

Meena Natarajan (she/her), playwright and director, is co–artistic director of Pangea World Theater, a progressive international ensemble space creating at the intersection of art, equity, and social justice since 1995. Meena has cocurated and designed many of Pangea's professional and community-based programs, and written some ten works, from poetry and mythology adaptations to original pieces about war, spirituality, and memory.

Una Osato (Una/they/she), a queer Japanese Jewish performer, writer, stripper, and educator born in NYC, dynamically merges art and politics. Una is a cofounder of the troupe brASS: Brown RadicalAss Burlesque and has taught for fifteen years at every level of education throughout the United States and South Africa. Una's work as an educator is an extension of Una's artistic work, all of which explores and addresses social justice issues through embodying knowledge, performance, and storytelling.

Linda Parris-Bailey (she/her) creates story-based plays with music, focusing on themes of transformation and empowerment in the African Diaspora. She is president and CEO of the newly formed Parris-Bailey Arts, Inc. and emeritus executive/artistic director of the Carpetbag Theatre in Knoxville, Tennessee. She is a 2019 Creative Capital awardee and the recipient of the 2015 Doris Duke Artist Award in Theater.

Daniel Park (he/him) is a queer biracial theater and performance artist based in Philadelphia. His work is interdisciplinary, combining live performance and game design to create interactive experiences that explore the boundaries of human agency.

Coya Paz (she/her), a writer/director, was raised in South America and the United States. She is artistic director of the Free Street Theatre and was founding co–artistic director of Teatro Luna. An associate professor in the Theatre School at DePaul University, Coya is coauthor (with Chloe Johnston) of *Ensemble-Made Chicago: A Guide to Devised Theater.*

Marty Pottenger (she/her) is a solo performance artist, director, and founder/director of Art At Work, a national initiative piloted with Portland, Maine's departments, unions, and elected officials to improve municipal government through strategic arts projects. Pottenger's arts practice puts creativity to work addressing social challenges with multiyear collaborative projects that focus on labor, race, equity, and care of the environment.

Kathy Randels (she/her) has created and performed theater in New Orleans' streets, her flooded and gutted childhood home, the levees of St. Bernard Parish, with incarcerated women in the Louisiana Correctional Institute for Women, and with some of those released through The Graduates (a theater ensemble) program. She has also led ArtSpot Productions, an interdisciplinary performance ensemble in New Orleans, for twenty-six years.

Bill Rauch (he/him) is the inaugural artistic director of the Perelman Performing Arts Center. His theater direction has been seen across the nation, from low-income community centers to Broadway. Bill was artistic director of the Oregon Shakespeare Festival (2007–2019) and cofounder of the Cornerstone Theater Company, serving as its artistic director from 1986 to 2006.

Michael Rohd (he/him) is founding artistic director of the ensemble-based Sojourn Theatre. He wrote *Theatre for Community, Conflict, and Dialogue.* He is lead artist for the Center for Performance and Civic Practice. His honors include a Castillo Award for Political Theater and the Robert Gard Foundation Award for Excellence. He recently partnered with planning commissions utilizing civic practice in public engagement settings. Michael teaches at Arizona State University.

Holly Sidford (she/her) is codirector of the Helicon Collaborative, providing strategy development, program management, research, and facilitation for arts and cultural organizations and funders. Her previous positions include founding president of Leveraging Investments in Creativity (LINC), a ten-year national initiative to expand support for creative artists, and program director for arts, parks, and adult literacy at the Lila Wallace–Reader's Digest Fund.

Peggy Shaw (she/her) is a performer, writer, and teacher of writing and performance. She is a 2019 Guggenheim Fellow, a 2016 United States Artist Fellow, and 2014 recipient of the Doris Duke Artist Award. Peggy is a veteran of Hot Peaches and Spiderwoman Theater, cofounder of Split Britches and WOW Café Theatre, and has collaborated with Lois Weaver since 1980.

Nick Slie (he/him) lives and works on the disappearing wetlands of coastal Louisiana. An actor, director, writer, educator, and community activist, he is cofounder and co–artistic director of the New Orleans-based performance collective Mondo Bizarro. Nick's performance work ranges from physical theater to multidisciplinary solo work, from digital storytelling to collaborative ensemble productions.

Erik Takeshita (he/him) has long advocated for the role of art and culture in building stronger communities. His positions include senior fellow at ArtPlace America, Community Creativity Portfolio Director at the Bush Foundation, and Senior Program Officer at the Local Initiatives Support Corporation. Erik ran an arts center in Honolulu, Hawaii, and served as a senior policy aide to the mayor of Minneapolis.

Cristal Chanelle Truscott (she/her), Ph.D., is a playwright, director, scholar, culture worker, creator of the SoulWork method for generative performance and analysis, and founder of Progress Theatre. She is a recipient of the Doris Duke Impact Artist Award, the Creative Capital Award, and the MAP Fund Award, and has received grants from the NPN Creation Fund and the NEFA National Theater Project. She is an associate professor of Performance Studies and Graduate Acting at Northwestern University.

Carlton Turner (he/him) is an artist, agriculturalist, researcher, former executive director of Alternate ROOTS, and founder of the Mississippi Center for Cultural Production (Sipp Culture). Sipp Culture uses food and story to support rural community, cultural, and economic development in his hometown of Utica, Mississippi, where he lives with his wife, Brandi, and three children.

Roberta Uno (she/her) is a theater director and the director of Arts in a Changing America. She was program officer for Arts and Culture at the Ford Foundation from 2002 to 2015. From 1979 to 2002, she was founder and artistic director of New WORLD Theater and also a professor of directing and dramaturgy at the University of Massachusetts at Amherst.

Carlos Uriona (he/him) is co–artistic director of Double Edge Theatre and has worked with DE since 1996. He moved to rural Ashfield, Massachusetts, to join DE from Argentina, where he was cofounder of the seminal puppet theater, Diablomundo. A bridge builder, Carlos has forged the way for DE's audience and grassroots involvement and infused DE's work, through acting, training, and creation, with a deep sense of optimism.

Mark Valdez (he/him) is artistic director of Mixed Blood Theatre. His work has been produced at the Alliance Theatre, the Cornerstone Theater Company, East West Players, La Peña Cultural Center, the Mark Taper Forum, MACLA, and Teatro Vision. From 2007 to 2014, he led the Network of Ensemble Theaters (NET), a community of artists committed to cocreation.

viBe Theater Experience provides Black girls, young women, and gender-expansive youth (ages thirteen through twenty-five) in New York City with free, high-quality artistic leadership and academic opportunities. Through its performing arts and training programs, viBe works to empower its participants to write and perform original theater, video, and music about the real-life issues they face daily.

Lois Weaver (she/her) is an artist, activist, facilitator, and professor of Contemporary Performance at Queen Mary University of London. She is a 2014 Guggenheim Fellow and a 2016–2019 Wellcome Trust Engaging Science Fellow. Lois is a founding member of Spiderwoman Theater and cofounder of Split Britches and WOW Café Theatre. She has collaborated with Peggy Shaw since 1980.

MK Wegmann (she/her) was a founding staff member of New Orleans' Contemporary Arts Center and managing director of Junebug Productions. She recently retired as president and CEO of the National Performance Network. She has more than thirty-five years of experience in organizational development, artists' services, presenting, and producing for nonprofit visual and performing arts organizations, and is currently a consultant with artist-focused organizations.

Caroline Woolard (she/her) is an interdisciplinary artist who, in making her art, becomes an economic critic, social justice facilitator, media maker, and sculptor. Since the financial crisis of 2007–2008, Woolard has catalyzed barter communities, minted local currencies, founded an arts-policy think tank, and created sculptural interventions in office spaces. Woolard has inspired a generation of artists who wish to create self-organized, collaborative, online platforms alongside sculptural objects and installations.

Rhiana Yazzie (she/her), founder of the New Native Theatre, is a Navajo playwright, producer, director, actor, and filmmaker based in Minnesota. She is a 2018/2019 Bush Leadership Fellow, a 2017 Sally Award Winner for Vision, a 2016/2017 Playwrights' Center McKnight Fellow, and a two-time Playwrights' Center Jerome Fellow (2010/2011 and 2006/2007).

About the Authors

Jan Cohen-Cruz (she/her) wrote *Local Acts, Engaging Performance,* and *Remapping Performance,* edited *Radical Street Performance,* and, with Mady Schutzman, coedited *Playing Boal* and *A Boal Companion.* She worked with A Blade of Grass, an organization that supports socially engaged artists, from 2013 to 2019, eventually serving as director of Field Research and cofounding its magazine. From 2007 to 2012, she directed Imagining America: Artists and Scholars in Public Life, a consortium of colleges and universities committed to civic engagement, and cofounded its journal, *Public.* Cohen-Cruz earned her Ph.D. in Performance Studies at New York University and was a longtime professor in the Drama Department, initiating its minor in Applied Theatre. In 2012, she received the Association for Theatre in Higher Education's Award for Leadership in Community-Based Theatre and Civic Engagement. Jan was an evaluator for the U.S. State Department/Bronx Museum cultural diplomacy initiative smARTpower and for numerous initiatives of New York City's Public Artists in Residence (PAIR) project. With Pam Korza, she researched and wrote a field guide for artist/municipal agency partnerships. She continues to teach at NYU, CUNY, and Touchstone Theatre/ Moravian University. Jan and her family operate the Smokehouse Food Truck in rural Pennsylvania. She is the grandmother of Islay Cohen-Cruz.

Rad Pereira (they/them) is a cultural worker, performing artist, healer, and educator from Pindorama (Campinas, São Paulo, Brazil), with a home base in Lenapehoking (Brooklyn). Their creative practice ranges from social sculpture to popular theatrical and TV/film performance to participatory liberatory art making and healing that weaves together an Afro-futurist longing for transformative justice and queer (re)Indigenization of culture. With their community, they have created *The (Im) Migrant Hustle* and produced *Bang Bang Gun Amok I + II at* Abrons Art Center. With their artner at You Are Here, LILLETH, they created Media Tools for Liberation at JACK, *Decolonization Rave,* and *Cosmic Commons.* In 2017, Rad was a NYC PAIR (Public Artist in Residence) at the Department of Cultural Affairs and Children's Services, working with LGBTQIA2+ foster youth with their collaborators Keelay Gipson, Josh Adam Ramos, and Britton Smith. They have taught theater and performance at Pace University, Interlochen Arts Academy, and The Door. As an actor and director, Rad has contributed to stories at HBO, CBS, MTV, National Black Theatre, Nowness, MITU350, the Public Theater, La MaMa, the Shakespeare Theatre Company in Washington, D.C., the Pittsburgh Public Theater, the New York Theatre Workshop, ART Boston, the Bushwick Starr, the Target Margin Theater, Ars Nova, the New Ohio Theatre, Clubbed Thumb, Sesame Street, Theatre 167, the Watermill Center, and more. As a cultural strategist and community connector, Rad has worked with the Queens Museum, the Rio de Janeiro Museum, the United Nations, the Instituto República, SITI Company Thought Center, A Blade of Grass, SUPERBLUE, the Broadway Advocacy Coalition at Columbia University, the New School, The 8th Floor, Working Woman of Color Conference, Dance/NYC Symposium, and Culture/Shift. Rad is eternally grateful for the support and love of their kin, partner, family, and friends.

www.ingramcontent.com/pod-product-compliance
Lightning Source LLC
LaVergne TN
LVHW012340100826
845148LV00018B/2866

* 9 7 8 1 6 1 3 3 2 1 5 4 6 *